WALT DISNEY WORLD WITH KIDS

1995

The Unofficial Guide

Kim Wright Wiley

Prima Publishing
P.O. Box 1260BK
Rocklin, CA 95677
(916) 632-4400

Copy editing by Kathy Darling
Production by Archetype Book Composition
Typography by Archetype Book Composition
Interior Design by Judith Levinson
Maps by Misty Berry
Cover design by The Dunlavey Studio, Sacramento

Library of Congress Cataloging-in-Publication Data

Wiley, Kim Wright.
    Walt Disney World with kids: the unofficial guide—1995 ed.
        p.   cm.
    Includes index.
    ISBN 1-55958-557-9
    1. Walt Disney World (Fla.)—Guidebooks.   2. Family recreation—Florida—Orlando Region—
Guidebooks.   I. Title
GV1853.3.F62W349   1993
    791´,06.´875924—dc20   93-34368
                                                        CIP

94 95 96 97 RRD 10 9 8 7 6 5 4 3 2 1

Printed in the United States of America

How to Order:
Single copies may be ordered from Prima Publishing, P.O. Box 1260BK, Rocklin, CA 95677; telephone (916) 632-4400. Quantity discounts are also available. On your letterhead include information concerning the intended use of the books and the number of books you wish to purchase.

To my husband, Royallen,
the Coaster Warrior

WALT DISNEY WORLD

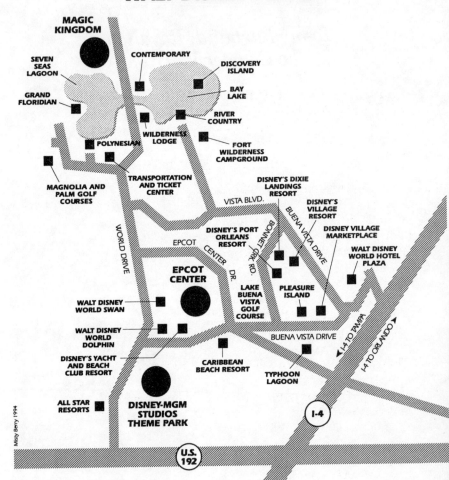

MAGIC KINGDOM

SEVEN SEAS LAGOON

CONTEMPORARY

DISCOVERY ISLAND

GRAND FLORIDIAN

BAY LAKE

RIVER COUNTRY

WILDERNESS LODGE

POLYNESIAN

FORT WILDERNESS CAMPGROUND

MAGNOLIA AND PALM GOLF COURSES

TRANSPORTATION AND TICKET CENTER

VISTA BLVD.

DISNEY'S DIXIE LANDINGS RESORT

DISNEY'S VILLAGE RESORT

WORLD DRIVE

EPCOT CENTER DR.

DISNEY'S PORT ORLEANS RESORT

DISNEY VILLAGE MARKETPLACE

BONNET CREEK RD.

BUENA VISTA DRIVE

WALT DISNEY WORLD HOTEL PLAZA

EPCOT CENTER

WALT DISNEY WORLD SWAN

LAKE BUENA VISTA GOLF COURSE

PLEASURE ISLAND

WALT DISNEY WORLD DOLPHIN

I-4 TO TAMPA

I-4 TO ORLANDO

DISNEY'S YACHT AND BEACH CLUB RESORT

CARIBBEAN BEACH RESORT

BUENA VISTA DRIVE

TYPHOON LAGOON

I-4

ALL STAR RESORTS

DISNEY-MGM STUDIOS THEME PARK

U.S. 192

Misty Berry 1994

Contents

SECTION 6: DISNEY–MGM STUDIOS THEME PARK   153

SECTION 7: THE REST OF THE WORLD   177

SECTION 8: DISNEY AFTER DARK   209

What Makes This Guide Different?

Once upon a time, people with kids didn't travel. Parents lucky enough to have supportive relatives or nannies may have taken off and left the children behind, but more often people with children stayed home, figuring geographic paralysis was the price of parenthood. Tour buses all over the world are filled with people in their 60s who deferred their dreams of Maui or Moscow or even Miami until their kids were grown and married.

Things have changed. No one is surprised anymore by the sight of an infant snoozing away in a four-star restaurant, and a recent letter to *Travel and Leisure* magazine inquired about the difficulty of locating Pampers in Nepal. Today people take their kids everywhere, and they especially take them to Orlando, Florida.

Walt Disney World is the most frequently visited man-made tourist attraction on the planet, and at first glance it seems designed to cater specifically to families with young children. But it's not a small world after all, and actually circumnavigating the three major theme parks, four minor parks, sixteen on-site hotels, and a shopping plaza requires as much organization and fortitude as a safari.

Guidebooks abound but they rarely address the questions the parents of young children ask: Which restaurants are suitable for evening dining with a pooped

5-year-old? Where can we get a sitter? A Band-Aid? How can you cut down on waiting in line by making reservations in advance? Will Epcot bore the kids? Is it worth the extra cost to stay at a hotel on the grounds? Is it OK to take the kids out of school for the trip? Where can I breast-feed? Do the men's restrooms have changing tables? Is the Haunted Mansion really all that scary?

This guidebook will take into account the pace and pocketbook of a couple traveling with young kids. It will feature those attractions, such as the character breakfasts with Mickey and the gang, that first-timers can easily miss, but that can make all the difference to a starstruck toddler. Preplanning is essential since, as you well know, a two-hour wait that would be merely annoying to a lone business traveler can be downright disastrous to a single parent with hungry kids in tow. Nonetheless, some families try to wing it. You know the ones; you see them every morning standing flat-footed in the middle of Main Street, kids bouncing in the strollers and parents huddled over their maps debating how to get to Splash Mountain. This approach is akin to attempting to learn Lamaze after the contractions have begun.

To minimize problems and maximize fun, you must be oriented before you arrive. If you follow this guide you'll learn how to get tickets, maps, and reservations in advance and plot your family path. Over the past five years I have passed out hundreds of questionnaires and interviewed dozens of families—their helpful comments and tips are incorporated throughout the book.

With just a little bit of forethought, you'll be able to go against the crowds—moving clockwise while the thundering hordes are moving counterclockwise, touring Epcot while most people are in the Magic Kingdom, and even the ultimate crowd-busting move, planning your trip during the off-season. If you manage to zig while everyone else zags, you can cut waits to a minimum and see twice as much as you would mindlessly drifting from queue to queue.

The basic rule when traveling with young children is to prepare without overplanning. You want to be familiar enough with the layout of Disney World that you can find a restroom fast, but not so driven by a timetable that you don't allow plenty of time for resting and savoring spontaneous pleasures. Fun stuff pops up all around the parks, and if you're grimly trying to make it from Fantasyland to Liberty Square on schedule you'll miss the key delights of this amazing attraction.

And pleasures are what this guide is all about. The three bugaboos of the World—the crowds, the heat-exhaustion, and the expense—are especially tough on young families, and no amount of preparation will totally eliminate these problems. Walt Disney World, after all, is a 43-square-mile complex in the middle of Florida, visited by as many as 150,000 people a day. It costs a family of four up to $130 bucks just to get through the gate. You're going to get hot, tired, and spend a lot of money. That's a given.

So why go at all? There's only one reason—it's the most fun place on earth!

What Makes Walt Disney World So Special?

The answer to this question is, in a word, detail. The entire Disney World fantasy is sustained through painstaking attention to detail.

In an attraction such as Pirates of the Caribbean, the atmospheric mischief begins in the queue, where you wind down into the bowels of a stucco fortress that grows danker and darker with every turn. The ride combines Audio-Animatronics, a catchy theme song, and an attention to detail so relentless that even the hair on the pirates' legs is real. You emerge seven minutes later, blinking in the sunlight that spills through the market stalls of the Caribbean Plaza, fully understanding why Disney insists that its "rides" be referred to as "attractions." (The illusion holds up just as well at Epcot, where the Disney people have presented themselves a bigger challenge: this time they're out to snooker adults into believing they're in Norway . . . or the land of the dinosaurs . . . or the human bloodstream.)

The theme parks were designed with the same precision that Disney animators brought to the classic films. Walt was such a perfectionist that he never let four frames per second suffice if eight were possible. Now his successors are successful because of the same sumptuousness. Why not fly in some monkey-puzzle trees for the Japan pavilion? Hire George Lucas as creative con-

sultant for the ride based on his *Star Wars* film series?
Buy the Teenage Mutant Ninja Turtles? Who says 11,000
dolls are too many for It's a Small World?

The authors of some guidebooks seem immune to the
Disney magic, which is why they can describe Dumbo as
a "sporadically loading ten unit cycle ride of the sort
common to most midways," and advise you to pass it up.
But it isn't a sporadically loading cycle ride at all—it's
Dumbo, and no 4-year-old worth his salt is going to let
you pass it up. The special charm of Walt Disney World
is that once we pass through those gates we're all 4-year-
olds—impulsive, impatient, curious, easily duped, essentially cheerful, and ready to believe in magic.

Abbreviations and Terms Used in This Book

WDW	Walt Disney World
MK	the Magic Kingdom
Epcot	Epcot Center
MGM	the Disney–MGM Studios Theme Park
the major parks	the Magic Kingdom, Epcot Center, and Disney–MGM Studios
the minor parks	Typhoon Lagoon, River Country, Pleasure Island, and Discovery Island
TTC	Ticket and Transportation Center: the monorail version of a train station, where riders can transfer to monorails bound for Epcot, the MK, or monorail-line hotels. You can also catch buses at the TTC bound for the parks, the on-site hotels, and the Disney Village Marketplace.
on-site	the Disney-owned hotels that are on the WDW property: the Contemporary, the Polynesian, the Grand Floridian, the Vacation

	Club, Disney's Village Resort, the Caribbean Beach Resort, Fort Wilderness, the Yacht and Beach Clubs, Port Orleans, Dixie Landings, Wilderness Lodge, the All-Star Resorts, the Disney Swan, and the Disney Dolphin
off-site	hotels that are not located on WDW ground or owned by the Walt Disney Co.
on-season	the busiest touring times, including summer and the weeks surrounding major holidays
off-season	less busy times of the year, most notably spring and fall
the MK resorts	the Grand Floridian, the Polynesian, the Contemporary, and Wilderness Lodge
the Epcot resorts	the Yacht and Beach Clubs, Caribbean Beach Resort, Disney Swan, and Disney Dolphin
Village Resorts	Port Orleans, Dixie Landings, Disney's Village Resort, the Vacation Club

1

★★★★★★★★★★★★★★★★★★★

*Before You
Leave Home*

WHAT TIME OF YEAR SHOULD WE VISIT?

1. September through mid-December is the best time of year for families with young children to visit. Crowds are light—around 30,000 visitors a day, as compared to 85,000 in the summer months—and many area hotels offer discounted rates. Even the weather cooperates, with highs in the 80s and lows in the 60s.

There are disadvantages to a fall visit. You may not want to take your children out of school, and the theme parks do close earlier at this time of year. The Magic Kingdom and MGM often close as early as 7 P.M., although Epcot generally remains open later. These earlier closings mean that some of the special evening presentations, such as the electric light parades, are suspended during the off-season.

Fall is also hurricane season in Florida, so there's some risk you'll schedule your trip for the exact week Hurricane Laluna pounds the coast. But Orlando is an hour inland, meaning even the worst coastal storms usually yield only rain. Furthermore, rainy days reach their peak during the summer months, not the fall, so the advantages of autumn touring far outweigh the disadvantages.

2. If fall isn't possible, spring is nearly as nice. With the exceptions of the holiday weeks around Washington's Birthday, spring break, and Easter, springtime crowds average around 45,000—not as low as in the fall but still far better than in summer. And the weather is sublime, with highs in the 70s, lows in the 60s, and less rainfall in spring than in any other season of the year.

Disney runs longer park hours in spring than in fall, but schedules vary widely in the weeks between January and May. To check projected hours of operation, dial (305) 824-4321 before you leave home.

3. If you must visit in summer, the first two weeks of June and the last two weeks of August are your best bet. Temperatures and attendance peak in July.

4. The absolute worst times are holidays. Christmas, New Year's, the Fourth of July, and other major holidays can pull in 150,000 visitors per day, which is six times as many people as you'll find on a typical day in October. Extended hours can't compensate for crowds of this size. Although special parades and shows are always planned, you're better off watching them at home on the Disney Channel.

Note: WDW is fetchingly decorated at Christmas, no doubt about it. But the decorations go up just after Thanksgiving, so if you can work in an early-December visit, you'll have all the trees and wreaths and carolers you could wish for—as well as a nearly deserted theme park. The special "Jolly Holidays" packages, which include price breaks on lodgings, a party with the characters, and access to the Christmas parades and shows, run from the end of November to mid-December.

5. Somewhat surprisingly, Fridays and Sundays are the least crowded days of the week. Mondays, Tuesdays, and Wednesdays draw the heaviest traffic.

HOW LONG SHOULD WE STAY?

1. It will take at least four days for a family with young kids to tour the MK, Epcot, and MGM. In acknowledgment of this, Disney did away with the standard 3-day ticket in 1989 when MGM opened. Now 4- and 5-day tickets are offered and, since the 5-day ticket also admits holders to Pleasure Island, Typhoon Lagoon, Discovery Island, and River Country, it is the best buy.

Note: Your admission into the minor parks is unlimited and free only within seven days of the first day the ticket is used. In other words, buying a 5-day ticket does not allow you entrance into Typhoon Lagoon for life.

2. If you plan to take in any of the minor theme parks, schedule five days. Five days are also necessary for families who enjoy boating, tennis, swimming, or golf—or those who'd like to tour at a more leisurely pace.

3. If you wish to visit other area attractions such as Sea World or Universal Studios, allow at least a week.

SHOULD WE TAKE THE KIDS OUT OF SCHOOL?

Even if you're sold on the advantages of fall and spring touring, you may be reluctant to take your children out of school for a week. Here are some ways to temper your guilt.

1. Kids remember what they see, so a single day at Epcot can be just as educational as a week of science and geography classes. "That's a Viking ship," my 4-year-old casually observed while we were watching a movie one evening. "You know, like at Epcot." Another mother reports that her son's award-winning science fair project on drip irrigation was inspired by touring the Land pavilion.

2. Since you'll have weeks of advance warning before a trip to Orlando, ask your children's teachers if they can do at least some of the lessons they'll miss before you leave. Coming back to piles of makeup work after a vacation can be profoundly depressing.

3. Perhaps your children can work out a deal with their teachers whereby they'll do special reports or projects relating to subjects they'll encounter at Epcot or MGM. Some suggestions:

- Into dinosaurs? Check out the Universe of Energy pavilion.

- Students of the natural sciences will find much of interest in the Land pavilion.

- Marine biology is the theme of the Living Seas.

- Missing health class? The Wonders of Life pavilion is devoted to that greatest of all machines, the human body, and even has hands-on exhibits inside.

- Interested in geography? Some students have done reports on the cultures of countries represented in the World Showcase.

- Art students are bound to pick up pointers during the Animation Tour at MGM.

- Drama students or even budding engineers will learn a lot "behind the scenes" at MGM's Backstage Studio Tour.

- "Kidventure," a four-hour guided tour of Discovery Island, Disney's zoological park, is open to kids 8–14. Park admission, transportation, lunch, and supplies to make a nature-themed craft are included in the $27 cost. For more details, or to make reservations, call (407) 824-3784.

4. Along with formal reports on the subjects listed above, your child might also want to make a scrapbook or collection display. The mother of one preschooler helped him create an "ABC" book before he left home, and he then spent his WDW week collecting souvenirs for each page—Goofy's autograph on the "G" page, sugar

packages from restaurants for the "S" page, and so on. An older child might gather leaves from the various trees and bushes imported from the countries represented in the World Showcase. Or a young photographer could illustrate his proficiency with various lighting techniques by photographing Cinderella Castle in early morning, at noon, at sunset, and after dark.

5. If your child is between 10 and 15, and you think he or she might benefit from a more formal type of instruction, try one of WDW's three seminars, collectively titled "The Wonders of Walt Disney World." Some schools will accept these one-day seminars for class credit.

At the day's start, students meet in a classroom and receive a book on the subject they'll be studying, as well as any needed classroom materials. Then the students board a special van with their instructor and begin a six-hour tour. At the end of the day participants receive a "Wonders" certificate of completion and a book with follow-up activities designed to help them expand the knowledge they gained during their program. The three programs are listed below.

- *Exploring Nature:* During this tour young people visit Discovery Island, Disney's 7,500-acre zoological park, study the ways animals and birds become endangered, and learn what they can do to protect their own environment. Seeing wildlife in a natural setting brings home the importance of ecology and the preservation of wilderness areas. Students have use of binoculars, but also have many chances to see birds, apes, and alligators up close. Exploring Nature is offered on Tuesdays and Thursdays from 8:45 to 2:45. Groups leave from a special marked area near the Guest Relations booth at Epcot.

- *Art Magic:* Students get a first-hand look at the artistic process at work in WDW productions; examine the basic shapes in character animation; and study a Disney attraction to see how sets, costumes, and color combine to create atmosphere. The highlight of the tour is a meeting with a Disney animator who demonstrates how to draw a character and then helps the students sketch the Disney gang. Students leave with their own hand-painted Mickey Mouse cel and a sketchbook to encourage them to keep practicing their new skills. Art Magic is offered on Mondays, Wednesdays, and Fridays from 8:45 to 2:45. Groups meet in front of the MGM gates at the far right side.

- *Show Biz Magic:* Described as a "behind the scenes look at the hard work, dedication, and pixie dust it takes to put on a great show every time," Show Biz allows students to meet Disney musicians, dancers, and singers. After watching an audition and rehearsal at MGM, students will meet with performers and technicians, watch a show, then go underground into the famous-but-little-seen tunnel area where costumes and props are stored and the huge Disney cast rehearses. Show Biz is offered on Mondays through Thursdays from 9:30 to 3:30. Groups meet in front of the MGM gate at the far right side.

General Information About the "Wonders of Walt Disney World" Programs

1. Reservations are accepted at (407) 354-1855 and should be made weeks in advance, preferably at the same time you book your hotel room. Class size is limited to 14 students per session.

Classes are subject to change, so be sure to verify times, prices, meeting places, and course content when you call.

2. You can get brochures that completely outline the programs by writing:

   WDW Seminar Productions
   P.O. Box 10000
   Lake Buena Vista, FL 32830-1000

   If you want your child to apply for classroom credit for participating in the program, request an extra brochure for your school principal.

3. Cost for one seminar is $75.00. Some packages include seminar fees, so be sure to check.

4. Students are considered to be on a supervised field trip and will not need an admission ticket during the program.

5. Parents need to drop kids off in the morning and pick them up in the afternoon but are otherwise free to do what they please while the seminars are in session.

6. Lunch is provided.

7. Students 16 and older are welcome on the adult tours, which are also outlined in the "Wonders of Walt Disney World" brochure.

Note: In the interest of offering guests even more varied and unique educational options, Disney will be offering a new program, dubbed "The Disney Institute," in the fall of 1995. Housed in a self-contained resort located near the Disney Village Marketplace, the Institute will combine a spa-like atmosphere with educational and cultural opportunities. Guests can book time with a personal trainer, use the elaborate fitness center, and then work out their minds by taking courses in animation, interior and landscape design, and the arts. Visiting lecturers and performance artists will round out the programs. As the Institute's offerings are developed in more detail, a brochure will become available. In the meantime, call (407) 827-4230 for information.

Other Orlando Educational Programs

Other Orlando attractions also offer educational programs.

* *Sea World:* (407) 351-3600. Ask about the 90-minute "Backstage Information" guided tour on marine life. At a price of $6 for adults and $5 for kids, this tour is a very worthwhile introduction to the problems facing endangered species, and explains how Sea World has helped its animals adapt to life in an artificial environment. If your kids are younger or more restless, the 45-minute "Let's Talk Training" tour, which demonstrates how the animals learn to do those dazzling tricks, or the 90-minute "Animal Lover's Adventure," which takes you all over the park into the animal's habitats, are a bit lighter on content but still quite educational. Since Sea World is easily toured in 5 to 6 hours and the guided tours run several times a day, it is easy to work one into your plans. You'll be amazed by how much your kids retain months after the tour.

* *Orlando Science Center:* (407) 896-7151. This impressive facility has oodles of hands-on exhibits, many of them designed to be interesting to kids as young as 4, as well as regular evening planetarium shows. The highly innovative one-day programs range from "Dirt Safaris" geared toward 4-year-olds

to "Gator Watches" for kids 11 and up. The Center even sponsors "Camp-In" sleepovers at the museum, with subjects ranging from Lego Mania to Silly Science, a set of pleasingly messy physics experiments using silly putty and slime. Not every class is offered every week, so request the brochure. You'll find that something is happening all the time and that the prices are reasonable. All programs must be booked in advance.

- *Spaceport USA:* (407) 452-2121. Orlando is only about an hour from Kennedy Space Center, so it's an easy day trip. Kids will enjoy a ride through the Rocket Garden, which holds eight rockets from the Mercury through Apollo programs. They'll also enjoy the films, projected on the five-story-high screen in the IMAX theater. Call the Center at 1-800-KSC-INFO before you leave home to see if a launch is scheduled during the time you'll be in Florida. If so, plan your trip for that day. The crowds will be heavier, but your kids will experience a rare thrill.

IS IT WORTH THE EXPENSE TO STAY ON-SITE?

Staying at one of the Disney-owned hotels is very convenient—and with rates as low as $69 a night at the new All-Star Resorts, staying on-site is becoming more affordable each year.

Off-site hotels are fighting back with special price promotions and perks—such as free child care—of their own, arguing that the Disney hotels still cost more and bring you only slightly closer to the action. On-site or off-site? The questions below should help you decide.

1. *What time of year are you going and how long are you staying?*

If you're going in summer or during a major holiday, you'll need every extra minute, so it's worth the cost to stay on-site. (Another reason to book on-site in summer: In the Florida heat it's nearly a medical necessity to keep young kids out of the sun in midafternoon. A nearby hotel room makes that easier.) Likewise, if your visit will be for less than three days, you can't afford to waste much time commuting, so staying on-site is worth considering.

If you're going at one of the busier times of the year, note that guests at Disney hotels are guaranteed admission to the parks, even on the days when they are so swamped with people that they're closed to day guests. On-site guests also have access to "Surprise Mornings," a special perk that allows them to enter the major theme parks an hour ahead of everyone else—a huge advantage on extra-busy days.

2. *What are the ages of your kids?*

If your kids are still young enough to take naps, staying on-site makes it much easier to return to your room after lunch for a snooze. If they're preteens who are up to a full day in the parks, commuting time is less of a factor.

3. *Are you flying or driving?*

If you're flying and doing only Disney, it may make more economic sense to stay on-site. The WDW transportation system is so efficient that you can manage without a rental car. But if you're driving to Orlando, consider an off-site location. You'll be able to drive into the parks at the hours that suit you without being dependent on those sometimes-less-than-prompt off-site buses.

4. *How strapped are you for cash?*

If money isn't a major issue, stay on-site.

If money is a primary consideration, you'll find your best deals at the budget hotels along I-4. Exits 25 and 27, which flank the Disney exit, are chock-full of chain hotels and restaurants. Exit 27 alone has three Days Inns within two blocks of each other.

5. *How much do your kids eat?*

Food is expensive at WDW, both in the parks and at the on-site hotels. If you're staying off-site you can always eat at the numerous fast-food and family-style restaurants along I-4, 192, and International Drive. If you book a suite, fixing simple meals in your room is even cheaper, and kids can really load up at those complimentary buffet breakfasts so frequently offered at the off-site hotels.

6. *Do you plan to visit other attractions?*

If you'll be spending half your time at Sea World, Universal Studios, or the other non-WDW attractions, stay off-site. There's no need to pay top dollar for proximity to Disney if you're headed for the Kennedy Space Center.

7. *Will there ever be times when your party will be splitting up?*

Does Dad want to play golf in the afternoon? Do you have teenagers who can head for Typhoon Lagoon on their own? Will there be times when it would make sense for Dad to take the younger kids back to the hotel while Mom stays in the park with the older ones? Is your 5-year-old raring to go at dawn while your 15-year-old sleeps until noon? If so, stay on-site where the use of the WDW transportation system makes it easy for you to all go your own way.

8. *What's your hassle quotient?*

If you simply don't want to be bothered with interstate commutes, parking lots, carrying cash, and maps . . . stay on-site. Let someone else be responsible for getting you around. On-site guests can charge nearly everything to their rooms, including meals and purchases inside the theme parks. For further details on on-site perks see "The Advantages of Staying On-Site" in Section 2.

THINGS TO ASK WHEN BOOKING AN OFF-SITE HOTEL

1. Does the hotel provide in-room baby-sitters? What are their qualifications? What's the cost? How far in advance should I reserve a sitter? Do you have on-site child care? (Several of the larger hotels have their own version of a kids' club, a drop-off child care center with planned activities for the youngsters. See "Off-Site Hotels: Good Choices for Families" in Section 2 for details.)

2. Do you provide bus service to the Magic Kingdom, Epcot, and MGM? The minor parks? How often? How early—and how late—do the buses run? Is there any charge? Are the buses express or do they stop and pick up riders at other hotels?

3. Do kids stay free? Up to what age?
   Note: This can be vitally important. On-site Disney hotels allow kids under 18 to lodge free with parents. The policy at off-site hotels varies.

4. Does the hotel provide a free buffet breakfast?

5. What fast-food or family-style restaurants are nearby?

6. Do you have any suites with kitchens?
   Note: No one would suggest you should spend a vacation cooking, but many Orlando hotels have villa-style lodgings and, obviously, if you can eat ce-

real and sandwiches in your room, you'll save significant bucks. Some hotels, like the Holiday Inn Sunspree, have mini-kitchens with small refrigerators and a microwave—all you need for simple meals. And the cost is no more than that of a regular room.

7. Does the hotel provide airport pickup?

8. Is there a laundromat on the premises?

9. Can I buy tickets to area attractions through the hotel's Guest Services desk? Are the tickets discounted? *Note:* Many Orlando hotels offer discounts to Universal Studios, Sea World, and area dinner shows. Not only do you save dollars, but you save the time you'd otherwise spend waiting in line.

10. Do you offer any sort of package? (Several of the larger hotels put together their own simple packages, including discounted theme park tickets. It never hurts to ask.)

SHOULD WE BUY A PACKAGE?

This is a toughie. There are advantages to package trips, most notably that they can save you a good deal of money. It's also helpful to know up front what your vacation will cost. Often packages require hefty prepayments, which are painful at the time, but at least you don't return home utterly maxed out on your Master-Card.

However, package trips can have drawbacks. You may find yourself paying for options you don't want and don't need. Packages are often padded with perks such as reduced greens fees, which are of interest to only a few families, or rental cars, which you may not need if you're

staying on-site. Be doubly wary of the very cheap packages offered in Sunday papers. If a deal sounds too good
to be true, it probably is.

Common Types of Packages

Disney's "Be Our Guest" Resort Package Vacations

Several families responding to the survey were sold on
Disney's own packages, such as the Grand Plan, which
houses guests in the swank Grand Floridian or the
almost-as-swank Yacht and Beach Clubs, and includes
all food, all tickets, unlimited golf, boating, and other
sporting facilities . . . as well as such extras as baby-sitting, stroller rental, tuition in one of the "Wonders of
Walt Disney World" programs, and a "Fantasia" alarm
clock. If you want the top of the line, trust me, this is the
top of the line.

Such luxury, needless to say, doesn't come cheap. A
family of four staying five days at the Grand Floridian on
the Grand Plan can expect to pay $3,700. Another draw-
back is that since all meals are included in the plan, you
may find yourself gorging as a cruise ship mentality
takes over: "We gotta eat it—it's free." But families who
want to sample a wide variety of Epcot cuisine, who have
kids who'd love to rent those $11-a-half-hour sailboats for
a whole afternoon, or who want child care every night,
may decide that it's worth it.

If all this sounds a bit too much, Disney also offers a
variety of less expensive packages such as Festival
Magic, which lodges families at one of the on-site budget
hotels (Dixie Landings, Port Orleans, or Caribbean
Beach Resort) and includes tickets. Five days for a family of four would be about $1,100. Call (407) W-DISNEY

for details on the "Be Our Guest" packages and all on-site hotel reservations.

Magic Kingdom Club Gold Card Packages

Those who hold a Magic Kingdom Club Gold Card have a wide variety of packages developed solely for them, ranging once again from the all-inclusive to the more affordably priced. The difference is that the Magic Kingdom Gold Card packages are 10 to 20% cheaper than comparable "Be Our Guest" packages, so if you're seriously considering booking a package, get thee posthaste to a telephone and dial 1-800-248-2665. Paying the $49 for the two-year club membership would be smart, especially if you're traveling during the off-season when the deepest discounts are in effect. *Note:* Once you purchase your Gold Card, you're in the Magic Kingdom Club automatically; Disney uses the terms "cardholder" and "club member" interchangeably, so it's a bit confusing.

The advantages of having the Magic Kingdom Gold Card are not limited to special packages, and, as is further explained in the next chapter, discounts of 10 to 30% on on-site hotel rooms are available to members year-round, even if they're not booking a package. Disney cruises are also cheaper. You'll get the brochures and benefits package automatically by joining. Club members book rooms and packages through their own number, so call (407) 824-2600 when you've made up your mind.

Delta Dream Vacations

If you're flying, check out the Delta packages, which include airfare, theme park tickets for both Disney and other Orlando attractions, car rental, and lodging at either on-site or off-site hotels. Again, there's a huge range of amenities—you can have valet parking, character breakfasts, and use of a camcorder if you're willing to pay for them. And again, the packages can be fine-tuned to meet your needs. If you'll be flying to Orlando, call 1-800-872-7786 and request a brochure. The package prices don't fluctuate as rapidly as airfare prices, and if you're traveling during a time when airfare rates are climbing you may get a good deal.

Cruise Packages

As of this writing, the Walt Disney Co. is making changes in its family cruise program, but under the new system there will still be some variation of the very popular cruise and Disney week. Families may opt to spend three or four nights at sea, and the remainder of the week in Orlando. Park admissions are included in the packages, as is airfare, a rental car, and your meals while on board ship. Also on board you'll find a staggeringly full program for children, including dawn-to-dusk kids' clubs, toddler pools, special menus, parties and mixers geared toward teens and preteens, and the Disney characters. Youth counselors squire the kids around, giving worn-out parents the chance to collapse on deck chairs or wander into the casinos and dance clubs if they find the strength.

You can book the cruises through your travel agent; or, if you have a Gold Card, dial (407) 824-2600.

Travel Agents

Once upon a time, Disney paid no commission to travel agents for booking guests into Disney-owned hotels. Ergo, travel agents would try to talk clients out of staying on-site. With the opening of seven new hotels in five years, however, Disney suddenly has a lot more rooms and more vacancies, so policy has changed. Disney now pays an agent's commission, and agents are much more likely to recommend packages which include on-site lodging.

Agents are also aware of other Orlando hotels that offer packages and are a good source of comparative rate-shopping for families who want to stay off-site. Large travel agencies sometimes put together their own packages, including airfare, lodging at an off-site hotel, and a rental car. If you need all three of these components, you'll probably come out cheaper buying a package through your local agent than trying to book all three separately.

Cheapie Deals

These are frequently seen in the travel sections of major newspapers and offer extremely low rates. Proceed with caution, however. The hotels are sometimes as far as 30 miles away from the Disney gates. (With a rental car and an alarm clock even this obstacle can be overcome—but you should know what you're up against.) Other pitfalls include tickets that can only be used at certain times of the year or extremely inflexible touring arrangements that require you to ride from attraction to attraction in slow-moving, overloaded buses.

Another consideration is that the hotels featured may not be in a very desirable area of town. Orlando has not suffered the degree of tourist-targeted crime that we've read about in other Florida cities, but unless either you or your travel agent are familiar with the area where the hotel is located, be wary. A family trying to save money would probably be better off driving and camping at Fort Wilderness or trying the All-Star Resorts than signing up for one of these packages.

THE ULTIMATE COST-SAVING TIP: ORDER A MAGIC KINGDOM CLUB GOLD CARD

If your family is really dizzy for Disney, it makes economic sense to order a Magic Kingdom Club Gold Card. Cardholders receive a variety of benefits, most notably discounts of up to $8 on theme park tickets and discounts of up to 30% on Disney-owned hotels. You can order a Magic Kingdom Club Gold Card by dialing 1-800-248-2665. The cost of a two-year membership is $49, or $39 for Disney stockholders.

The biggest perk, of course, is the substantial discounts on rooms in Disney-owned hotels. The deepest discounts coincide with the least crowded times of the year, so membership in the Club is doubly attractive to families with young kids. Although the weeks in which the discounts apply vary somewhat from year to year, the 1994 schedule is typical:

30% discount off the regular rates from mid-August to mid-December and from January 2 to mid-February at the following resorts:

- Disney's Yacht and Beach Clubs
- The Contemporary
- The Polynesian
- The Village Resort Villas
- Wilderness Lodge
- Fort Wilderness Trailer Homes and Campgrounds
- The Vacation Club

From mid-April to mid-June, club members receive an additional 10% off the already discounted Value Season rates at the resorts listed above, a combined discount of nearly 20%.

If your touring plans call for a summer, Easter, or Christmas trip to WDW, you still get a flat 10% discount on the listed resorts.

Club members get a 10% discount year round at the Disney Swan, Disney Dolphin, and the hotels of the Disney Village Hotel Plaza.

Club members also get a 15% discount on the Disneyland Hotel in California.

But like the Fairy Godmother told Cinderella, there's one catch: If you are planning to visit either WDW or Disneyland next year, you should order your card as soon as possible, since you must have it in hand when you make your reservation.

Magic Kingdom Club members receive other benefits: discounts of 30% on National car rentals; 10% discounts on Delta airfares to Orlando or Los Angeles; price breaks on the use of sporting facilities, most notably the greens fees at WDW courses; and 10% savings on WDW dinner shows. Cardholders have their own travel agency that offers special packages to WDW, Disneyland, and Euro-Disney and discounts on all Royal Caribbean and Norwegian Cruise Line cruises.

Other perks include a two-year subscription to *Disney Magazine,* the most timely source of information on upcoming films and theme park attractions, and membership in *Travel America at Half-Price,* which entitles you to 50% savings at hundreds of hotels. (*Note:* Hotels in the Anaheim and Orlando area are "blacked out" to cardholders, but *Travel America* can really come in handy when you're off to see Grandma in Omaha.) Cardholders also receive 10% discounts on merchandise at Disney stores nationwide and merchandise advertised in the Disney catalog.

Get more information on the Magic Kingdom Club by writing:

Magic Kingdom Club
P.O. Box 10160
Lake Buena Vista, FL 32830-0160

Or call: (407) 824-2600.

Note: If you're really lucky, you can receive most of the goodies listed above without having to pay the $49 to order the card. Many corporations hold Magic Kingdom Club Gold Cards, which qualify their employees for the discounts listed above. Check with your personnel or employee benefits department to see if your company is a member.

WHAT KIND OF TICKET DO WE NEED?

This decision, believe it or not, needs to be made long before you get to the theme park gates. There are several options, varying widely in cost, and some hotels offer their own version of a hybrid multiday pass, further complicating the decision.

Four-Day Super Pass (admitting holder to the three major parks)
Adult: $142 plus tax   Child (3–9): $113 plus tax

Five-Day Super Duper Pass (admitting holders to the three major parks, as well as the four minor ones)
Adult: $190 plus tax   Child (3–9): $151 plus tax

One-Day Ticket (admitting holder to one park only)
Adult: $38 plus tax   Child (3–9): $31 plus tax

Children under 3 are admitted free.

Note: Holders of the five-day pass have unlimited access to Typhoon Lagoon, Discovery Island, Pleasure Island, and River Country for seven straight days after the first date they use the ticket. Considering that a one-day ticket to Typhoon Lagoon is $22 for adults and $18 for kids, the Five-Day Super Duper Pass is clearly your best buy if you're visiting in the summer and want to hit the water parks several times during the week. Not interested in swishing around the water parks or dancing at Pleasure Island? The four-day pass will suffice.

It's also worth noting that the four- and five-day tickets do not have to be used on consecutive days and, in fact, never expire. If you come back in two years you can still use the unused days on your multiday ticket, although your access to the minor parks will have expired.

Guests at the on-site hotels have another option: the Be Our Guest Pass, which is good for a stay of any length from one day to ten days. The pass offers unlimited access to both the major and minor parks during the time you're staying at a Disney hotel and is slightly cheaper than the Super Duper Pass. More significantly, the Be Our Guest Pass means that guests staying at a Disney hotel have the park-hopping benefits of the Super Duper Pass even if they're only going to be around for a long weekend. Prices obviously are linked to how long you're staying, but to give you some idea, a five-day Be Our Guest Pass is $186 for an adult and $148 for a child.

True Disneyophiles might want to opt for the annual passports at a price of $216 for adults, $188 for kids. These cost scarcely more than the five-day ticket. The minor parks also offer annual passports: the $84 Typhoon Lagoon pass is popular with locals.

One final word of caution: the Guest Services desk at off-site hotels may not be run by your hotel at all, but by a separate company that exists solely to sell tickets and bus fares to tourists. Many off-site hotels offer their own multiday ticket, which they hawk aggressively, usually by telling you that it is much cheaper than the Disney ticket. It isn't. If you are offered a four-day ticket with access to River Country, Discovery Island, and Pleasure Island, this is a good buy *only* if you're sure you'll never use that extra day provided on the five-day pass and you don't plan to visit Typhoon Lagoon.

Also be wary of buying bus rides into the parks. Many hotels offer free shuttle service, so if you've chosen your hotel carefully there's no reason you should have to pay for transportation. The agents at the desk may tell you that you'll save the "horrendous" cost of Disney parking by taking their shuttle, but the truth is that it costs $5 to park, and the bus tickets run anywhere from $3 to $7 a person. Also, the shuttles offered by these independent services generally stop at several hotels, making your commute time much longer than if you stayed at a hotel offering a direct shuttle or drove your own car. Don't pay for this abuse.

ADVANCE RESERVATIONS AND TICKET PURCHASES: CALL NOW, AVOID LINES LATER

1. Get maps of the theme parks and general touring information by writing:

> WDW Information
> P.O. Box 10040
> Lake Buena Vista, FL 32830-0040

2. Tickets to the theme parks can be purchased by calling (407) 824-4321. MasterCard, Visa, and American

Express are all accepted, and the tickets will be mailed to you. If you'd prefer to pay by check, call first to confirm prices, then mail payment to:

WDW Tickets
P.O. Box 10030
Lake Buena Vista, FL 32830-0030

Many area hotels, including all Disney hotels, allow guests to purchase theme park tickets through Guest Services. Inquire when you make reservations.

Theme park ticket prices have spiraled in the last two years, changing about every six months. *Always* call to confirm prices. Once you purchase tickets, however, the price is fixed, so buy in advance when you can. If you live near one of the Disney stores you can buy theme park tickets there.

2. **Room reservations for on-site hotels should be made at least two months in advance.** Dial (407) W-DISNEY for information on all Disney-owned hotels. The line is open seven days a week from 8 A.M. to 10 P.M., but you'll have better luck getting through on evenings and weekends.

Room reservations for off-site hotels can usually be made later, perhaps a few weeks before you plan to arrive. Only the wildly optimistic should arrive in Orlando with no reservations at all.

Booking mistakes are rare, but it never hurts to call and confirm room reservations before you leave home.

3. **Disney dinner show reservations should also be made from home.** Reservations are accepted up to 30 days in advance, or upon receipt of confirmed reservations for those staying in the on-site hotels. Since on-site guests get first crack at reservations, off-site guests may find themselves shut out of the most popular shows and

restaurants. If you're going during a busy time of the year and want to see the Hoop-Dee-Doo Revue, be sure to call 30 days in advance.

To reserve seats for the Polynesian Revue or Mickey's Tropical Revue at the Polynesian, or the Hoop-Dee-Doo Revue at Fort Wilderness, call (407) W-DISNEY. Magic Kingdom Club members receive a 10% discount at the Polynesian Revue, and can make their reservations by calling (407) 824-2600.

4. Two of the character breakfasts also accept reservations up to 30 days in advance or upon receipt of a confirmed reservation at an on-site hotel. To reserve seats for Breakfast à la Disney on the *Empress Lilly* riverboat at the Disney Village Marketplace, call (407) 934-7639. If you'd rather try Minnie's Menehune at the Polynesian, dial (407) 824-1391. The other character breakfasts are buffets and in general accept no reservations, although during the very busiest times—such as the week between Christmas and New Year's—policy may change and reservations will be accepted three days in advance. If you're visiting during a holiday, check with Guest Services at your hotel the minute you arrive to see if you can book a seating time and save yourself a bit of hassle.

The character breakfasts should be scheduled for the last day of your visit. The children will have had time to get used to the characters, who are large and a bit overwhelming at first. In addition, you won't be rushing to get to the theme parks, and the breakfasts are a nice send-off for the trip home. The breakfasts cost about $10–$12 for an adult and $6–$9 for a child. The Sunday brunches are more elaborate and more expensive. For more information on locations and times see "Disney Extras" in Section 8.

5. If you're staying at one of the Disney hotels, dinner reservations for restaurants within the theme parks can be made up to three days in advance either by phone or through Guest Services in your hotel. If you're not staying on-site, you'll need to make reservations on the day you plan to visit, either in person at the MGM and MK restaurants or at the WorldKey Information System under Spaceship Earth at Epcot.

6. Call 1-900-89MAGIC a few weeks before you leave home to request a Magic discount card and general information about Orlando hotels. The Magic card is free—the call is $3—and entitles holders to discounts on area hotels, restaurants, and attractions. If you're staying off-site and planning to spend some time at non-WDW attractions, the card is definitely worthwhile.

If you are a member of the Entertainment Club, you may be surprised to learn that some spiffy area hotels, such as the Hotel Royal Plaza, Marriott Orlando, and Delta Orlando offer 50% discounts to cardholders, making an upscale resort as inexpensive as an interstate cheapie. But reservations must be made in advance to get the discounts. (Becoming a member of the Entertainment Club is as simple as buying one of the discount coupon books in your hometown. The books generally cost between $35–$50 and are best known for their restaurant coupons. Few people seem to realize that a nationwide directory of hotels offering 50% discounts can be found in the back of the books.)

If you're just not the kind of person who makes calls and buys coupon books before you leave home, a last-minute savings alternative is to drop by the Official Visitor Information Center at the Mercado Mediterranean Shopping Village on International Drive. The kind people there can help you with reservations and book hotel rooms. The Center also offers a wide variety of discounted tickets for family-style dinner shows, water parks, and theme parks, and gives you handfuls of printed material on the umpteen area attractions. The freebie visitor magazines you can pick up in restaurants also have pages of discount coupons.

THINGS TO DISCUSS WITH YOUR KIDS BEFORE YOU LEAVE HOME

1. *The trip itself*

There are two schools of thought on just how far in advance of the trip you should let the kids in on the plan. Since many families make reservations six months in advance or more, it's easy to fall into a "waiting for Christmas" syndrome, with the kids nearly in a lather of anticipation weeks before you leave. In order to avoid the agony of a long countdown, one couple packed in secret, then woke the children up at 5 A.M. one morning and announced "Get in the car, we're going to Disney World." Probably the best method is somewhere between the two extremes. Tell the kids at the time you make your reservations, but don't begin pouring over the brochures in earnest until about two weeks before the trip.

2. *Height requirements*

Get out your yardstick. If your kids fall under the height requirement for riding Space Mountain and Splash Mountain (44 inches) or Big Thunder Mountain Railroad (40 inches), you should break it to them now. Disney vigilantly enforces these requirements, and there is nothing worse than waiting in line for an hour only to have little Nathan unceremoniously ejected just as you approach the ride.

3. *The layout of the parks*

Kids 7 or over should have some idea of the layout of the major parks, and if you're letting preteens and teens roam about on their own they definitely should be briefed on the location of major attractions.

Among the more than 200 families surveyed or interviewed for this book, there was a direct correlation between the amount of advance research they had done and how much they enjoyed the trip. Visitors who showed up at WDW without any preparation still had fun, but their comment sheets were sprinkled with "Next time I'll know . . ." and "If only we had . . ."

The pleasures of being prepared extend to preschoolers. If you purchase a few WDW coloring books to enjoy on the trip down to Orlando or watch one of the Disney Channel specials featuring the park, even the youngest child will arrive able to identify the Swiss Family Robinson Treehouse and Living Seas pavilion. A little knowledge prior to entering the gates helps you decide how best to spend your time and eliminates those "Whadda-we-do-now" debates.

4. *The classic stories of Disney*

If your children are under 7, another good pre-trip purchase is a set of Disney paperbacks with audiotapes. Even though parental eyes may glaze over when "Dumbo" rewinds for its 34th straight hearing, these tapes and books help to pass the time and familiarize kids with the characters and rides they'll be seeing once they arrive. (If you find kiddie tapes too annoying you can always bring along a Walkman for the children to use.) Some families rent Disney movies just before the trip as well; the videotape "Disneyland Fun" is especially good for getting the whole family revved up and in the mood. The park featured is Disneyland in California and not the Magic Kingdom in Florida, but the attractions are similar enough to make the tape an exciting preview.

The Disneyland Game is also a fun way to orient kids age 2–10 to the general layout of the theme parks. Players are required to move about the board gathering cards from different attractions, and the goal of the game—to visit as many rides as possible before the park closes—is considerably like that of the real-life game you'll play when you hit Orlando.

5. *Special academic projects*
See "Should We Take the Kids Out of School?" earlier in this section for ideas on special projects.

6. *Souvenirs and money*
Will you save all souvenir purchases for the last day? Buy one small souvenir every day? Are the children expected to spend their own money, or will Mom and Dad spring for the T-shirts? Whatever you decide will depend on your pocketbooks and your particular interpretation of fiscal responsibility, but do set your rules before you're in the park. Otherwise the selection of goodies will lure you into spending far more than you anticipated.

One excellent technique for limiting impulse buys is to request Disney Dollars at the time you order your theme park tickets. Disney Dollars come in denominations of $1 (Mickey), $5 (Goofy), and $10 (Minnie) and are accepted throughout the theme parks, shops, restaurants, and resorts of WDW. Some wily parents have managed to convince their tots that these bills are the only currency accepted and have given them a certain number of Disney Dollars before leaving home, explaining that this money and this money alone is for souvenirs.

Purchase Disney Dollars by writing to:

Walt Disney World Ticket Mail Order
P.O. Box 10030
Lake Buena Vista, Florida 32830-0030

DON'T LEAVE HOME WITHOUT ...

1. Comfortable shoes. This is no time to be breaking in new Reeboks.

2. Minimal clothing. Many hotels have laundromats, and you can always use Woolite to wash out underwear in your sink. Most families make the mistake of over-packing, not figuring in all the souvenirs they'll be bringing back. Disney T-shirts are not only great for touring but can serve as swimsuit cover-ups and pajamas. And, unless you're planning a special evening out on the *Empress Lilly* or at Victoria and Albert's, casual clothing is accepted everywhere.

3. Lightweight jackets, preferably water-resistant.

4. Disposable diapers, film, blank VCR tapes, baby formula. All these are available within WDW, but at premium prices.

5. Sunscreen. Keep a tube with you and reapply it often. Sunburn is the number one complaint at the First Aid Clinic in the MK. *Note:* You need sunburn protection all through the year in Orlando, not just during the summer.

6. Juiceboxes. Not only are they handy in the car for the trip down, but you might want to keep a couple in your diaper bag while touring. There are few places in the parks where you can grab a healthy drink fast, and kids can become dehydrated rapidly.

7. A waist pouch or fanny pack. It's a good alternative to dragging along a purse while touring and frees up your hands for boarding rides, pushing strollers, and holding on to your kids.

8. Sunglasses. The Florida sun is so blindingly bright that more than once I've reached into my purse for my sunglasses only to realize I already had them on. Kids too young for sunglasses need wide-billed caps to cut down on the glare.

9. Strollers. Earlier versions of this guide suggested renting strollers at the theme parks, because they're rather a hassle on the monorails and boats. But since Disney has raised its stroller rental fee to an unconscionable $6 a day, you're better off bringing a stroller from home. If you're staying at one of the more sprawling resorts, such as the Caribbean Beach Resort, Dixie Landings, or the Fort Wilderness Campground, you'll need your own stroller just to get around your hotel.

10. A credit card. It's no joke. The Sun Bank, with locations throughout WDW, gives cash advances on most major cards, which can be a lifesaver.

HELPFUL PHONE NUMBERS

All Orlando numbers have a (407) area code.

General WDW information	824-4321
General accommodation information	W-DISNEY
Magic Kingdom Club information	824-2600
Dinner show and character breakfast reservations	W-DISNEY

Typhoon Lagoon	560-4141
Pleasure Island	934-7781
River Country	824-2760
Discovery Island	824-2760
Disney Village Marketplace	825-3058
Fort Wilderness	824-2900
Contemporary Resort	824-1000
Polynesian Resort	824-2000
Grand Floridian Resort	824-3000
Wilderness Lodge	824-3200
All-Star Sports Resort	939-5000
All-Star Music Resort	939-6000
Dolphin	939-4000
Swan	939-3000
Yacht Club	934-7000
Beach Club	934-8000
Port Orleans	934-5000
Caribbean Beach Resort	934-3400
Dixie Landings	934-6000
Disney Vacation Club	827-7000
Disney Villas	827-1100

2

★★★★★★★★★★★★★★★★★★★★

*Choosing
a Hotel*

THE ADVANTAGES OF STAYING ON-SITE

Surprise Mornings

Under the new "surprise morning" program, Disney allows on-site guests into one designated theme park a day a full hour earlier than day guests. When you check into your hotel you will be given a brochure on this perk that will read something like "Epcot—Tuesday, MGM—Wednesday, Magic Kingdom—Thursday," etc. You should plan your touring schedule around the surprise mornings. Since visitors are almost always admitted to the theme parks 30 minutes before the stated opening time, this program means that on-site guests may be within the Magic Kingdom as early as 7:30 on mornings when the official opening time is 9 A.M.

Generally only part of the park is opened during the first hour. For example, in the Magic Kingdom it might be Fantasyland and Tomorrowland, which means you can ride Space Mountain and the other attractions in these two sections with minimal waits. Then, when the ropes drop allowing you into the other sections at the official opening time, you're already deep within the park. You can dash straight for Splash Mountain or any other attractions that will be crowded later in the day, beating the surge of people who are still coming down Main Street.

At MGM the shows don't begin until the stated opening time, but the continuous-loading attractions are operative—including the Great Movie Ride, the Tower of Terror, and Star Tours—so you can ride them and still be in line for the first showing of *Voyage of the Little Mermaid* far ahead of the day guests.

Be Our Guest Passports

These tickets, which can be tailored to fit the length of your stay, offer you unlimited access to the major and minor parks and are slightly cheaper than comparable multiday passports.

Restaurant Reservations

On-site guests can dial for reservations at the sit-down restaurants both within the theme parks and at the other on-site hotels up to three days in advance from their hotel rooms. You should make all desired reservations for the first three days of your stay on the night you check in, thus ensuring you can eat where you want when you want, and eliminating standing in line. *Note:* Since there are so many on-site guests, this perk has the effect of freezing off-site visitors out of the most popular restaurants at the most popular times.

Transportation

On-site guests have unlimited use of the monorails, buses, and boats of the WDW transportation system, which is so efficient that it is your best bet for getting to the major parks. You may save a few minutes driving your own car if you're headed toward the minor parks or another on-site hotel, since such a journey may involve a bus switch at the TTC, but on-site guests generally conclude that it's less of a hassle to leave the driving to Disney.

Use of Other On-Site Hotel Facilities

If you want to use the child care or sporting facilities of other Disney hotels, or dine at their restaurants, you'll receive preferential treatment over off-site guests. (Although each hotel, reasonably enough, allows its own guests first shot at its services.) This means that even if you're staying at the budget Dixie Landings, you can leave your kids at the Neverland Club at the Polynesian or take a tennis lesson at the Grand Floridian.

Access to Parks

The parks are never closed to on-site guests, although when they are filled to capacity they may close the gates to day guests. This is only a factor if you're visiting during the week between Christmas and New Year's, Easter week, or in the middle of summer, when Typhoon Lagoon and the Magic Kingdom may reach capacity as early as 10 A.M.

Charging Privileges

If you're staying on-site everyone in your party will be issued a resort ID the day you arrive. The ID entitles you to full use of the WDW transportation system and also allows you to charge all food at your resort—even fast food and drinks by the pool—as well as food at the sit-down restaurants in the theme parks, purchases in the shops, tickets, sporting equipment, and child care. It's certainly easier not to have to carry huge amounts of cash all the time, especially at the pools and marinas.

It's up to you whether or not your older kids have charging privileges. It makes it easier to send Johnny up to the snack bar for a round of Cokes, but if you do opt to give the minors charging privileges be sure to impress upon them that these IDs work like credit cards—and are not an open invitation for the kids to ingratiate themselves with other kids in the arcade by ordering pizza for everyone, purchasing all seven dwarfs from the hotel gift shop, or, heaven forbid, obtaining cash advances. If an ID with charging privileges is lost it should be reported to the front desk immediately to avoid unauthorized charges.

RATING THE ON-SITE DISNEY HOTELS

Not content with merely dominating the entertainment market, the Walt Disney Company has begun turning its attention to lodging the ten million visitors who stream into Orlando each year. Orlando has 100,000 hotel rooms, more than any other U.S. city, and an increasing percentage of these rooms are Disney-owned— that is, on-site.

The majority of the new hotels added by Disney fall into the budget category. In the past five years, Port Orleans and Dixie Landings have joined the mammoth Caribbean Beach Resort to bring the total of rooms in the $89–$109 price category to well over 5,000. The All-Star Sports and All-Star Music resorts will be opening in sections over the next five years; upon completion Disney will have another 5,000 budget rooms, these in the $69–$79 category. Up until now cost has been the primary reason that visitors opt to stay off-site; with the advent of the on-site budget resorts, Disney is working to eliminate even that objection. Each time Disney opens a new resort your options increase.

So do your decisions. All this expansion means that even if your family has decided to stay on-site, you still face a bewildering number of choices. Does the convenience of being on the monorail line justify the increase in price? Do you want to stay amid turn-of-the-century Victorian splendor or is a fort more your style? Is it important to be near the swimming facilities, golf courses, stables, and other sporting activities, or do you plan to spend most of your time in the parks? Do you need on-site baby-sitting? As in all of WDW, making the best choice hinges upon your awareness of what your particular family really needs.

Magic Kingdom Hotels

The Grand Floridian

Modeled after the famed Florida beach resorts of the 1800s, and possibly the prettiest of all Disney hotels, the Grand Floridian has 900 rooms encased amongst its gabled roofs, soaring ceilings, and broad white verandas.

Proximity to MK: Excellent, via direct monorail or launch.

Proximity to Epcot: Good, via monorail with a change at the TTC.

Proximity to MGM: Fair, via bus.

Pluses:

1. Convenient location on the monorail line.
2. A private beach on the Seven Seas Lagoon and numerous water sports.
3. Excellent dining choices, including 1900 Park Fare, which serves a dinner buffet with the characters.
4. On-site child care center.
5. On-site health club.
6. Exceptionally pretty rooms. The Grand Floridian is a favorite with honeymooners and others seeking a romantic ambiance.

Minuses:

1. Extremely pricey, with rooms about $235–$435 a night. Magic Kingdom Club Cardholder and other

discounts rarely apply, and only the most expensive packages include the Grand Floridian.

2. The elegance puts off some families who feel funny trooping past a grand piano in dripping bathing suits.

Overall Grade: B. Expensive but luxurious.

The Contemporary Resort

You'll either love or hate the Contemporary, which has 1,050 rooms surrounding a mammoth high-tech lobby full of shops and restaurants. This place is always hopping.

Proximity to MK: Excellent, via direct monorail.

Proximity to Epcot: Good, via monorail with a change at the TTC.

Proximity to MGM: Fair, via bus.

Pluses:

1. Located on the monorail line.
2. Fairly easy to book, and discounts are available.
3. Disney movies are shown nightly. The Contemporary is also home to the Fiesta Fun Center, a giant arcade.
4. The standard water sports are available, along with tennis and a spa.
5. The Contemporary Cafe is one of the best restaurants in all of WDW for families, offering diners a chance to visit with the characters while enjoying an all-you-can-eat buffet.

Minuses:

1. It's loud, with a big-city feel that is exactly what many families come to Florida to escape. "Like sleeping in the middle of Space Mountain," wrote

one mother. *Note:* The Garden wings are both quieter and cheaper than the main building.

2. Like the other hotels on the monorail line, the Contemporary is expensive. Expect around $195–$270 a night, unless discounts apply.

Overall Grade: B. Convenient and lively. Perhaps a little too lively.

The Polynesian Resort

Designed to emulate an island village, the Polynesian is relaxed and casual. The main desk as well as most of the restaurants and shops are in the Great Ceremonial House amidst orchids, parrots, and fountains. Guests stay in one of the 863 rooms in the sprawling "long houses." The Polynesian enjoys a loyal repeat business, with many of the families surveyed raving about the laid-back ambiance and pretty lagoon views.

Proximity to MK: Excellent, via direct monorail, launch, or ferryboat.

Proximity to Epcot: Good, via monorail with one change at the TTC.

Proximity to MGM: Fair, via bus.

Pluses:

1. The Poly offers the most options for transport. You're on the monorail line but are also within walking distance of the ferryboats. Launches leave from the docks regularly, as do buses from the Great Ceremonial House. Your best route to the MK depends on the location of your room. Near the lagoon? Take the launch. Near the Great Ceremonial House? The monorail is faster. On the beach? Walk to the ferryboat.

2. Private beach with an especially attractive pool and numerous water sports available. Like the beach at

the Grand Floridian, the Polynesian has canvas shells which provide shade for napping babies and toddlers digging in the sand.

3. On-site child care.

4. Numerous discounts apply in the off-season, including cardholder discounts.

Minuses:

1. Without a discount, expect to pay $185–$275 a night.

Overall Grade: A. An outstanding resort, and your best choice if you're willing to pay the bucks required to be on the monorail line.

Wilderness Lodge

Disney opened the Wilderness Lodge beside the Contemporary in 1994. The rustic-looking western-spirited resort is aimed at filling the gap between the budget and expensive hotels.

As is typical with the newer resorts, the theme of Wilderness Lodge is extended into every aspect of the hotel's design—the pool begins as a hot spring in the lobby, flows into a meandering creek, and culminates in a waterfall that spills into the rocky caverns of the outdoor pool. The totem poles and stone fireplaces, the geysers in the spa area, the quilted bedspreads and Indian wallpaper of the guest rooms, and even the cowboy menus in the Whispering Canyon Cafe all combine to evoke the feel of the National Park Service lodges built a hundred years ago.

Proximity to the MK: Good, via launch.

Proximity to Epcot: Fair, via bus.

Proximity to MGM: Fair, via bus.

Pluses:

1. The lodge is brand new, and looks it. The pool area is especially dramatic.

2. You have close access to River Country and all the down-home fun of Fort Wilderness without having to camp. For those who just like to appear to be roughing it, Wilderness Lodge is perfect—you can jump into the spa right after your trail ride.

3. On-site child care.

4. Wilderness Lodge is small for a Disney resort—760 rooms, in contrast to the budget hotels that have as many as 2,000—which gives it a more intimate feel and makes it easier to get around.

Minuses:

1. At $150–$190 a night, it's still not cheap.

2. This is the only Magic Kingdom resort without monorail access to the MK. The boat takes slightly longer.

3. The rooms sleep four people, while the other full-priced resorts sleep five.

Overall Grade: B+.

On-Site Budget Hotels

"Budget" is somewhat of a misnomer, because both the price and the quality are higher than a typical chain hotel in Orlando. For paying about $30 more a night than a comparable off-site hotel, you get a mood that's pure Disney. As you sip a drink by the pool bar and watch your kids zoom down the tongue of the beloved sea serpent slide at the Port Orleans pool, you certainly won't feel like you're slumming. The hotels are well maintained and beautifully landscaped, with gobs of atmosphere thrown in to carry their motifs to the nth degree.

Port Orleans and Dixie Landings

These penny-new budget hotels are both based on an Old South theme and offer unbeatable amenities and ambiance for the price. Port Orleans transports guests to the heart of the French Quarter, with lawn croquet amid manicured gardens, wrought-iron railings, and street names such as Rue d'Baga. The Mardi Gras mood extends to the pool area, dubbed the "Doubloon Lagoon," where alligators play jazz while King Triton sits atop the water slide regally surveying his domain.

Dixie Landings is a bit more down-home, with a steamboat-shaped lobby, general stores run by gingham-clad girls in braids, and "Ol' Man Island"—a swimming area based on the Disney film *Song of the South*. A bit schizophrenic in architecture, with white-columned buildings encircling fishin' holes and cotton mills, Dixie Landings manages to mix in a variety of Southern clichés without losing its ditzy charm. If Huck Finn ever married Scarlett O'Hara, this is where they'd come on their honeymoon.

Comparatively speaking, Port Orleans is only half the size of Dixie Landings, which is the major reason why it gets our nod as the best. At Port Orleans the odds are you'll be close to the pool, lobby, food court, and shuttle bus station—at Dixie Landings getting around is more of a headache. Both resorts have a fast-food court, a sit-down restaurant, and a bar that offers live entertainment. The food court at Dixie Landings is more complete, but the sit-down restaurant at Port Orleans is quieter and more relaxing. If you're in a rush, the creole munchies in the Port Orleans bar and the Cajun snacks at the Dixie Landings bar make an adequate meal.

Proximity to MK, Epcot, and MGM: Fair, via bus.

Pluses:

1. Great water areas, which can easily keep the kids entertained for a full afternoon.

2. So cleverly designed and beautifully maintained that you won't believe you're paying as little as $95 a night.

3. Both hotels have marinas with the standard selection of watercraft.

4. The Sassagoula Steamboat offers both resorts easy water access to the Disney Village Marketplace and Pleasure Island.

5. More dining options than Disney's first budget hotel, the Caribbean Beach Resort.

Minuses:

1. Unless you drive your own car, you are dependent upon buses for transport to the major and minor parks, and this means a slightly longer commuting time.

2. No on-site child care.

Overall Grade: A+. You get a good deal here in more ways than one.

Fort Wilderness Trailer Homes and Campground

A resort unto itself, Fort Wilderness offers campsites for tents and RVs as well as air-conditioned trailers for rent. The wide-open spaces, perfect for volleyball, biking, and hiking, are a relief for families with children old enough to explore on their own.

Proximity to MK: Good, via bus or launch.

Proximity to Epcot: Fair, via bus or bus to the monorail line.

Proximity to MGM: Fair, via bus.

Pluses:

1. Fort Wilderness offers a huge variety of activities for kids, such as hay rides, horseback riding, bike trails, and a petting zoo with ponies, pigs, goats, and geese.

2. Proximity to River Country and Discovery Island.

3. You have access to the MK via a private launch. Shuttle buses run to Epcot, MGM, and the minor theme parks.

4. Proximity to the Hoop-Dee-Doo Musical Revue.

5. This is your least expensive on-site option, with hookups and tent sites as low as $5 a night. The trailers rent for about $185 a night but sleep six people and offer full kitchens. Groceries are available at the on-site trading posts.

6. Daily maid service is free in the rental trailers.

7. The *Fort Wilderness Gazette* keeps you up to date on campground amenities, special happenings, and your somewhat confusing transportation options.

Minuses:

1. Camping may not seem like a vacation to you.

2. A large number of people are sharing a relatively small space, and the beach, marina, and pools can get crowded.

3. The place is so spread out that it requires its own in-resort bus system just to get campers from area to area. You can also rent golf carts or bikes, but make no mistake: Fort Wilderness is large and hard to navigate.

Overall Grade: B. If you like to camp, and are willing to put up with a little inconvenience for great savings, this is a good option.

Caribbean Beach Resort

This family-priced 2,112-room resort is located on 200 acres with a private lake and white sand beaches. Each section of this mammoth hotel is painted a different tropical color and named after a different Caribbean island. Each "island" has its own shuttle bus stop, private beach, and pool. The rooms, although small, are attractively decorated.

Proximity to MK, Epcot, and MGM: Fair, via bus.

Pluses:

1. The price is right, at $89–$119 a night.

2. Parrot Cay, a man-made island with a playground, climbing fort, and small aviary is especially fun for young kids.

3. Water sports abound, and the Toobies—small, motorized bumper boats that can be rented at the marina for $10 per half-hour—are especially popular.

4. This is one of the best places in all of WDW to explore by bike. Bikes can be rented at the marina for $3 an hour or $7 a day, with specialty bikes like tandems costing a bit more. (If you're driving to Orlando and plan to bike a lot, it's definitely cost-effective to bring your own wheels.)

5. Inexpensive food can be found in the fast-food plaza called Old Port Royale. Geared toward kids, the plaza even offers a kid's breakfast of cereal, juice, and a prize.

Minuses:

1. The fast-food plaza is the only restaurant on the grounds and it is always swamped with people. For more elaborate fare or faster fast food, you'll have to leave the hotel. Why on earth didn't the hotel

planners put at least a burger-and-fries stand in each section?

2. Although the buses are regular, they're not as swift as the water-taxis or monorails. Expect a longer commuting time.

3. The place is huge. It may be a major hike from your hotel room to the food plaza or marina. If you have young kids, bring your own stroller.

4. No on-site child care.

Overall Grade: A. Lots of bang for the buck.

All-Star Sports and Music Resorts

Phase One of what will ultimately be a 5,000 room resort complex opened in 1994, providing Disney's cheapest rooms to date. We're talking as low as $69 a night here. All-Star Sports will contain ten buildings, devoted to five different sports—tennis, football, surfing, basketball, and baseball, with the decor themed appropriately. At the Music Resort, you'll ultimately have your choice between jazz, rock and roll, country, calypso, and Broadway tunes.

Proximity to MK, Epcot, and MGM: Fair, via bus.

Pluses:

1. In a word, cost.

2. Despite the low price, Disney is pumping in plenty of atmosphere—the pool in the surfing section of the sports resort will look like a beach, the one in the baseball section looks like a diamond. Over in the music section you can swim in a guitar or piano.

3. The shuttle buses are a good transportation option considering the price. When you get into this price

range at the off-site hotels, you often have to pay for a shuttle.

Minuses:

1. Food options are limited. Fast-food courts only, with no restaurants or indoor bars.
2. Sporting options are limited. Swimming is about it.
3. The rooms are very small. They sleep four but you'll be bunched.
4. Upon completion, these resorts will be enormous. It's hard to predict just what the final verdict will be; Disney is striving to eliminate that sleeping-in-the-middle-of-Penn-Station feel by breaking each resort into five separate sections. But there's no way around the fact that it takes more effort to get around a huge hotel than a small one.

Overall Grade: B.

Epcot Center Resorts

The Disney Swan and Disney Dolphin

This convention/resort complex is connected to Epcot and MGM by water-taxi and bridges. The Swan and Dolphin are "twin" hotels (like the nearby Yacht and Beach Clubs), meaning that although they have separate check-ins (and are in fact owned by separate companies) the resorts are alike in architecture and mood and share some facilities. Both the Swan and the Dolphin have an emphatically sophisticated feel, but since their openings both have also made great strides to become more family-oriented and offer amenities directed toward the parents of young children.

Proximity to MK: Fair, via bus.

Proximity to Epcot: Excellent, via water-taxi, tram, or a moderate walk.

Proximity to MGM: Excellent, via water-taxi.

Pluses:

1. Disney is aggressively going after the convention trade with the Swan and Dolphin. If a working parent is lucky, she can score a free family vacation here.

2. Transportation to MGM by water-taxi and Epcot by shuttle tram takes less than ten minutes from lobby to theme park gate, with a slightly longer shuttle ride to the MK. These hotels offer extremely easy access to Epcot, with a private entrance into the back of the World Showcase, allowing Dolphin and Swan guests to completely avoid arriving and departing crowds. (You even have your own stroller rental booth at the World Traveler Shop—and breakfast at the Boulangerie Patisserie in the nearby France pavilion is sublime.) If you like MGM and Epcot, it's hard to beat the location of these two.

3. Camp Swan and Camp Dolphin offer excellent on-site child care. Planned activities range from tennis programs to craft classes, are geared for kids as young as 3, and are reasonably priced.

4. The new, expanded beach area offers a playground, kiddie pools, water slides, and a small marina with paddleboats.

5. Bike rentals, tennis courts, and health clubs are also available. *Note:* The Body by Jake health club at the Dolphin is by far the most inclusive gym in the whole Walt Disney World complex.

Minuses:

1. Expensive, at $185–$315 a night.

2. Because of the proximity to Epcot and MGM and the fact that they're gunning for the convention

trade, these are adult-oriented resorts, with a citi-
fied atmosphere.

Overall Grade: B. A great place to go if the company is
picking up the tab. Otherwise, try the Yacht and Beach
Clubs first.

The Disney Yacht and Beach Clubs

Designed to resemble a turn-of-the-century Nantucket
seaside resort, the Yacht and Beach Clubs are situated
on a 25-acre freshwater lake. The Yacht Club, with 635
rooms, is the more elegant of the two, but the sunny
gingham-and-wicker-filled Beach Club, with 580 rooms,
is equally charming. The Yacht and Beach Clubs hit the
perfect balance for families with young kids in tow—
homey, lovely, and not one bit fancy.

Proximity to MK: Fair, via bus.

Proximity to Epcot: Excellent, via a short stroll over a
bridge.

Proximity to MGM: Excellent, via water-taxi.

Pluses:

1. Stormalong Bay, the water recreation area that sepa-
   rates the two resorts, is almost like being next door to
   a private water park. The bay contains pools of varying depths, water slides, and a wrecked ship for atmosphere. It's especially fun to climb the shipwreck
   nearly to the top of its rigging, then zoom through a
   long tube into the middle of the pool. In fact, the
   water areas at the Yacht and Beach Clubs are so nice
   you'll have no trouble convincing the kids to return
   "home" for a dip in lieu of a more time-consuming
   trek to Typhoon Lagoon or River Country.

2. Like the Dolphin and Swan, the Yacht and Beach
   Clubs are literally on the doorstep of the Epcot

World Showcase and an easy boat commute to
MGM as well.

3. The Sandcastle Club offers on-site child care for
   children 3–12. It's open from 4:30 P.M. until midnight at a cost of $4 an hour, with a $2-an-hour
   add-on for siblings.

4. Disney characters are on hand for breakfast at the
   Cape May Cafe in the Beach Club. Ariel's, named
   after the heroine of *The Little Mermaid* and featuring a huge aquarium, is also popular.

5. The two resorts share an on-site health club.

6. Bayside Marina offers paddleboats, pontoons, and
   toobies.

Minuses:

1. Rates run about $215–$335 a night, but cardholder
   discounts do apply in certain seasons.

Overall Grade: A+. A welcome addition to the Disney family. If your kids like water sports and you all like Epcot,
try the Yacht or Beach Resort on your next trip down.

Villa Style Accommodations

Disney Vacation Club Resort

Designed to be sold as time shares, the villas of the
brand-new Vacation Club are available for nightly
rentals. You'll get all the standard amenities of a Disney
resort—plus a lot more room.

Proximity to MK, Epcot, and MGM: Fair, via bus.

Pluses:

1. If you have more than two children and need to
   spread out, or if you'd like a kitchen where you can

prepare your own meals, the Vacation Club is your best on-site option. The villas are new, bright, cheery, and beautifully decorated with a Key West theme.

2. Tennis, pools, a cute sand play area with a permanent castle, and a marina are on-site. There's an arcade and fitness room, and free Disney movies are shown nightly.

3. You can pick up groceries at the Conch Flats General Store, and a full service restaurant and snack bar are also available.

4. Prices run from $190 for a studio with a kitchenette to $725 for a three-bedroom Grand Villa, which could easily accommodate 12 people. A roomy two-bedroom villa with full kitchen is about $340, which is comparable to the price for a room at the Grand Floridian or Yacht Club. If you're willing to swap proximity to the parks for more space and the chance to cook your own meals, the Vacation Club is a good option.

Minuses:

1. Still much pricier than off-site villas such as Embassy Suites.

2. Quieter, with less going on than the resorts.

3. No child care options.

Overall Grade: B.

Disney's Village Resort

Designed for families—and for large families—the Village Resort is far from the madding crowd, tucked behind the Disney Village Marketplace, and offers one-, two-, and three-bedroom villas.

Proximity to MK, Epcot, and MGM: Fair, via bus.

Pluses:

1. Proximity to Disney Village Marketplace and Pleasure Island.
2. Proximity to golf.
3. Best choice for those traveling with a huge brood, such as a family reunion; several villas easily sleep up to 12 people.
4. Some of the villas are designed like treehouses, others have lofts and skylights.
5. Each villa has a complete kitchen with coffee-maker, microwave, and wet bar.
6. As well as great access to golf, you'll find tennis, boating, biking, six small swimming pools, and a health club nearby.

Minuses:

1. You're a fairly long way from the theme parks, even by bus.
2. There's only one restaurant, although if you're cooking in your villa a lot this may not be a problem. You also have access to plenty of eating places at the nearby Disney Village Marketplace and Pleasure Island.
3. The villas, although well maintained, are much older than those at the Vacation Club.
4. It's quite expensive, with villas ranging from $185 to $775 a night. Average villas run about $300, and far cheaper suites can be found off-site.
5. This place is very quiet. You may have trouble keeping older kids entertained.

Overall Grade: C. Lots of space, but you have to rely on buses or your own car to get to where the action is.

Disney Village Hotels

The Disney Village Hotels include Buena Vista Palace, Grosvenor Resort, Guest Quarters Suite Resort, Hilton, Royal Plaza, Howard Johnson Resort Hotel, and Travelodge Hotel.

Since they're not owned by Disney or built on Disney property, the Disney Village Hotels are somewhat of a hybrid between the on-site and off-site lodgings. Located just across the road from the Disney Village Marketplace and Pleasure Island, these seven hotels are also considered to be "official" WDW hotels, meaning they run very frequent shuttles to all Disney theme parks, offer access to the restaurant reservation system, and give price breaks on admission tickets.

Proximity to MK, Epcot, and MGM: Fair, via bus.

BEST ON-SITE CHOICES AT A GLANCE

Best Magic Kingdom Resort: The Polynesian
People who come here always seem to come back, and that says something.

Best Epcot Resort: The Beach Club
You like Epcot? It's a stroll away.

Best Budget Hotel: Port Orleans
The best of both worlds—all the charm and intimacy of a full-priced hotel at budget prices.

Best Villa: Vacation Club
Bright and airy villas—like staying in the Key West condo you always wished you owned.

Best Disney Village Hotel: The Hilton
Great child care program, great restaurants, and lots of extra activities and freebies for youngsters.

GENERAL INFORMATION ABOUT THE ON-SITE DISNEY HOTELS

1. A deposit equal to the price of one night's lodging is required within 21 days after making your reservation. You may pay by check or with MasterCard, Visa, or American Express.

2. Refund of your full deposit will be made if your reservation is canceled at least 48 hours prior to arrival.

3. All Disney hotels operate under the family plan, meaning that kids 18 and under stay free with parents. The rooms at the budget hotels, the Swan and the Dolphin, and Wilderness Lodge are designed for four people; the other on-site hotels can easily sleep five in a room. If your family is larger, consider a Village Resort villa, Vacation Club villa, or Fort Wilderness trailer home.

4. Check-in time is 3 P.M. at most Disney resorts, but 4 P.M. at the Village Resort villas and Vacation Club. However, you can drop off your bags and pick up your tickets and resort IDs in the morning, and tour until mid-afternoon. Then return to your hotel to check in.

5. Check-out time is 11 A.M., but once again, you needn't let this interfere with touring. Check out early in the morning and either store your bags with the concierge or take them to your car. Then enjoy your last day in the parks.

6. You'll be issued a resort ID when you check in that allows you to charge meals, drinks, tickets, and souvenirs to your room, and also gives you access to all WDW transportation.

7. If you can't manage to get booked on-site, you will find many of the same policies and amenities at the seven hotels of the Disney Village Hotel Plaza.

8. "Value Season" usually runs in January, from mid-April to mid-June, and from mid-August to mid-December. All guests booking rooms during this time will receive a slightly reduced rate—about $20 off per night—even if they don't qualify for cardholder discounts or are not buying a package. The budget hotels—Port Orleans, Dixie Landings, the All-Star Resorts, and the Caribbean Beach Resort—do not qualify for value season.

9. If you won't be purchasing your tickets by mail in advance, request that they be waiting for you at the front desk on the morning you check in. (The alternative is to wait for Guest Services to open at 9 A.M., but there is nearly always a line the first hour after the desk opens, which just slows you down in getting to the parks.) Remember that Disney hotel guests qualify for the "Be Our Guest" passports.

10. Room service at the Disney hotels is painfully slow, with 45-minute waits not uncommon. Breakfast, which can be ordered the evening before by hanging a request card outside your door, is a bit more prompt, but even then it is faster to get your own food. Nearly every hotel has a fast-food restaurant or snack bar on-site that is open very early; one parent can go out for muffins or cereal and take the food back to the room so that the kids can munch while they dress.

11. Now that Disney has so many rooms on-site, it is quite possible you'll be able to stay on-site even without reservations. So if you get to Orlando and aren't satisfied with your off-site hotel, dial W-DISNEY and see what's available.

OFF-SITE HOTELS: GOOD CHOICES FOR FAMILIES

There's a huge variety of lodging in Orlando, with a wide range of prices and amenities. To make sure you're getting top value for your dollar, consult "Things to Ask When Booking an Off-Site Hotel" in Section 1—and take nothing for granted. Some $250-a-night hotels charge you for shuttle service; some $75 hotels do not. Some hotels count 11-year-olds as adults, and others consider 19-year-olds to be children. Some relatively inexpensive resorts have full-fledged kids' clubs; some larger and far more costly places are geared to convention and business travel and don't even have an arcade. Use the questions on the list to help you ferret out the best deal.

Two things to be aware of: An extremely cheap hotel rate, say $50 or less, generally means that the hotel is located in a less-desirable part of town, both with regard to proximity to the theme parks and general security. Unless you are personally familiar with the location and quality of the hotel, proceed with caution.

Also, many hotels sell a special hybrid ticket called a Four-Day Super Duper Pass that is not available at the Disney gates. The ticket offers access to both the major and minor parks, but is sometimes priced only a few dollars cheaper than the Five-Day Super Duper Pass. If you can get an extra day in the theme parks for $3 or $4 bucks it would be foolish not to buy the Five-Day pass, especially when you consider that the tickets are good indefinitely. Some of the hybrid tickets also do not include admission to Typhoon Lagoon. If you have very young kids or are going in winter, this won't matter; but if you're taking older kids in the summer, you'll need a ticket offering unlimited access to Typhoon Lagoon. The moral is to make sure the "discounted" tickets offered at the off-site hotels are truly your best buy before you purchase them.

Also note that most of the kids' clubs, in compliance with Florida law, require that children be 4 years old and potty trained before they can participate in the planned activities. All of the hotels listed below can arrange baby-sitting in your room for younger children.

1. *Hilton at Disney Village Hotel Plaza*

Conveniently located with shuttle service to nearly all area attractions, the Hilton has the additional boon of a kids' club, called Vacation Station, for kids 4–12. It's open from 5 P.M. until midnight with a charge of $4 an hour, and a $2 add-on for siblings. Kids who need to eat dinner while their folks are on the town will be escorted to the Soda Shoppe next door. (The Hilton is a mere stroll away from Pleasure Island; or, you might want to try the hotel's own Florida Fin Factory, a funky seafood restaurant.) There's a playroom, large-screen TV with Disney movies, video games, and even a six-bed dormitory complete with teddy bears so sleepy preschoolers can be bedded down.

The Hilton concierge has a lending library of games— even Gameboys!—and kids get a Family Fun Kit with freebies and discount coupons when they check in. Rates are $160–$280. Call 1-800-782-4414 or (407) 827-4000.

2. *The Hyatt Regency Grand Cypress Resort*

The Grand Cypress isn't a hotel, it's an event. With 750 rooms, an enormous pool and grotto area with waterfalls and caves, golf courses, lakes, and riding trails, you could spend a vacation here without ever leaving your hotel. (But should you decide to venture out, WDW is only three miles away.) The Grand Cypress is home to Camp Hyatt, a child care center that plans daily activities for children 5–15, and the new and totally unique

Rock Hyatt. An evening program that gives teenagers the chance to hang out with other kids their age, Rock Hyatt provides specially trained counselors to oversee volleyball and ping pong games, video tournaments, and "field trips" to area attractions. The Grand Cypress also boasts five restaurants—including Hemingway's, a Key West–style getaway perched dramatically atop the resort waterfall—and a stellar Sunday brunch that's widely conceded to be the best in town, even by the staffs at other hotels.

Rates are $170–$245 and suites begin at $275. Call 1-800-233-1234 for reservations and (407) 239-1234 for information about Camp Hyatt and Rock Hyatt.

3. *Sonesta Villa Resort Orlando*
While the Disney hotels advertise themselves as being "in the middle of the magic," not everyone wants to spend 24 hours a day in a revved-up, go-go atmosphere. If you'd like to return "home" each evening after touring to a place that seems far, far off the beaten path, try the Sonesta Villa Resort, a virtual hamlet of townhomes surrounding a 300-acre lake. Sand Lake offers boating, jet skiing, windsurfing, and a panorama of other water sports, including my personal favorite: lying on the beach watching the snowy egrets. The townhomes have kitchenettes so you can fix your own meals.

The Sonesta has an elaborate kids' club with free T-shirts to prove it. This isn't just daycare in the sun—trained counselors lead children 4–12 through volleyball, crafts, sack races, and other camp-like events. Amazingly, the Club is free to all guests, and kids and parents can drop by the lobby each morning to discuss what's on tap for the day with one of the counselors. Evening activities run two nights a week in the off-season and up to six nights during the on-season. Again, there is no fee unless the children are fed as part of the activity—then the cost is a reasonable $5. Hotel mascot Sunny the Seal will visit your villa with a bedtime snack and tuck in the kids.

Rates are $110–$250, and Sonesta offers a wide variety of packages that include rental cars and theme park tickets. Call 1-800-SONESTA or (407) 352-8051.

4. *The Peabody Orlando*

Despite having nearly 900 rooms, the Peabody has the feeling of a small, elegant hotel. Kids adore the daily Royal Duck March, when the famed Peabody ducks are escorted by the tuxedo-clad DuckMaster down a red carpet to their personal wading pool in the hotel lobby. *Note:* As the most special of all special perks, you may be able to arrange for your child to serve as honorary Duck-Master one afternoon during your stay. Request information when you book your room. (Even if you're not staying at the Peabody, it's worth dropping by for the afternoon tea and 5 P.M. duck march.)

The Peabody is home to one of the finest restaurants in Orlando, Dux—which serves, not surprisingly, no duck on its menu. Children will prefer the '50s-style B-Line Diner, which serves such kid-pleasing specialties as peanut-butter-and-jelly milkshakes 24 hours a day.

Rates are $180–$250. Call 1-800-732-2639 or (407) 352-4000.

5. *Delta Orlando Resort*

Located just across from Universal Studios and convenient to both Wet 'n Wild and the Mystery Fun House, the Delta Orlando offers resort-style amenities at budget prices. Wally's Kids Club, named after resort mascot Wally Gator, provides free daily activities for children 4–12 from 10 A.M. to 5 P.M. In addition to scavenger hunts, pool games, and crafts, one special activity is highlighted daily: it might be a cooking lesson with the resort chef (the kids return wearing chef hats and clutching sacks of chocolate cookies that they made themselves), a scuba demonstration in the pool, a tennis clinic, or a magic class taught by a professional magician. There's a small fee for these special activities—usually about $4. Each evening from 6:30 to 9:30 there's a themed Kid's Night Out featuring dinner, games, and movies for the very low price of $10 per child.

The Delta also offers The Oasis, a recreation area in the center of the resort with an enormous pool, three hot tubs and saunas, two kiddie pools, a small putt-putt course, volleyball, and two playgrounds. Children ages 1–7 and their parents can even participate in a learn-to-swim program called the Delta Dolphin; youngsters earn badges as each swimming milestone is reached.

The commitment to pleasing families shows through in small ways, such as the free meals in the food court for kids under 6 or the weekly resort newsletter, which keeps you up to date on scheduled sandcastle building contests, frisbee golf, and water volleyball. Kids get to check in separately and receive a grab bag of goodies and coupons. Wally Gator is frequently on hand for the activities and will come to your room at night for tuck-in service. All in all, the Delta is an outstanding value in an off-site hotel and a clear winner in its price range.

Rates are $69–$99. Call 1-800-776-3358 or (407) 351-3340.

6. *The Holiday Inn Sunspree and Holiday Inn Maingate*

Located less than 2 miles from the Disney gates, these Holiday Inns provide a minikitchen with refrigerator, microwave, and coffeemaker in every room. It's a nice option for families who don't need a full suite (and who don't want to pay suite prices) but who'd like to save a few bucks by eating cereal and sandwiches in their room. The Sunspree offers a Kids-Only restaurant with an all-you-can-eat buffet and big screen TV that continuously plays cartoons and kiddie movies for guests under 12. (Kids eat for free here when their parents dine at the adjacent restaurant, Maxine's.) Children also have their own special check-in where they receive a bag full of small gifts and surprises, which is a fun way to start the vacation and makes the kids feel terribly special.

Each evening from 5–10 P.M. free activities are provided for kids 2–12 at Max's Magic Castle. Hotel mascot Max the Raccoon and his friends supervise Bingo games, magic shows, and movies. (Note that the Holiday Inn is licensed to take kids in the 2–4 range, a rarity.) Beepers are available for rental, adding to parental peace of mind, and daytime child care is also available on-site for $3 per hour. Max will also come to your room to tuck tired toddlers in after a tough day in the parks.

Rates are $79–$119 per night. Call 1-800-HOLIDAY or (407) 239-4500. The Holiday Inn Sunspree often fills up weeks in advance at peak seasons.

The Maingate Holiday Inn also offers an excellent (and free) child care program and a hotel mascot named Holiday Hound. All the perks are still there—Camp Holiday, the food court, the beeper service, the minikitchens in each room—but because the Maingate is a little older and located on U.S. 192, a slightly less toury exit, it's cheaper. Rates start as low as $60. Call 1-800-366-5437 or (407) 396-4488 for details.

7. *Embassy Suites Resort Lake Buena Vista*

This relatively new resort, with a dramatic coral stucco exterior and an even more dramatic open-air atrium decorated in Caribbean shades of teal and purple, offers dramatically good deals for families. The 280 suites have kitchens with microwaves, fridges and coffeemakers, and pleasant sitting areas. Suites can sleep as many as six people easily. A full range of sporting activities—an indoor-outdoor pool, tennis, basketball, volleyball, shuffleboard, and a jogging trail with exercise stations—is close at hand. The resort also offers several significant freebies to guests: shuttle service to the Disney parks, drinks at the manager's daily cocktail party from 5–7:30 P.M., and a bountiful breakfast buffet. (What many hotels advertise as a free breakfast often turns out to be a paper cup of orange juice and a wrapped roll, but this spread features a fruit bar, sausage, bacon, eggs, pancakes, french toast, and made-to-order omelets.)

The Cool Cat Kids' Club cranks up each evening at 4 P.M., with crafts (a $6 fee to cover materials) and dinner ($8 for the food), and wraps up at 9:30 P.M. with movies and ice cream. Beeper service is provided for parents, and the Club has plenty of video games, a video wall with five separate TV sets for high-tech viewing, a crawl castle, and a small ball pit. Kids get fingerprinted for a resort ID on their first visit and subsequently receive newsletters and birthday cards from Garfield, the resort mascot, throughout the year. Poolside games such as egg tosses, relay races, and the popular "Daddy Splash"—a contest in which the Dad with the most impressive belly flop wins a prize for his kid—keep things hopping all day. The guests at this resort are almost exclusively families, so it is easy for a child in any age group to meet new friends.

At $135–$235 for a suite, and so many perks included in the price, the Embassy Suites offer great value and a great location—just off exit 27 on I-4, a mere 10-minute ride from the Disney parks. Call 1-800-EMBASSY or (407) 239-1144.

3

★★★★★★★★★★★★★★★★★★

Touring Plans

GENERAL WALT DISNEY WORLD TOURING TIPS

Most of the tips below assume you'll be visiting WDW for more than one day. If you aren't staying longer, see "A One-Day Touring Plan" later in this section.

1. Come early! This is the single most important piece of advice in this entire book. By beating the crowds you can not only visit attractions in quick succession, but you also avoid the parking and transportation nightmares that occur when the parks fill to peak capacity around 11 A.M.

For families with kids it is especially important to avoid the exhaustion that comes with just trying to get there. If you're staying off-site it can take a full two hours from the point you leave your hotel to the point where you board your first ride, which is enough to shatter the equanimity of even the best-behaved kids. They've been waiting for this vacation a long time, and flying and riding a long time; you owe it to them to get into the parks fast.

2. On the evening you arrive, dial 824-4321 to confirm the opening time of the theme park you plan to visit the next day. If you learn, for example, that the Magic Kingdom is scheduled to open at 9 A.M., be at the gate by 8:30. Frequently—for no apparent reason—the gates open a half-hour early. This is a gift from the gods, and you should be prepared to capitalize on it. On the mornings the park is opened ahead of the stated time, you can ride a dozen attractions while the other 50,000 poor saps are still out on I-4.

Note: Guests at Disney hotels are admitted an additional hour early under the "Surprise Mornings" program. Guests Services at your hotel can tell you which park is slated to open early on a given day; there's usually printed material on the program in your check-in package as well.

3. Even if the park doesn't open ahead of the stated time, guests are frequently ushered into one section early. This means you can get maps and entertainment schedules before you enter the body of the park, and even eat breakfast if you order something simple and eat fast.

In the MK, visitors are usually allowed to travel the length of Main Street before the park actually opens. You can window-shop, grab a muffin at the Main Street Bakery, and still be at the ropes blocking the end of Main Street by 9 A.M., far ahead of the throngs outside the main turnstile. Similarly, at MGM visitors are often allowed onto Hollywood Boulevard to browse the shops and nibble a bite at Starring Rolls before the main park opens. If you have young kids and a special morning showing of the red-hot *Voyage of the Little Mermaid* is scheduled, you should go there first. Older kids? Try the Twilight Zone Tower of Terror first, then head for *Voyage of the Little Mermaid*.

At Epcot, the advantages of an early arrival are even greater. Spaceship Earth (aka the Big Ball) stands silent and empty at the day's beginning. A family can get strollers, ride Spaceship Earth, make dinner reservations at the WorldKey Information System behind the Big Ball, and have a quick breakfast at the Stargate Restaurant—all before the park officially opens. As an added bonus, the Disney characters, dressed in nifty spacesuits, appear in the Stargate Restaurant early in the morning and happily pose for pictures.

4. Plan to see the most popular attractions either early in the day, late at night, or during a time when a big event siphons off other potential riders (such as dur-

ing the 3 P.M. parade in the MK). The newer attractions—such as the Wonders of Life pavilion at Epcot, Splash Mountain in the MK, or the Twilight Zone Tower of Terror and *Voyage of the Little Mermaid* at MGM—are always crowded, so hit these first.

5. Eat at "off" times. Some families eat lightly at breakfast, have an early lunch around 11 A.M., and eat supper at 5 P.M. Others eat a huge breakfast, have a late lunch around 3 P.M., then have a final meal after the parks close. If you tour late and you're really bushed, all on-site and many off-site hotels have in-room pizza delivery service.

6. Be aware that kids usually want to revisit their favorite attractions. (My daughter insisted on riding Dumbo every single day the first time we visited WDW, something I hadn't foreseen and that radically restructured our touring plans.) Parents who overschedule to the point where there is no time to revisit favorites risk a mutiny.

One way to handle this dilemma is to leave the entire last day of your trip free as a "greatest hits" day, so you can go back to all your favorites at least one more time. If you only feel like lugging the camcorder around once, make this the day.

7. Use the touring plan to cut down on arguments and debates. It's a hapless parent indeed who sits down at breakfast and asks "What do you want to do today?" Three kids will have three different answers, and the indecision and bickering waste valuable time.

8. When making plans, keep the size of the parks in mind. MGM is small and can be easily crisscrossed to take in various shows. The MK is larger, and while some cutting back and forth is possible, you'll probably want

to tour one "land" thoroughly before heading to another. Epcot is so enormous you're almost forced to visit attractions in geographic sequence or you will spend all your time and energy in transit.

9. If you're going to be in the MK for two days or longer, plan to visit the most popular attractions on different days. Many families arrive in the MK determined to take in Space Mountain, Splash Mountain, Big Thunder Mountain, the Jungle Cruise, and Pirates of the Caribbean their first day . . . then wind up spending hours in line. Better to try to see a couple of the biggies during the first hour after the park opens. After that, move on to less popular attractions, saving the other biggies for subsequent mornings.

10. If you leave a park and plan to return to either that park or another, save your stroller receipt and have your hand stamped. You won't have to pay another stroller deposit at the new park if you can show a receipt, and you can reenter the new park swiftly by showing your stamped hand and ticket. (Don't worry if you're leaving to swim . . . the hand stamps are waterproof, although sunscreen can smear them if rubbed directly on the back of the hand.)

Likewise, if you're staying off-site and using your own car to visit more than one park in a day, save your parking receipt so you won't have to pay the $5 fee more than once.

11. Plan to visit more than one park a day. Many families with a multiday ticket figure "We'll spend Monday in the MK, Tuesday at MGM, Wednesday at Typhoon Lagoon, and Thursday at Epcot." Sounds logical, but it can lead to burnout. A day in the MK is too much riding, 12 hours at Epcot is too much walking, a whole day at

MGM is too much sitting, and anyone who stays at Typhoon Lagoon from dusk to dawn will wind up waterlogged. It's far better to break up the day, using the ever-present WDW transportation system to allow you to follow a morning spent plunging down Space Mountain or bodysurfing at Typhoon Lagoon with more passive pleasures like seeing an MGM show or Epcot film.

12. If you're trying to predict how crowded a ride or show will be, take these four factors into account:

The newness of the ride—In general, the newer the hotter, particularly if it's a thrill ride like Splash Mountain or the Twilight Zone Tower of Terror.

The quality of the ride—Space Mountain, Star Tours, IllumiNations, and other Disney "classics" will be mobbed five years from now.

Speed of loading—Dumbo has to be completely stopped and emptied before a new cycle of riders can board; thus, huge lines can develop. It's a Small World can load whole boatfuls of tourists while other boats are unloading, so lines never become unbearable. Continuous-loading attractions such as Pirates of the Caribbean, Spaceship Earth, and the Great Movie Ride can move thousands of riders through in an hour. The lines at the start-and-stop rides such as 20,000 Leagues Under the Sea, Astro Orbiter, and the Mad Tea Party move much more slowly.

Capacity—Movies like *O Canada!* at Epcot, shows like *MuppetVision 3-D* at MGM, and even the Country Bear Jamboree in the MK can seat large crowds at once. Lines form then disappear rapidly as hundreds of people enter the theaters. For this reason, theater-style attractions are good choices in the afternoon when the park is crowded.

13. At some rides you might opt to do a "baby swap." "Baby swap" does not mean you can trade your shrieking 2-year-old for that angelically napping infant behind you! It enables the family that has some coaster-warriors and some uneasy-riders to enter the line together, rather than split up or go through the lines twice.

As you approach the ride inform the attendant that you'll need to swap off the baby or younger kid. One parent rides, then the waiting parent passes the baby through and rides himself. (Older kids often are allowed to ride back-to-back with Mom and Dad if the lines aren't too bad.)

If you're unsure whether a ride is too intense for your kids, you can use the "baby swap" as a test: let one parent ride, then return with the verdict. If the first parent thinks it's OK, the second parent can them immediately board the ride with the child.

14. When planning your touring days, take time to familiarize yourself with the TTC (the Ticket and Transportation Center). Located near the MK, the TTC is the main station for the monorails and buses, and is where you'll make all your transfers.

If you're staying on-site you'll be able to take a direct bus, boat, or monorail to any of the three major theme parks, but if you're trying to get to a minor park you'll have to go through the TTC.

Off-site visitors can drive directly to Epcot, MGM, or any of the minor parks, all of which have their own parking lots and shuttle trams. But the parking lot for the MK is so far from the actual park that off-site visitors will have to park, catch the shuttle tram, and then go through the TTC in order to catch a monorail or ferryboat to get to the Magic Kingdom. (This is why we recommend that off-site visitors allow 45 minutes to get to

the MK, even if their hotel is close to the park.) Likewise, if you're park hopping, you'll need to go through
the TTC to get from Epcot to the MK, for example, or
from the MK to Typhoon Lagoon.

It may sound like a big bowl of alphabet soup, but
everything is very well marked and there are always
plenty of Disney employees on hand to answer your
questions. Once you get the hang of the system you'll
find using the WDW transportation services easier than
trying to get around on your own.

15. If you'll be at WDW for more than four days, plan
a day "off" in the middle of your vacation. Families
sometimes feel so compelled to do it all that they come
back from their trip exhausted and irritable. A day in
the middle of the trip devoted to sleeping in, hanging
around the hotel pool, taking in a character breakfast, or
visiting a minor park can make all the difference. You'll
start the next day refreshed and energized.

16. Tickets are expensive, so use them wisely. Each
time you enter the gates of a major park you get a day
marked off your multiday ticket, even if you only visit
for a couple of hours. Thus, on the days when you'll be in
a major park, make sure that the hours spent warrant
losing a day of your multiday pass. In other words, on
Monday visit the MK in the morning, take a rest, then
visit MGM that evening—you will still only get one day
marked off your ticket. Tuesday you can visit Typhoon
Lagoon in the morning and Pleasure Island at night
without having any days marked off your multiday
ticket. If you visit MGM on Monday morning and Pleasure Island at night, then the MK Tuesday morning and
Typhoon Lagoon at night, you will lose two days on your
ticket, not one.

TOURING TIPS FOR VISITORS STAYING ON-SITE

1. By far the greatest advantage of staying at one of the hotels found within WDW is the easy commute to the theme parks. Visitors with small kids can return to their hotels in midafternoon, then reenter the parks at about 5 or 6 P.M. Remember the mantra: Come early, stay late, and take a break in the middle of the day.

If you arrive early, you'll have been touring for five or six hours by 2 P.M. and will be more than ready for a rest. Have a late lunch either at one of the Main Street restaurants, which are reasonably empty at midday, or back at your hotel. (Neither the shuttle buses nor the monorail is crowded in midafternoon, but if you're staying at the Polynesian or Grand Floridian, taking the launch or the ferryboat is even faster.) Once "home," nap or take a dip in the pool.

At least one day you'll want to remain in the Magic Kingdom until 3 P.M. for the Main Street parade. Be sure to watch near the Railroad Station, at the Main Street hub, so you'll be close to the main gates and can make a clean getaway once the parade has passed.

2. Never order breakfast through room service at a Disney hotel—it can take forever! Service at the sit-down restaurants in Disney hotels also can be maddeningly slow, so either try the snack bar or food court at your hotel or get through the gates early and eat breakfast at the parks.

3. In the off-season the MK and MGM sometimes close at 6 P.M., but Epcot stays open later, even during the least crowded weeks of the year. The solution? Spend mornings in the MK or at MGM, return to your hotel for

a break, and then spend late afternoons and evenings at Epcot. This buys you more hours per day in the theme parks—and the best places for dinner are all at Epcot anyway.

4. It's hard to over-emphasize the importance of taking advantage of the "Surprise Mornings." If Epcot is the featured park on Tuesday, go to Epcot on Tuesday. By getting in the park an hour and a half ahead of the stated time you can easily ride the most popular attractions before the crowds arrive. During Christmas week of 1993 my family was able to ride nine rides in the Fantasyland and Tomorrowland sections of the MK during our first hour. Later in the day we noticed that some of those same rides were posting 90-minute waits.

TOURING TIPS FOR VISITORS STAYING OFF-SITE

1. Time your commute. If you can make it from your hotel to the theme park gates within 30 minutes, it may still be worth your while to return to your hotel for a midday break. This is a distinct possibility for guests of the hotels at the Disney Village Hotel Plaza and some I-4 establishments. If your hotel is farther out, it's doubtful you'll want to make the drive four times a day.

2. If it isn't feasible to return to your hotel, find afternoon resting places within the parks. (See the list "Afternoon Resting Places" in our discussions of each theme park.) Sometimes kids aren't so much tired as full of pent-up energy. If you suspect that's the case, take preschoolers to the playground in Mickey's Starland in the MK or let older kids run free among the forts and backwoods paths of Tom Sawyer Island. The Honey, I

Shrunk the Kids Adventure Zone at MGM is also perfect for burning off excess energy.

3. If you're willing to leave the parks in the middle of the afternoon, you have even more options. Cool off at River Country, Typhoon Lagoon, or in the 10-screen movie theater beside Pleasure Island. *Note:* River Country is an easy commute from the MK, since it runs its own launch. If you stash your bathing suits in one of the lockers under the railroad station in the MK, you can retrieve them around lunchtime and go straight to River Country without having to return to your car.

The hotel restaurants in the MK resorts are never crowded at lunch, and the dining is much more leisurely than in the parks. An early dinner (around 5 P.M.) can also effectively break up a summer day, when you may be staying at the park until midnight. A good bet is 1900 Park Fare at the Grand Floridian, which offers a buffet dinner, appearances by the characters, and a giant carnival organ called Big Bertha. The Contemporary Cafe in the Contemporary Resort also offers an evening buffet, which is one of the most reasonably-priced meals in all of WDW. *Note:* If you take the monorail, be sure to line up for the train marked "Monorail to the MK Resorts." Most of the monorails are expresses back to the TTC.

4. If you'll be touring all day, get strollers for all preschool age kids. Few 5-year-olds can walk through a 14-hour day.

5. Staying for a late evening show such as IllumiNations at Epcot or SpectroMagic in the MK? Either choose a location near the main exit so you can get the jump on the rest of the departing crowd, or stop for shopping and a snack after the show and exit the park about

20 minutes behind the main surge of people. Not staying for the late show? Leave the park while it's in progress and you'll miss the departing crowd altogether.

HOW TO CUSTOMIZE A TOURING PLAN

There's no substitute for a good touring plan. Unfortunately, the generic touring schedules included in many guidebooks assume that all visitors are equally interested in all attractions, which simply isn't true. If your 7-year-old is sold on stegasophagi, for example, you may spend an entire morning in the Universe of Energy pavilion at Epcot. On the other hand, if no one in your group likes anything remotely scary, you can cross certain attractions off your list from the start.

In creating a personalized touring plan, your first step is to familiarize yourself with the overall map of WDW and the maps of the three major theme parks so you can arrive in Orlando with some sense of proximity and the location of major attractions. Getting to Big Thunder Mountain Railroad early is considerably easier if you know where Big Thunder Mountain Railroad is. Next, poll your family on which attractions they most want to see and build these priorities into the plan.

Third, divide each day of your visit into three components: morning, afternoon, and evening. It isn't necessary to specify where you'll be every hour—that's too confining—but you need some sense of how you'll break up each day. Check out the plan below, which is an adaptation of the perfect four-day touring plan described later. This plan is custom-designed for a family with a 4-year-old girl and 7-year-old boy who will be at WDW for five days in October, staying at the on-site Caribbean Beach Resort. The younger child is sold on the characters and most yearns to meet Minnie Mouse up close and personally. She still naps in the afternoon. The older child likes action rides, is pretty fearless when it comes to special effects, and especially wants to see the Living Seas at Epcot. The husband asks only that one after- noon be left open for golf. The wife would like some time in the parks without the kids to get an early jump on Christmas shopping and wants to get a sitter one evening for a parents' night out.

A touring plan for this family might look something like this:

Wednesday A.M.:	The Magic Kingdom—tour Fantasyland, Mickey's Starland, and Tomorrowland.
Wednesday P.M.:	Return to hotel for lunch and naps around 2 P.M.
Wednesday night:	Epcot—tour Future World, includ- ing the Living Seas.
Thursday A.M.:	MGM Studio Theme Park.
Thursday P.M.:	Return to hotel after the Aladdin parade. Mom supervises swim- ming and naps while Dad golfs.
Thursday night:	Hoop-Dee-Doo Musical Revue at Fort Wilderness; afterward watch Electrical Water Pageant.
Friday A.M.:	The Magic Kingdom—ride Big Thunder Mountain Railroad and Splash Mountain first, then tour Adventureland, Liberty Square, and Frontierland. Lunch late at King Stefan's in Cinderella Castle, then take in 3 P.M. parade.

Friday P.M.:	While Dad takes kids to River Country via the launch, Mom stays behind to shop.
Friday night:	Sitter comes to hotel room for kids while Mom and Dad visit Pleasure Island.
Saturday A.M.:	Return to Magic Kingdom and re-ride all favorites.
Saturday P.M.:	Lunch at Mexico pavilion at Epcot. Tour World Showcase, encouraging kids to rest and/or nap during films, since this is the only day they won't be returning to the room for an afternoon nap. Meet characters at late afternoon show near the lagoon.
Saturday night:	Dinner at Coral Reef restaurant. Then tour the rest of Future World and see IllumiNations.
Sunday A.M.:	Take in character breakfast at the Yacht Club Resort. Return to room to check out, then leave bags with the concierge or go ahead and load car. Return to MGM to see anything missed on first morning.

This touring plan has much to recommend it:

1. You can get an early start every day.
2. Naps, or at least down-time, are built into the afternoons.
3. You see the characters every day.

4. Minimal time is spent waiting in lines. Certain reservations such as the Hoop-Dee-Doo Revue and character breakfasts can be made before you leave home. Other reservations, such as the final dinner meal at the Coral Reef, can be made from your hotel room.

If your kids are older, the plan can be easily adapted. Substitute the wilder rides for the tamer, opt for Typhoon Lagoon over River Country, cut out the naps and character breakfasts, and you still have the prototype of a workable plan.

THE PERFECT TOURING PLAN FOR FOUR- OR FIVE-DAY VISITS

This touring plan assumes that you're staying off-site, have a multiday pass, and are visiting at a time when all three parks are open past 8 P.M.

Day 1

Be at the end of Main Street in the MK by the stated opening time. When the ropes drop (assuming that your kids are 7 or older and up to it) head directly for Space Mountain.

After you ride Space Mountain, go to Fantasyland. (If your children are younger or frightened by coasters, go to Fantasyland first.) If you want to eat lunch inside the castle, make your reservation at King Stefan's Banquet Hall. Visit these Fantasyland rides in rapid succession:

Dumbo
Cinderella's Carousel
Snow White's Adventures

Peter Pan's Flight
It's a Small World
Mr. Toad's Wild Ride (optional)
20,000 Leagues Under the Sea (optional)
Mad Tea Party

After you exit the Tea Party teeter on to Mickey's Starland. The kids can enjoy the petting zoo and playground while you wait for the next show. (Starland is also one of the best places in the park to take pictures.)

When the show is concluded and you've met Mickey, stop for a snack before you head toward Adventureland. It's a fairly long walk.

In Adventureland, visit Pirates of the Caribbean, the Jungle Cruise, and the Swiss Family Robinson Treehouse. By now it should be midday and some of the lines may be prohibitive. If you face a wait of more than 20 minutes at an attraction, skip it. You'll need to be back out on Main Street by 2 P.M., and you'll be returning to the MK on other days.

As you exit Adventureland and head toward Main Street, stop at either the Crystal Palace, Plaza Restaurant, or Tony's and eat a hearty lunch. (If you've made lunch reservations for King Stefan's in the Cinderella Castle, go there now.)

Watch the 3 P.M. parade from the Main Street hub.

After the parade, exit the theme park. It is now time for your well-deserved midday break. Be sure to have your hand stamped as you exit the park.

About 6 P.M., go to MGM. Pick up an entertainment schedule at Guest Services as you enter. You should easily be able to catch the Indiana Jones Epic Stunt Spectacular, Superstar Television, and *MuppetVision 3-D*.

Eat last of all; the restaurants stay open after the attractions close down.

Enjoy the fireworks presentation. (Times for this finale show vary, so consult your entertainment schedule.)

Day 2

Spend the morning at Typhoon Lagoon. Exit the park midday, take a break in your hotel room if needed, then head for Epcot.

Enter Epcot around 4:30 P.M. If you want a sit-down meal, stop by the WorldKey Information System and see which restaurants still have seating times left. Avoid booking a time just before IllumiNations—you don't want to miss the show.

Catch the late afternoon character show at the World Showcase.

Tour the Living Seas and Land pavilions, and Journey Into Imagination. See *Honey, I Shrunk the Audience.* Eat dinner, then watch the closing presentation of IllumiNations.

Day 3

Be through the MK gates early. This time when the ropes drop, hoof it to Big Thunder Mountain Railroad and Splash Mountain.

Tour the Haunted Mansion in Liberty Square.

See the Country Bear Jamboree.

If you missed any Adventureland or Fantasyland attractions on the previous day, tour them now. If the kids are restless, you might opt to visit Tom Sawyer Island and have a snack at Aunt Polly's while they explore.

Visit the Tomorrowland Grand Prix and any other Tomorrowland attractions that appeal to your kids. Eat a fast-food lunch.

Be on the Main Street side of Cinderella Castle for the midday character show. (Starting times vary, so consult your entertainment schedule.)

Exit the park and take an early midday break. Consider taking the launch from the MK over to either Discovery Island or River Country for your midday break.

Either take in a family style dinner show such as the Hoop-Dee-Doo Revue, go shopping at the Disney Village Marketplace, or try out the Water Sprites or some other sort of boating activity.

Day 4

Start your day at MGM. If you dare, ride the Twilight Zone Tower of Terror immediately upon entering. If an early showing of *Voyage of the Little Mermaid* is scheduled, go there next. Make lunch reservations for either the Prime Time Cafe or SciFi Drive-In at the reservation booth on Hollywood Boulevard.

See Star Tours and the Great Movie Ride.

Visit the Turtles and the Honey I Shrunk the Kids Adventure Zone.

See the Beauty and the Beast stage show.

Take the Animation Tour.

See the Aladdin parade.

Have lunch, then take the Backstage Studio Tour. Visit the Monster Sound Show.

Exit the park around 4 P.M. for swimming and resting.

This is parents' night out. If your hotel does not have a kids' club, or if you plan to be gone past 10 or 11 P.M., you should arrange for a sitter in advance. Orlando has many elegant restaurants (some of them inside Epcot), or you may prefer a rowdier evening at Pleasure Island.

Day 5

Start your day early at Epcot. With any luck, you should be able to make lunch reservations and tour Spaceship Earth before the ropes are dropped.

Head straight for the new and popular Wonders of Life pavilion. Ride Body Wars first, then proceed to Cranium Command.

Tour Horizons and World of Motion.

Head toward the World Showcase Lagoon.

Ride El Rio del Tiempo in Mexico and Maelstrom in Norway, then have lunch in either pavilion.

Continue circling the World Showcase Lagoon. The presentations at the China, U.S., France, and Canada pavilions are all compelling and extremely well done, as are the comedy street shows in Italy and the United Kingdom. Take in as many of these as time and your child's stamina permit. Finish with the Universe of Energy pavilion on your way out of the park.

Exit Epcot. Enjoy an afternoon rest.

Enter the MK in early evening. Revisit a couple of favorite rides—Splash Mountain and Big Thunder railroad are especially fun at night. See SpectroMagic, Tinkerbell's Flight, and the fireworks at closing.

A ONE-DAY TOURING PLAN

If you're going to be in WDW only one day, your task is challenging indeed. A one-day ticket entitles you to the use of a single Disney park, so select carefully. Time will be at a premium, so you'll probably want to forgo your midday break, opting instead for finding afternoon resting places inside the theme park.

1. If you only have one day it is imperative that you be at the park and through the gates a half-hour before the stated opening time. (In the MK, with its convoluted transportation system, this will mean leaving your hotel 60 to 75 minutes before the stated park opening time.)

2. Turn to the section of this book that refers to your theme park and read the section on your first hour in the park.

3. See as many attractions as possible in the morning, moving swiftly from one to the next. If any attraction has a line requiring more than a half-hour wait, skip it for now. You can try it again just before park closing when lines are usually shorter.

4. Have lunch, then move on to theater-style attractions that allow you to sit, or consult the "Afternoon Resting Places" list for your theme park.

5. The parades and character shows are quite worthwhile, even on a packed schedule. They're what make Disney, Disney.

6. Around 6 P.M. crowds thin out a bit. Eat a snack supper, then return to any sections of the park you missed or that had long lines earlier. Save the most popular attraction for last.

7. At park closing one parent should stake out a spot as near as possible to the main exit where you can watch the closing festivities while the other parent takes the kids to pick out a souvenir. Turn in your strollers and make a final potty run. It may also be a good time to grab a dessert or ice cream while waiting for the parade/fireworks/laser show to begin.

8. As soon as the closing festivities conclude, head directly out of the park. Don't look back—the crowds behind you will be the scariest thing you've seen all day.

A ONE-DAY TOURING PLAN FOR THE HIGHLY ENERGETIC

The following is an eclectic but efficient touring plan for families with multiday tickets who are driving their own cars.

This plan works well as a wrap-up on your final day since it allows you to visit two major parks, revisit favorite attractions, eat in an Epcot restaurant, and see as many as three major presentations. Admittedly this plan requires a lot of energy and probably shouldn't be attempted with preschoolers. But for families determined to see as much as possible in the smallest amount of time, it can't be beat!

1. Epcot is much easier to access by car than the Magic Kingdom. Early-arriving visitors can park very close to the main entry gate and simply walk in, often circumventing even the need for a tram.

2. Drive to Epcot at least 30 minutes before the stated opening time, get strollers and maps, and make your evening dinner reservation at the WorldKey Information

Center in Earth Station Spaceship Earth. Have breakfast if you haven't eaten, and ride Spaceship Earth.

3. Tour Future World until about 11 A.M., then exit Epcot, turning in your stroller and keeping the receipt. Take the monorail to the TTC and transfer to the MK monorail. You'll be running just behind the surge of visitors that usually glut the MK main gates between 10 and 11 A.M. Use your receipt to get a new stroller at MK and have lunch on Main Street.

4. Tour the MK until 2:45. Return to the Main Street hub and watch the 3 P.M. parade.

5. Exit the MK immediately after the parade. Again, monorail traffic should be light since most MK visitors are still watching the parade snake its way through the rest of the route. Go back to the TTC and take the monorail to Epcot. You should be back there in time for the afternoon character show at the World Showcase Lagoon. Then eat at the Epcot restaurant where you made your reservations that morning and tour the World Showcase until the closing presentation of IllumiNations.

6. After IllumiNations is over, you'll feel mighty smug as you bypass the horrendous crowds in line for the monorails and parking trams. Walk to your car and exit the park.

Note: An alternative to this plan is to exit Epcot around lunchtime via the "backdoor" located between the France and United Kingdom pavilions in the World Showcase. Walk to the Yacht and Beach Club marina and catch the water-taxi to MGM. Tour MGM until 4 P.M., then return to Epcot via the same water-taxi for your evening activities.

4

★★★★★★★★★★★★★★★★★★★★

The Magic Kingdom

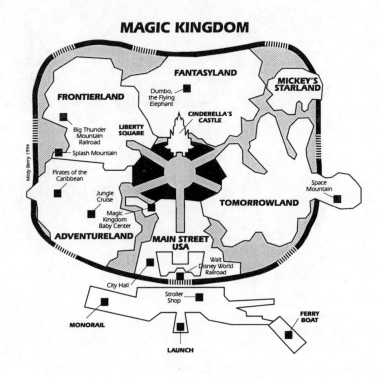

MAGIC KINGDOM

FANTASYLAND

MICKEY'S STARLAND

FRONTIERLAND

Dumbo, the Flying Elephant

CINDERELLA'S CASTLE

LIBERTY SQUARE

Big Thunder Mountain Railroad

Splash Mountain

Pirates of the Caribbean

Space Mountain

Jungle Cruise

TOMORROWLAND

Magic Kingdom Baby Center

ADVENTURELAND

MAIN STREET USA

Misty Berry 1994

City Hall

Walt Disney World Railroad

Stroller Shop

FERRY BOAT

MONORAIL

LAUNCH

GETTING TO THE MAGIC KINGDOM

1. If you're staying off-site, prepare for a complicated journey. Either drive or take a shuttle bus to the Ticket and Transportation Center (TTC). From the TTC you can cross the Seven Seas Lagoon by ferryboat or monorail. *(Note:* Make it a habit each time you board the monorail to ask if the driver's cab is vacant; people who'd like to ride up front wait in a special holding area. Since monorails run every three minutes during the peak times, you shouldn't have to wait long and the view is spectacular.) As you enter the front gates, the turnstiles to the right are usually less crowded than those to the left.

2. If you're staying at the Contemporary, you can bypass the TTC and take the monorail directly to the MK.

3. Likewise, if you're staying at the Grand Floridian, the monorail will have you in the MK within minutes. Or you can take the launch from the marina dock.

4. Guests at the Polynesian have the most choices of all: the launch, the monorail, or the ferryboat. If your room is on the lagoon, walk to the ferryboat. If you're in one of the buildings near the Great Ceremonial House, the monorail is a better bet. If your room is close to the pool, take the launch.

5. From Fort Wilderness or Wilderness Lodge, take the launch.

6. Guests at Disney hotels that are not on the monorail line can take direct shuttle buses that deliver them directly to the MK, bypassing the TTC. This saves you at least 10 minutes of commuting time—more during the morning rush hour.

When leaving at the end of the day, visitors staying off-site should pause for a second as they exit the gates. If a ferryboat is in the dock to the far left, that's the fastest route back to the TTC. If there's no boat in sight, off-site guests are probably better off queuing up for the monorail, which runs directly back to the TTC.

Guests at Disney hotels should return to the shuttle bus station.

Guests at the Contemporary should always exit via the monorail, making sure they take the one designated for the resorts.

Those staying at the Polynesian or the Grand Floridian should glance down at the launch dock, which is straight ahead through the MK exit gates. If a launch is in the dock, it's the best way back to the hotel; otherwise, the resort monorail is the best choice.

GETTING AROUND THE MAGIC KINGDOM

Walking is by far the fastest means of transport in the MK. The trolleys, vintage cars, and horse-drawn carriages are fun, as are the skyways. But think of these as pleasant rides that offer charming views, not as serious means of getting around the park.

The railroad, which leaves from the entrance gate and stops near Splash Mountain in Frontierland and Mickey's Starland, can save you a bit of time and effort if you happen to hit it right. Don't think, however, that catching the train to Splash Mountain in the morning is your fastest way there. The railroad station is busy in mid-morning, and you may have to wait for a second or third train; by this time you could have walked. If you're entering in the afternoon or some other time when the station is less crowded, the odds are you can catch the next train. This may save you a few steps, especially if you're headed toward Mickey's Starland.

Be prepared to make frequent rest stops while touring the MK. You won't walk as much as you do at Epcot, but you're likely to spend more time waiting in lines. Standing still is ultimately harder on the feet—and the nerves—than walking.

YOUR FIRST HOUR IN THE MAGIC KINGDOM

1. Be through the gates 20 minutes earlier than the stated opening time, 40 minutes if you plan to have breakfast on Main Street. Get strollers, pick up a map and entertainment schedule at City Hall, and, if you'd like, make reservations for the Diamond Horseshoe Jamboree at the Hospitality House.

2. Be at the end of Main Street by the stated opening time. When the ropes drop, if your kids are 6 or older, head for Splash Mountain, then Big Thunder Mountain Railroad, then across to Space Mountain.

3. If your kids are under 6, head straight through Cinderella Castle to Fantasyland. When most people reach the end of Main Street they tend to either veer left toward Adventureland or right toward Tomorrowland, and thus begin touring in a clockwise or counterclockwise fashion. If you go straight to Fantasyland first, you'll not only be able to tour five or six attractions before 10 A.M., but you'll also spend the rest of your day moving against the crowds.

4. If there's a gap in the ages of your children and the 9-year-old is ready for the coasters but the

4-year-old isn't, split up. Mom can take one child, Dad the other, and you can meet up again in an hour.

MAIN STREET TOURING TIPS

1. Although you might want to spend a few minutes mingling with the characters who greet you as you enter, don't stop to check out the shops or minor attractions of Main Street in the morning; you need to hurry on to the big rides.

2. Return to Main Street to shop in midafternoon. Especially worthwhile are Disney Clothiers, Uptown Jewelers, and the Emporium. Main Street is also a good place for lunch.

3. If you're looking for souvenirs, be aware that there's no point in comparison shopping within the confines of WDW. A $22.50 stuffed Dumbo at the Emporium will also be $22.50 at a gift shop in the Polynesian Resort or the Disney Village Marketplace.

4. After shopping, stow your purchases in the lockers underneath the railroad. If you're not planning to see the parade, be sure to be off Main Street by 2:30 P.M. After that, it's a mob scene.

5. A fun diversion for kids is having their bangs trimmed amid the old-fashioned splendor of the Harmony Barber Shop beside the flower market on Main Street. The barbers are jovial, even by Disney employee standards, and happy to explain the history of the moustache cups, shaving mugs, and other paraphernalia.

6. If you're touring the MK late and your party splits up, make sure you choose a spot on Main Street as

your meeting place. Disney employees clear people out of the other sections of the park promptly at closing time, remaining firm even if you explain that you were supposed to meet Lauren by Dumbo at 10:00. But Main Street stays open up to an hour after the rides shut down, and is the best place to reassemble the family before heading for the parking lot.

FANTASYLAND

The aptly named Fantasyland, located directly behind Cinderella Castle, is a cross between a Bavarian village and a medieval fair. Most of the kiddie rides are here, and it is the most congested section of the Magic Kingdom.

Fantasyland Attractions

It's a Small World
During this 11-minute boat ride, dolls representing children of all nations greet you with a song so infectious you'll be humming it at bedtime. *Note:* The ride loads steadily, so the lines move fast, making this a good choice for afternoon. And it's one of the best of all attractions to film with a camcorder.

Peter Pan's Flight
Tinkerbell flutters overhead as you board miniature pirate ships and sail above Nana's doghouse, the sparkling night streets of London, the Indian camp, and Captain Hook's cove. Of all the MK attractions, this one is most true to the movie that inspired it.

Skyway to Tomorrowland

This overhead cable car offers great views, particularly at night.

Magic Journeys

An 18-minute 3-D film with startlingly lifelike effects. Kids unfamiliar with the 3-D concept love the glasses, and often reach out in an attempt to grasp the kites and balloons that appear to drift out toward the audience. This is one of the few places in Fantasyland designed for resting.

Note: Since the lines disappear every 20 minutes, it's rarely necessary to wait long for this attraction. Ask the attendant at the door how long until the next showing begins, and don't line up unless the wait is five minutes or less.

Mr. Toad's Wild Ride

Cars careen through a funhouse, narrowly missing a chicken coop, an oncoming train, and a teetering grand-father clock. *Note:* Although the special effects are nowhere near those of Peter Pan's Flight, younger kids may enjoy the ride.

Cinderella's Golden Carousel

Seventy-two white horses prance while a pipe organ toots out "Chim-Chim-Cheree" and other Disney classics. *Note:* This ride is gorgeous at night. Benches nearby let Mom and Dad take a breather.

Snow White's Adventures

As you ride mining cars through the dark, the Wicked Witch appears several times quite suddenly, giving a few toddlers the willies. The acid test: How well did your kids handle the scene in the movie when Snow White is chased through the forest? My 4-year-old liked the ride while she was on it, but, perhaps significantly, didn't want to try it again the next day.

20,000 Leagues Under the Sea

This is a submarine ride featuring sunken treasure, octopi, and other marine life, and culminating in an attack by a giant squid.

Note: The ride boards slowly and doesn't compare to the real-life adventures of the Living Seas at Epcot. Unless the queues are short, skip it.

Dumbo, the Flying Elephant

This happy little elephant has become the center of some controversy: Is he worth the wait or not? Although the lines do indeed move slowly, making a one-hour wait possible for a 90-second ride, there's something special about this attraction. It's frequently featured in the ads, so it has become an integral part of our collective Disney consciousness. And since riders make Dumbo fly by pressing a button, it's one of only two Fantasyland rides that aren't totally passive. Obviously, if you visit this ride first thing in the morning you can cut the wait down substantially, perhaps to only a few minutes.

Note: Go for it. If you weren't the sort of person willing to invest an hour of agony for 90 seconds of joy you probably shouldn't have had children in the first place.

The Mad Tea Party

Spinning pastel cups, propelled by their riders, swirl around the Soused Mouse who periodically pops out of the teapot. Since you largely control how fast your teacup spins, this ride can be enjoyed by people of all ages.

Note: Rider volume ebbs and flows at this attraction. If the line looks too daunting, grab a drink at the nearby

Tomorrowland Terrace. By the time you emerge, the crowd may have dispersed.

FANTASYLAND TOURING TIPS

1. Visit Fantasyland either before 11 A.M., after 5 P.M., or during the 3 P.M. parade.

2. Don't eat or shop in Fantasyland. Similar food and toys can be found elsewhere in far less crowded areas of the MK.

3. Park your strollers in one spot and walk from ride to ride. Fantasyland is geographically small, so this is easier than constantly loading and reloading the kids only to push them a few steps.

4. Dumbo can have long lines and loads slowly. The waiting area is completely exposed to the sun, which can be sweltering for an adult and even worse for a 3-year-old. One parent should stand in line while the other makes a potty stop with the children. As the queue makes its last turn before boarding, simply hand the kids back over to the parent who has been waiting in line.

5. Stay alert. Because the kiddie rides tempt kids to wander off, this is the most likely spot in all of WDW to lose your children.

MICKEY'S STARLAND

More like a single, unified attraction than a "land," Mickey's Starland was opened in 1989. Mickey's house dominates the miniature town of Duckburg, which also contains an unassuming petting zoo, and a playground with slides, "treehouses," and a maze. The unchallenged star of the petting zoo is a cow dubbed Minnie Moo whose spots form a perfect outline of Mickey Mouse. After cooing over the animals and playing awhile on the slides, the kids will undoubtedly want to meet some of the characters who regularly wander the streets of Starland, signing autographs and posing for pictures.

The main attraction of Starland is the musical stage show featuring the stars of the Disney Afternoon TV shows. File through Mickey's house and rest a bit while watching the cartoon clips, which are shown in the Starland tent. Within 20 minutes you'll be ushered into the theater and treated to a lively show. As the characters are hitting their last note, prepare to exit via the doors to your left and head for Mickey's Hollywood Theater, which is next door to the show tent. Many people leave the show without realizing they can visit Mickey in his personal dressing room; if you exit promptly now, you'll be the first in line. (You can always return to the interactive games and "Walk of Fame" in the tent later, after you've visited Mickey.)

Guests are taken in groups of 10 to meet Mickey. This is by far your best chance in all of WDW to meet the main mouse without getting mobbed. Families who have toured several days without yet snagging that obligatory picture of the kids posing with Mickey are almost in tears of gratitude as they enter the dressing room.

Mickey's Starland is a must if your kids are under 10, but probably skippable for others. Also, be advised that you can meet Mickey without taking in the show; just go straight to the Hollywood Theater and get in line.

Note: The WDW railroad runs between Main Street and Mickey's Starland, but arriving by train is no faster than walking and, in fact, since you detrain with a couple of hundred other passengers who all swarm the show tent en masse, it may even waste time. Take the train only if it's midday and you're looking for a chance to sit down.

TOMORROWLAND

A precursor to Epcot, and scheduled for a complete makeover, Tomorrowland has relatively few attractions that appeal to children under 7. With the exception of the area around Space Mountain, it's the least crowded section in the MK.

Tomorrowland Attractions

Space Mountain

This three-minute roller-coaster ride through inky darkness is one of the few scream-rippers in the MK. The cars move at 28 mph, a fairly tame pace compared to that of the monster coasters at some theme parks, but the entire ride takes place inside Space Mountain and it's impossible to anticipate the turns and dips in the blackness, which adds considerably to the thrill. Space Mountain is the most popular MK attraction with visitors between 11 and 21 years of age.

Children under 7 must be 44 inches tall and have an adult present to ride. Children under 3 and pregnant women are prohibited. Some kids 3–7 loved the ride, but most surveyed found it too scary. Only you know whether your children are up to this.

Grand Prix Raceway

These tiny sports cars circle a nifty-looking miniature racetrack, and although the ride isn't anything unusual, kids rated it very highly, perhaps due to the fact that even young drivers can steer the cars themselves. (If Jennifer's legs are too short to reach the gas pedal, Mom or Dad can handle the floor pedals while she steers.) Kids 52 inches and taller can drive solo.

Note: Try to convince your child not to rush through the ride; loading and unloading the race cars takes time and you may as well drive slowly, savoring the loops of the track, rather than sit for five minutes in the pit waiting to be unloaded.

Skyway to Fantasyland

You'll find pretty views, especially at night, but by the time you wait in line to board this ride you could have walked.

Delta Dreamflight

This is a happy, upbeat ride tracing the history of flight. Nothing terribly special, at least not in comparison to similar Epcot attractions, but it loads quickly and preschoolers like it.

Astro Orbiter

This circular thrill ride, a sort of Dumbo on steroids, is a bit too much for preschoolers and a bit too little for teens. Like Dumbo, it loads slowly; kids 7–11 liked the Orbiter, but others should skip it.

Transportarium

Transportarium is a new CircleVision 360 film that combines a variety of special effects with Audio-Animatronics for a time-travel theme. It replaces the old standard, *American Journeys.* The film is well done, but guests stand throughout the presentation and strollers are not allowed inside the theater, which means babies and toddlers have to be held during the 20-minute show—a condition that eliminates it for many families. *Note:* Lines disappear every 20 minutes, making *Transportarium* a good choice for the most crowded times of the afternoon.

WEDway PeopleMover

This little tram circles Tomorrowland and provides fun views, including a glimpse inside Space Mountain.

Carousel of Progress

This is another fairly long show (26 minutes), another high-capacity attraction, and thus another good choice for the crowded times of the afternoon. Kids under 10, however, may be bored by this salute to the uses of electricity, especially once they've seen the jazzed-up presentations of Epcot.

Alien Encounter

Due to open in 1995 where the old Mission to Mars was located, the Alien Encounter represents Disney's ambitious first step in a complete revamp of Tomorrowland. This will be a mixed-media show, with aliens appearing and disappearing into a giant screen. Despite the ominous previews—"It's coming . . . and there's nothing you can do about it"—humor is mixed in with the special effects, which include the sensation of someone blowing down the back of your neck.

TOMORROWLAND AND MICKEY'S STARLAND TOURING TIPS

1. If you plan to ride Space Mountain, make a beeline for it immediately upon entering the park gates. After 9:30 A.M. there are substantial lines.

2. If you don't plan to ride Space Mountain, save To-morrowland for afternoon touring when the park is at its most crowded. Several Tomorrowland attractions, such as *Transportarium* and Carousel of Progress, are high-capacity and relatively easy to get into even in the most packed part of the day. Others, such as the WEDway PeopleMover and Delta Dreamflight, board quickly and offer the added bonus of letting you sit for a while.

3. Looking for fast food during peak dining hours? To-morrowland food stands are rarely as busy as those in other areas of the MK.

4. The characters appear throughout the day in Mickey's Starland; your entertainment schedule gives specific times. It is easier to meet them here than on Main Street or in front of Cinderella Castle.

5. Like Fantasyland, Mickey's Starland can become unbearably crowded in midafternoon. By early evening, however, the crowds thin.

ADVENTURELAND

Thematically the most bizarre of all the lands—a kind of "Bourbon Street meets Trinidad by way of the Congo"—Adventureland still manages to convey an exotic mood.

Adventureland Attractions

Jungle Cruise
You'll meet up with headhunters, hyenas, water-spewing elephants, and other varieties of frankly fake wildlife on

this 10-minute boat ride. What distinguishes this attraction is the amusing patter of the tour guides—these young adventurers in pith helmets are unsung heroes of Disney casting genius.

The cruise is not at all scary and is fine for any age, but the lines move with agonizing slowness. It's skippable, but if you decide to take the cruise, go in the morning—or during the 3 P.M. parade.

Swiss Family Robinson Treehouse

There's a real split of opinion here—some visitors love this replica of the ultimate treehouse, others rate it as dull. One word of warning: This is a tough attraction to tour with toddlers. The steps are numerous and at times the climbing is a bit too precarious for unsteady little legs. Lugging a 2-year-old through the exhibit is tiring, but the real problem is that the bamboo and rigging look so enticing that kids want to climb on their own, and at their own pace. This may not sit well with the 800 people in line behind you.

The Enchanted Tiki Birds (aka Tropical Serenade)

Interestingly, these singing/talking birds, and the singing/talking flowers and statues around them, represent Disney's first attempt at the Audio-Animatronics that are now such an integral part of Epcot magic. The attraction is dated and boring in comparison to the newer robotics, however, and is quite skippable unless you're just looking for a cool, quiet place to sit down in midafternoon.

Pirates of the Caribbean

The Pirates inspire great loyalty, and a significant number of guests of all ages name this ride as their favorite in all the MK. Your boat goes over a small waterfall, and there is a bit of menace on the faces of some buccaneers, but very few kids leave the Pirates frightened. Most would agree with the 5-year-old who voted the ride "best reason to leave Fantasyland."

FRONTIERLAND

Kids love the rough-and-tumble, Wild West feel of Frontierland, which is home to several of the MK's most popular attractions.

Frontierland Attractions

Big Thunder Mountain Railroad

A roller coaster disguised as a runaway mine train, Big Thunder is considerably less scary than Space Mountain, but almost as popular. The glory of the ride is in the setting. You zoom through a deserted mining town populated with bats, rainmakers, and saloon denizens, all crafted Disney-style.

If you're wondering if the coaster may be too much for your kids, be advised that Big Thunder Mountain is more in the rattle-back-and-forth school than the lose-your-stomach-as-you-plunge category. Almost any child over 7 should be able to handle the dips and twists, and many preschoolers adore the ride as well. If you have doubts, see how your 5-year-old reacts to Pirates of the Caribbean or the Maelstrom at Epcot's Norway pavilion first.

Note: Children under 7 must ride with an adult, and no one under 40 inches tall is allowed to board.

Splash Mountain

Based on *Song of the South* and inhabited by Brer Rabbit, Brer Bear, Brer Fox, and the other characters from that film, Splash Mountain takes riders on a watery, winding journey through swamps and bayous, culminating in a 40 mph drop over a five-story waterfall. Zip-A-Dee-Doo-Dah, perhaps the most hummable of all Disney theme songs, fills the air, making the ride both charming and exhilarating—truly the best of both worlds.

Note: Splash Mountain has gotten a good deal of media attention, and it's crowded; ride early in the morning or in the last hour before closing. The intensity of that last drop, along with the 44-inch height requirement, will eliminate most preschoolers as riders. If your kids are unsure if they're up to it, watch a few cars make the final drop before you decide.

Diamond Horseshoe Jamboree

Sandwiches and punch are served during this 30-minute saloon show, which is full of hokey humor and lively dance. Some of the puns will go over the heads of younger children, but the material is delivered in the same broad style as the Hoop-Dee-Doo Musical Revue, so kids find themselves laughing even when they're not quite sure why.

Make reservations for the Jamboree at the Hospitality House as you enter in the morning. Between standing in line, eating, and watching the show, you'll end up devoting 90 minutes to the Jamboree. That may be an advantage if you have young kids who nap, if you're pregnant, or if you just want a midday place to rest. But it's a disadvantage if you're on a tight touring schedule. See the Jamboree only if (1) you'll be in the MK for more than one day, and (2) you aren't planning to see the similar

Hoop-Dee-Doo Musical Revue at Fort Wilderness Campground. *Note:* If you just want to see the show, you don't have to order food.

Frontierland Shootin' Arcade
Bring your quarters. This is a pretty standard shooting gallery, but a good place for the kids to kill a few minutes while adults wait in line at the Country Bear Jamboree.

Country Bear Jamboree
Kids of all ages fall for the funny, furry Audio-Animatronic critters featured in this 15-minute show. From the coy Teddi Barra to the incomparable Big Al, from Bubbles, Bunny, and Beulah (a sort of combination of the Andrews Sisters and the Beach Boys) to Melvin the Moosehead, each face is distinctive and lovable.

The Jamboree is popular, but you can slip in easily in the evening or during the 3 P.M. parade. (But don't, for heaven's sake, try to get in just after the parade, when thousands of tourists suddenly find themselves on the streets of Frontierland with nothing to do.)

Note: A different but equally charming show runs at Christmas.

Tom Sawyer Island
A getaway playground full of caves, bridges, forts, and windmills, Tom Sawyer Island is a good destination when the kids become too rambunctious to handle. Adults can sip a lemonade at Aunt Polly's Landing, the island fast-food restaurant, while the kids run free.

The only real drawback is that the island is accessible only by raft, which means you often have to wait to get there and wait to get back. If your kids are under 5, don't bother making the trip. The terrain is too rough and widespread for preschoolers to play without supervision, and young kids can better blow off steam at the playground in Mickey's Starland. But if your kids are 5–9 and beginning to resemble wild Indians, stop off at Tom Sawyer's Island, where such behavior is not only acceptable, it's de rigeur.

Davy Crockett Explorer Canoes

Like the riverboat and keelboats of Liberty Square, these crafts circle the Rivers of America around Tom Sawyer Island, affording you unusual views of Big Thunder Mountain Railroad and the other sights of Frontierland. Unlike the riverboat and keelboats, however, the canoes are human powered, which makes them appealing to some tourists, appalling to others. Don't board unless you're prepared to row.

Note: The canoes are in dock only during the summer and major holidays. Kids need to be able to pull their own weight—literally—to board, so if you have preschoolers choose another type of boat instead.

LIBERTY SQUARE

Walk on a few feet from Frontierland and you'll find yourself transported back another hundred years to Colonial America, strolling the cobblestone streets of Liberty Square.

Liberty Square Attractions

Liberty Square Riverboat

The second tier of this paddle-wheel riverboat offers outstanding views of Liberty Square and Frontierland but, as with the other Rivers of America crafts, board only if you have time to kill and the boat is in the dock. *Note:* There are some seats but most riders stand.

The Hall of Presidents

This attraction may remind you that one of the villains in the movie *The Stepford Wives* was a Disney engineer. The Hall of Presidents is indeed a Stepford version of the presidency, with eerily lifelike and quietly dignified chief executives, each responding to his name in the roll call with a nod or tilting of the head. In the background other presidents fidget and whisper. Bill Clinton made his debut in 1994, and Maya Angelou narrates the show.

The presidential roll call and the film on the Constitution that precedes it will probably bore kids under 10. Older children will find the 20-minute presentation educational. Babies and toddlers consider the Hall a fine place to nap. A good choice for afternoon.

Note: The theater holds up to 700 people, which means that lines disappear every 25 minutes. Ask one of the attendants at the lobby doors how long it is before the next show and amble in about 10 minutes before showtime.

Mike Fink Keelboats

These small boats follow the same route as the canoes and riverboat. But the riverboat holds more people at a time, so if you're in a rush, take the riverboat.

The Haunted Mansion

More apt to elicit a giggle than a scream, the Mansion is full of clever special effects—at one point a ghost "hitchhikes" a ride in your own "doom buggy"! The cast members, who dress as morticians and never smile, add considerably to the fun with such instructions as "Drag your wretched bodies to the dead center of the room." A significant number of kids 7–11 listed the Haunted Mansion as one of their favorite attractions, but the mothers of several children under 7 reported that their kids were frightened. The spooks are played for fun, but the entire ride does take place in darkness.

The Mansion is best viewed before noon or, if you have the courage, in the last two hours before closing.

ADVENTURELAND, FRONTIERLAND, AND LIBERTY SQUARE TOURING TIPS

1. If you have two days to spend touring the MK, begin your second in Frontierland, at Splash Mountain. Move on to Big Thunder Mountain Railroad, then the Haunted Mansion in Liberty Square. All three attractions are relatively easy to board before 10 A.M., and you can return to ride less-crowded Liberty Square and Frontierland attractions later in the day.

2. Because most visitors tour the lands in a clockwise or counterclockwise fashion, these three lands reach peak capacity around noon and stay crowded until around 4 P.M., when the people lined up to watch the 3 P.M. parade finally disperse. So if you miss Splash Mountain, the Jungle Cruise, the Haunted Mansion, or Big Thunder Mountain Railroad in the morning, wait until evening to revisit them.

3. Should you, despite your best intentions, wind up in one of these three sections in midafternoon, you'll find a bit of breathing space on Tom Sawyer Island, with the Enchanted Tiki Birds, in the Hall of Presidents, or among the shops in the shady Adventureland Pavilion. Surprisingly, Pirates of the Caribbean isn't that difficult to board in midafternoon. The lines look terrible, but at least you wait

inside—and this is one of the fastest-loading attractions in WDW.

4. As of this writing, Splash Mountain stays mobbed almost all day long. Any time you find a wait of less than 30 minutes you should queue up immediately and thank your lucky stars.

   Everyone dashes to Splash Mountain the minute the ropes drop, and on very busy days this means the line may be massive within minutes after the park opens. If you hustle straight to Frontierland and arrive only to find yourself facing a wait longer than 30 minutes, move on to Big Thunder Mountain Railroad; check Splash Mountain again immediately afterward, and you may find that the initial surge of people has moved through and the line is a bit shorter.

   The lines also shorten in the last hour before closing, especially on the nights when SpectroMagic is scheduled. Even if you've already ridden once, you'll find that Splash Mountain is a whole new experience after dark.

FULL SERVICE RESTAURANTS IN THE MAGIC KINGDOM

1. *Tony's Town Square Cafe*
Located in the Main Street Hub
This thoroughly enjoyable restaurant is dedicated to *Lady and the Tramp*, with scenes from the popular film dotting the walls and a statue of the canine romantics in the center. The cuisine, like that of the cafe where Tramp wooed Lady, is classic Italian, and the portions are generous.

Tony's is a terrific choice for breakfast because, along with the other Main Street eateries, it begins serving before the park officially opens. The *Lady and the Tramp* character waffles are a big hit with preschoolers, as are most of the other offerings on the kiddie menu.

The menus, which feature pictures of Lady and the Tramp to color, are handed out with crayons, and the wait at Tony's is rarely long, making it a good choice for families with toddlers in tow. Tony's is moderately priced, and open for breakfast, lunch, and dinner. Reservations are accepted at the door.

2. *The Plaza Restaurant*
Located on Main Street

The sandwiches, burgers, and salads served at the Plaza are very filling. Try the chicken pot pie, which is encased in a huge pastry puff, or the milkshakes, which are trotted over from the Sealtest Ice Cream Parlor next door. The Plaza is moderately priced and open for lunch and dinner. No reservations are accepted.

3. *Crystal Palace*
Located between Main Street and Adventureland

The MK's only cafeteria offers something for everyone and allows picky eaters a chance to pick. You can find a classic eggs-and-bacon breakfast here, salads and sandwiches at lunch, and nearly anything you please at dinner—even that most elusive of all MK foods, vegetables. And the setting is absolutely lovely.

One warning: Because of its central location and distinctive architecture, few visitors pass by the Crystal Palace without checking it out. The cafeteria is especially crowded from noon to 2 P.M., so you should aim to go around 11 A.M. or in midafternoon. The Crystal Palace is moderately priced and open for breakfast, lunch, and dinner. No reservations are accepted.

4. *Liberty Tree Tavern*
Located in Liberty Square
Crammed with antiques and decorated in a style reminiscent of Colonial Williamsburg, the tavern serves salads and sandwiches at lunch, along with more than passable clam chowder. The dinner menu offers classic American cuisine, such as turkey and dressing or pot roast stew, as well as prime rib, seafood, and chicken. Reservations are recommended, but, unlike King Stefan's Banquet Hall in the castle, there is no one at the door to take them until 11 A.M. Either plan to eat early, when you can usually walk in without a reservation, or make reservations as you leave Fantasyland midmorning. The Tavern is open for lunch and dinner—and it's expensive.

5. *King Stefan's Banquet Hall*
Located in Cinderella Castle, Fantasyland
Nestled high amid the spires of the castle, this restaurant—named, mysteriously enough, for Sleeping Beauty's father—is very popular. Make reservations at the restaurant door first thing in the morning, although even with reservations you can expect to wait for both your table and your food. Because the service is slow and the menu pricey, King Stefan's is not a place to drop in to casually.

Is it worth it? Yes, if your kids like Cinderella. She appears downstairs throughout the day to greet diners and pose for pictures. (Ask what times she is scheduled before you make your reservation.) Kids love the distinctive pumpkin-shaped kiddie menus, and often bring them back downstairs for Cinderella to autograph. The setting of the high-ceilinged, massive banquet hall is spectacular, and the leaded glass windows overlook the rides of Fantasyland, offering a stunning view, especially at night. King Stefan's offers a relatively ambitious menu, including a gorgeous fruit plate and yummy prime rib sandwiches. Open for lunch and dinner. Reservations are accepted—and required.

DECENT FAST-FOOD PLACES IN THE MAGIC KINGDOM

1. The Mile Long Bar in Frontierland is a good place for tame Tex-Mex, and lines move more swiftly than those at the Pecos Bill Cafe next door.

2. Tomorrowland Terrace is by far the fastest of the sandwich and fries places.

3. Columbia Harbour House in Liberty Square serves clam chowder in a scooped-out loaf of sourdough bread, a pleasant change from burgers and dogs.

4. Sleepy Hollow, also in Liberty Square, is a good place for the health-conscious, offering veggie sandwiches and meatless chili. The shady park across the street is a great place to relax while you eat.

5. If you feel like lighter fare, get a citrus swirl at the Sunshine Tree Terrace in Adventureland. Like Sleepy Hollow, this snack shop is tucked out of the way with its own quiet courtyard.

6. Families who demand healthy snacks will be pleased by the addition of the Liberty Square Market, where fresh fruits and juices are available.

7. Luminere's Kitchen in Fantasyland provides the Disney version of a Happy Meal, featuring a cartoon-covered box with a burger, fries, and a souvenir pin inside. If you buy one of these meals, carry the food into a less crowded part of the park and look for a bench.

In general, the fast-food places in Fantasyland are a must to avoid, as is the Adventureland Veranda, where you wait far too long for mediocre Chinese food.

AFTERNOON RESTING PLACES

* The WDW Railroad (you can rest while you ride)
* The small park across from Sleepy Hollow in Liberty Square
* The Diamond Horseshoe Jamboree
* The Hall of Presidents
* *Magic Journeys,* the 3-D film in Fantasyland
* Tom Sawyer Island
* Guests with a five-day ticket can take the launch marked "Campground and Discovery Island" to either River Country or Discovery Island. If it's hot, bring your suits along, or wear them under your clothes—an hour or two in River Country can cool you off and revive your spirits.
* If you want a leisurely, quiet lunch, take the resort monorail to one of the MK hotels. The coffee shops and snack bars are rarely crowded in the middle of the day.

BEST VANTAGE POINTS FOR WATCHING THE PARADES

1. The absolutely best location is at the very beginning of Main Street, along the hub in front of the Railroad Station. (The parade begins here, emerging from behind City Hall.) You do lose the vantage

point of the floats coming down Main Street, but it's worth it not to have to fight the crowds.

The crowds grow less manageable as you proceed down Main Street, and are at their worst in front of Cinderella Castle. In fact, if you find yourself four layers of people back on Main Street, send one of your party toward the entrance gate to check out the situation at the hub; you may find there's still curb space there when the rest of the route is mobbed.

2. If you find yourself deep in the bowels of the theme park at parade time, don't try to fight your way up Main Street to the hub. You'll never make it. Instead, go to the end of the route, in front of Pecos Bill Cafe in Frontierland. The crowds here are thinner than in front of the Castle or in Liberty Square.

3. On very busy days, the parade may run more than once—going from Main Street to Frontierland and then back from Frontierland to Main Street. Ask the nearest Disney attendant which direction the parade will be coming from and try to get as close as possible to the beginning of the parade route. Being near the beginning of the route saves the kids a 20-minute wait to see the show and also ensures that you won't be caught in the exit crowd.

BEST RESTROOM LOCATIONS IN THE MAGIC KINGDOM

By best I mean least crowded. You can get in and out of these rather quickly:

1. Behind the Enchanted Grove snack bar near the Mad Tea Party.

2. In the passageway between Adventureland and Frontierland. This one draws traffic, but it is so huge that you never have to wait long.

3. Near the Skyway to Fantasyland in Tomorrowland.

4. If you're in the Baby Services Center for other reasons, make a pit stop.

5. The sit-down restaurants have their own restrooms, which are never very crowded.

6. As you leave Pirates of the Caribbean, make a stop at the restroom located at the back of the market stalls. This one is so secluded that I only found it myself on my 17th fact-finding trip to WDW.

THE MAGIC KINGDOM DON'T-MISS LIST

If your kids are 7 or older:

- Space Mountain
- Splash Mountain
- Pirates of the Caribbean
- Big Thunder Mountain Railroad
- Haunted Mansion
- The parades
- Any of the Fantasyland rides that catch their fancy
- Alien Encounter

If your kids are under 7:

- Dumbo, the Flying Elephant
- Grand Prix Raceway
- Mad Tea Party
- It's a Small World
- Peter Pan's Flight

- Mickey's Starland
- Pirates of the Caribbean
- Country Bear Jamboree
- The parades
- Splash Mountain, if they pass the height requirement
- Big Thunder Mountain Railroad, if they pass the height requirement

YOUR LAST HOUR IN THE MAGIC KINGDOM

1. Some rides—most notably Big Thunder Mountain Railroad, Cinderella's Carousel, Dumbo, Splash Mountain, and the Skyway between Tomorrowland and Fantasyland—are particularly beautiful at night.

2. If you've missed any of the biggie rides earlier in the day, return in the last hour; lines are shorter just before closing, especially in Fantasyland.

3. If you're visiting on an evening when SpectroMagic is scheduled, move as far as possible up Main Street and stake your curb space near the hub. Turn in your strollers and make a final potty run before the parade starts, so you'll be ready to make a fast exit once the final float rolls by.

THE SCARE FACTOR IN THE MAGIC KINGDOM

Nothing at WDW is truly terrifying. In fact, young visitors raised on a steady diet of coasters called "Cork-

screw" and "Python" are apt to find Disney offerings
pretty tame.

But Disney plays on your emotions in more subtle
ways. Children who would seem to be anesthetized by
the violence of movies like *Halloween VIII* have been
known to sob inconsolably over the demise of Old Yeller.
And the attention to detail that is so much a Disney
trademark is especially evident in attractions like the
new Great Movie Ride at MGM—when the alien lunges
at you from above, he's believable.

It makes the scare factor tough to gauge. With the exception of Space Mountain, nothing at WDW will knock
off your glasses or shake out your fillings. But remember, Walt was the guy who bumped off Bambi's mother,
and preschool children may be shaken in a totally different way.

Snow White's Adventures

Don't expect to leave this attraction humming "Whistle
While You Work." Riders take the role of Snow White as
she flees through the woods, and the witch does leap out
at you several times. But the ride is a short one, and the
special effects are fairly simple.

Final verdict: Not too scary, fine for most kids over 4.

Mr. Toad's Wild Ride

Your car careens through a fun house. At one point you
make a wrong turn onto a railroad track with a train ap-
proaching.

Final verdict: Not scary at all.

Big Thunder Mountain Railroad

An exciting three-minute ride, one of the best-loved in
the Magic Kingdom. At no time does the train go very

high, although it does travel fairly fast. Riders exit giggly but not shaky.

Final verdict: Fine for the 7 and above crowd. Children must be 40 inches tall to ride, and some kids under 7 who rode with their parents loved Big Thunder. If you're debating which of the three "mountains" (i.e., Splash Mountain, Big Thunder Mountain, Space Mountain) is most suitable for a preschooler, Big Thunder is your best bet.

The Haunted Mansion

More funny than scary. The teenagers who load you into your black "doom buggy" are dressed like morticians and never smile or meet your eyes . . . the ceiling in the portrait hall moves up . . . and the mansion is home to ravens, floating objects, swirling ghosts, glowing crystal balls, and doors that rap when there's no one there.

Final verdict: Fine for any child over 7, and most younger kids. A few parents reported that their preschoolers got nervous.

Alien Encounter

A gruesome alien shows up in the theater when a transportation experiment goes awry. The sound effects are shiveringly real, and at one point someone taps you on the shoulder.

Final verdict: A rather intense show, best suited for kids 10 and over.

Pirates of the Caribbean

My 4-year-old daughter grew a bit apprehensive as we wove our way through the drafty, dungeonlike queue area, but she loved the ride that followed. Although there are gunshots, skeletons, cannons, mangy-looking buccaneers, and even a brief drop over a "waterfall" in the dark, the mood is decidedly up-tempo.

Final verdict: Fine for anyone.

Splash Mountain

The atmosphere inside the mountain is so happy and kid-oriented that it's a shame the final plunge over the waterfall is so steep. This last drop gives riders the feeling that they're coming out of their seats and momentarily takes your breath away. Nonetheless, the same 44-inch height requirement applies as at Space Mountain, meaning that many children under the age of 7 technically qualify to ride. The final verdict rests with the parents. The general consensus among the families we surveyed is that the ride is OK for any child 5 and over.

Note: Don't let the fact that Splash Mountain has the same height requirement as Space Mountain fool you—it's nowhere near as wild. The height requirement is partially due to the construction of the log boats, which are built with high walls to limit how much riders are soaked during the final drop. But an unhappy side effect of the log construction is that a child shorter than 44 inches wouldn't be able to see much—and might be tempted to stand.

Astro Orbiter

You can control how high your spaceship flies in this cyclic ride. A good choice for those not quite up to Space Mountain.

Final verdict: Fun for kids 7–11. This is the jazzed-up version of the old Starjets ride.

Space Mountain

It's not just the fact that this is a roller coaster, it's the fact that you plunge through utter darkness that makes Space Mountain unique. There are lots of sharp dips with very little warning time. Kids under 7 must be with an adult, and pass the 44-inch height requirement. Children under 3 cannot ride.

Final verdict: Forget it for preschoolers. Kids in the 7–11 age range in general like Space Mountain. Teens adore it.

5

★★★★★★★★★★★★★★★★★★★

Epcot Center

EPCOT CENTER

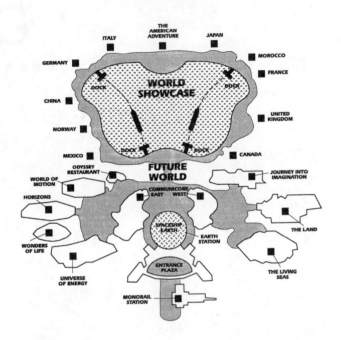

GETTING TO EPCOT CENTER

1. Epcot is easy to reach by car. If you arrive early in the morning, you can park very close to the main entrance gate and forgo the tram ride. If you arrive a bit later, however, the trams do run quickly and efficiently. Just be sure to write down the number of the row where you parked your car.

2. Many off-site hotels offer shuttle buses to Epcot. Fort Wilderness, Port Orleans, Dixie Landings, the Disney Villas, Wilderness Lodge, the All-Star Resorts, the Vacation Club, and the Caribbean Beach Resort all run direct shuttles as well.

3. If you're staying at the Polynesian, Grand Floridian, or Contemporary, your fastest route is to take the monorail to the TTC and then transfer to the Epcot monorail.

4. The Swan, the Dolphin, and the Yacht and Beach Clubs are connected to a special "backdoor" World Showcase entrance by bridge. Either take the shuttle tram, or, if you're staying at the Yacht or Beach Club, simply walk over the bridge.

GETTING AROUND EPCOT CENTER

As any Disneyophile can tell you, Epcot is an acronym for the Experimental Prototype City of Tomorrow. But as one of the players at the Comedy Warehouse on Pleasure Island suggests, maybe Epcot really stands for Every Person Comes Out Tired.

Epcot is indeed sprawling, but the FriendShips that crisscross the World Showcase Lagoon and the double-decker buses that encircle the lagoon should be viewed as fun rides, not serious transportation. Your fastest means of getting around is walking.

YOUR FIRST HOUR AT EPCOT CENTER

1. As soon as you enter the main gate, veer left to rent strollers. Then, if it's operative, ride Spaceship Earth.

2. One parent should take the kids and the camera and order breakfast at the Stargate Restaurant. The characters are often sighted here around 8:30 A.M. (Sometimes they're at the Sunrise Terrace, also near the entrance; appearances are noted on your entertainment schedule, and there's always a sign outside the door as well.)

   The other parent should enter the WorldKey Information center inside the Earth Station under Spaceship Earth, pick up an entertainment and special events schedule, and then make dining reservations.

3. After the ropes are dropped and you're allowed to enter the body of the park, veer sharply left to the Wonders of Life pavilion. Ride Body Wars first.

4. After Body Wars, leave the Wonders of Life pavilion—knowing you can always return for the films and interactive exhibits later—and move on to Horizons, then to World of Motion, and finally to the Maelstrom ride in the Norway pavilion.

EPCOT CENTER TOURING TIPS

1. Visit new attractions such as the Wonders of Life or the Norway pavilion first.

2. If you can't ride Spaceship Earth early in the morning, wait until evening.

3. Avoid the high-capacity shows such as Universe of Energy or *O Canada!* in the morning. Your time is better spent moving among the continuous-loading attractions such as Body Wars and Horizons, and the Land, World of Motion, Living Seas, and Journey Into Imagination pavilions. Save the theater-style attractions until afternoon.

4. Touring Epcot is easier if you zig when everyone else zags. Future World stays crowded from mid-morning until late afternoon, then empties as people head toward their dinner reservations in the World Showcase.

   You can avoid crowds by touring Future World until midmorning, then drifting toward the World Showcase in the afternoon, where you can escape to the films and indoor exhibits during the hottest and busiest times.

   Then, perhaps after the late afternoon character show at the mouth of the World Showcase Lagoon, or after dinner if you've made a reservation, head back into Future World. Attractions such as Journey Into Imagination and Living Seas are rarely packed in the evening.

5. If you are touring off-season and plan to spend mornings in the MK or at MGM and evenings at Epcot, make your Epcot dinner reservations for as early as possible, leaving yourself several hours to tour after dinner.

   Another alternative: If your children have had a good afternoon nap and can keep going until 10 P.M., make your dinner reservations very late. The restaurants accept their final seating just before the park shuts down, and all the transportation stays operative for at least 90 minutes after the official park closing time. Eating late buys you maximum hours in the park, assuming your kids can handle the schedule.

6. Upon entering a World Showcase pavilion that has a show or film—France, Canada, America, or China—ask the attendant how long you have until the show begins. If your wait is 10 minutes or less, queue up. If the wait is longer, browse the shops of the pavilion until about 10 minutes before showtime. The World Showcase theaters are large and everyone who shows up within 10 minutes of the film's starting time will be seated.

7. Most people circle the World Showcase Lagoon in a clockwise fashion, beginning with Mexico. You'll make better time if you move counterclockwise, beginning with Canada.

8. The interactive exhibits inside the CommuniCores and in the Wonders of Life, Journey Into Imagination, and World of Motion pavilions are very worthwhile, and a nice break from the enforced passivity of all the rides. But ride the rides first and save the interactive games for midafternoon or early evening.

9. If you're not staying for IllumiNations, begin moving toward the exit gates while the show is in progress.

   If you miss the chance to exit before the IllumiNations crowd or you've opted to stay for the show, don't join in the throngs that mob the exit turnstiles and shuttle buses just after the show has ended. Pick up dessert before the show and then, after IllumiNations, find a table, sit down, relax, and let the crowds pass you by. The trams and monorails will still be running long after you finish your snack, and the lines waiting for them will be shorter.

FUTURE WORLD

Future World comprises nine large pavilions, each containing at least one major attraction. It is rather like a permanent World's Fair, mixing educational opportunities with big doses of fun. Most visitors are drawn first to the rides, with their spectacular special effects, but don't miss the chance to play with the smaller, interactive exhibits. Many of these encourage young visitors to learn while doing, and stopping to try them out helps kids avoid what one mother termed "Audio-Animatronics overload."

Future World Attractions

Spaceship Earth

Few travelers, whatever their age, can remain blasé at the sight of Spaceship Earth, the most photographed and readily recognizable symbol of Epcot.

The ride inside, which coils toward the top of the 17-story geosphere, traces developments in communication from cave drawings to computers. The voice of Walter Cronkite booms in your ear as you climb past scenes of Egyptian temples, the Gutenberg press, and a performance of *Oedipus Rex*. Even preschoolers rated Spaceship Earth highly, probably due to the excitement of actually entering the "Big Ball" and the impressive finale, which flashes a planetarium sky above you as you swirl backward down through the darkness.

The Living Seas

The Living Seas features a saltwater aquarium so enormous that Spaceship Earth could float inside it. You begin with a short film that discusses the critical role of the ocean as a source of energy, then swiftly move on to board a gondola that takes you through an underwater viewing tunnel. Over 200 varieties of marine life, including stingrays, dolphins, barracuda, sharks, and an occasional scuba-clad Mickey, swim above you.

The most enjoyable part of the attraction, however, comes after you disembark at Seabase Alpha. You can remain here as long as you choose, wandering through two levels of observation tanks that allow you to view the fishes and the human divers at startlingly close quarters. (Interested kids sometimes get a chance to suit up in diving gear, but don't worry—despite teasing, the Disney cast has no intention of letting visitors in the tank.) The baby manatee is especially popular with the kids.

Note: It's easy to spend an entire afternoon at the Living Seas. But if you plan to devote a day to Sea World while in Orlando you'll find much of the same stuff there, so hold your time at the Living Seas to a minimum.

The Land

This cheerful pavilion is home to three separate attractions, as well as a rotating restaurant and fast-food court. Because it is the hub of so much activity, the Land pavilion is crowded from midmorning on. If you can't visit it before 11 A.M., wait until evening.

Living with the Land　The theme here is food and how we get it. Visitors travel by boat past scenes of various farming environments, ending with a peek at fish farming, drip irrigation, and other innovative agricultural technologies. Perhaps because there are few special effects and no cute "tour guide" like Figment, who lives in the Journey Into Imagination pavilion next door, this attraction is less interesting to preschoolers. But, as is the case in all of Future World, the ride moves swiftly and the educational aspects are winningly presented. In short, this won't be your children's favorite attraction, but they won't complain either.

Circle of Life (in the Harvest Theatre) This film, which graphically illustrates how easily man can ruin his own environment, is timely and terrific for adults and kids over the age of 11. Younger kids will be bored senseless, which isn't all bad. More than one youngster has napped during the presentation.

Food Rocks This funny, 15-minute presentation features famous rock 'n roll stars masquerading as foods. Information about nutrition is worked in among the jokes and songs. Food Rocks, which replaces the old Kitchen Kabaret show, takes place in a cool, dark, rarely-crowded theater and is a good choice for midafternoon.

Journey Into Imagination

One of the best pavilions in Future World for young kids, the ride inside features Dreamfinder and the charming purple Figment of his imagination. Together they take you through a variety of scenes celebrating art, literature, music, and other products of human creativity. Be forewarned—there's a sudden flash of light near the end of the ride. This pavilion is sponsored by Kodak and a wide-screen photograph of you in all your glory is waiting around the next turn.

Honey, I Shrunk the Audience is a 3-D movie using the theme from the *Honey, I Shrunk the Kids* films. (It replaces the popular—but suddenly controversial—Michael Jackson film *Captain EO.*) Kids love the 3-D effects!

After you disembark from Journey Into Imagination a huge digital clock tells you how many minutes until the next presentation of *Honey, I Shrunk the Audience*. While you wait, it's fun to explore the Image Works, a series of hands-on exhibits such as the Magic Palette, with an electronic paintbrush, or Stepping Tones, where kids can create music by jumping into different-colored puddles of light. Or, volunteers may get the chance to act as characters in a video short story told by the Dreamfinder himself: five or six children selected from the crowd are "inserted" into the background of a space adventure, and by following such simple commands as "jump" or "run in place" they appear to be interacting with the figures on-screen. Image Works is especially fun from 6 P.M. on, when the crowds disperse and kids don't have to wait in line to try everything out.

Image Works earned the ultimate praise—"This is better than an arcade"—from my 12-year-old niece. *Note:* Take time to check out Splashtacular, a fountain show full of special effects, as you leave the pavilion.

World of Motion
"It's Fun to Be Free," the major attraction inside the General Motors World of Motion exhibit, is described as "an Audio-Animatronics survey of the history of transportation." The description does nothing to convey the sheer joy of the ride. The robots here are the most humorous and lifelike in Future World—check out the exasperated expression on the Mona Lisa's face as Leonardo deserts her to conduct a flight experiment, or the astonishment of the rider whose stagecoach is under Indian attack. Best of all, there is rarely much of a wait at this fast-loading attraction. The TransCenter you'll find at the end of the line appeals to youngsters with motor fetishes, but contains mostly passive exhibits, with far

fewer opportunities for active play than Journey Into Imagination or Wonders of Life.

Horizons

How will the average family live in the future? General Electric takes riders into the next century, in which robots clean house, families "visit" via holographic telephone, and cities flourish on the ocean floor. Needless to say, Disney's predictions for the year 2020 are all sunny, and children love the final special effect, which allows them to press a button and choose whether their journey will end in space, on land, or under the sea.

Horizons, like World of Motion, loads fast and is rarely too crowded. These two pavilions are good choices when the new Wonders of Life next door is swamped.

Wonders of Life

Devoted to celebrating the human body, the Wonders of Life pavilion resembles a brightly colored street fair full of hands-on exhibits. You can check out your health profile via computer, get advice on your tennis or golf swing, and test your endurance on a motorized bike. Kids enjoy the film *Goofy About Health* and the Sensory Funhouse. (Despite the provocative name, this exhibit is devoted to only the most wholesome of tactile sensations.) Like the Land pavilion, Wonders of Life houses three major attractions and a food court, and is crowded by 11 A.M. Until the novelty of this new pavilion subsides, early morning touring is strongly advised.

Body Wars   As close as Epcot comes to a pure thrill ride, Body Wars incorporates the same flight-simulation technology found at MGM's Star Tours to take riders on a turbulent high-speed thrill ride through the human body. After being miniaturized to the size of a pinhead and injected into a patient, the crew is briefed to expect a routine medical mission for the purpose of removing a splinter from the "safe zone just under the skin." But when shapely Dr. Lair is sucked into a capillary, your crew is off on a rescue chase through the heart, lungs, and brain.

No expectant mothers or kids under 3 are allowed to board, and Body Wars does indeed have its queasy moments, due more to the accuracy of flight-simulation technology—and perhaps the subject matter—than the bouncing of the spaceship. Those prone to motion sickness should skip the trip, but others will enjoy it. *Note:* If you have any doubts about whether your child can handle it, ask attendants to help you do a "baby swap."

The Making of Me   This 15-minute film provides a fetus-eye view of conception, gestation, and birth. Martin Short travels back in time to show us his own parents as babies, then chronicles how they met and ultimately produced him. (One glaring anachronism: Martin must have been the only kid born in America in the fifties who was delivered through Lamaze.) Although the film is direct and unflinching, it's appropriate for any age.

If you're touring the Wonders of Life pavilion early in the morning, you should see Body Wars and perhaps Cranium Command first, then move on. Save *The Making of Me* for later in the day when you'll welcome a chance to sit down. *Note:* The line for the film is long, so let one parent queue up while the other takes the kids around to some of the interactive exhibits. Coach's Corner, which gives visitors a chance to have their golf, tennis, or baseball swing videotaped, replayed in slo-mo, and then analyzed by Nancy Lopez, Chris Evert, or Gary Carter, is especially fun.

Cranium Command   One of the funniest presentations at Epcot, Cranium Command mixes Audio-Animatronics with film. General Knowledge taps an unfortunate recruit, Fuzzy, to pilot "the most unstable craft in the fleet," the brain of a 12-year-old boy. If he fails in his mission, Fuzzy will be demoted to flying the brain of a chicken or, worse, a talk show host. Fuzzy tries to guide his boy through a typical day of junior high school without overloading his system—which isn't easy, especially when the body parts are played by this cast: Charles Grodin as the right brain, Jon Lovitz as the left brain, Hans and Franz from "Saturday Night Live" pumping it up in the role of the heart, Norm from "Cheers" as the stomach and, in a particularly convincing performance, Bobcat Goldthwait as adrenaline.

Universe of Energy

This technologically complex presentation can be enjoyed by any age and on any level. Kids are dazzled by the dinosaurs, and parents leave the pavilion muttering "How did they do that?"

A digital clock at the entryway keeps you posted as to how long it will be until the show begins. Don't file in until the wait is 10 minutes or less; this is a 32-minute presentation, and there is no point in wearing the kids out before you begin. After a pleasant preshow, you file into a conventional-looking theater for a second, shorter film about the development of fossil fuels during the prehistoric era. *Note:* There's no need to dash into the theater; latecomers stand the best chance of being seated on the ends of the rows and thus having the best views.

The Disney twist comes after the second film. The 97-seat theater begins to break apart in sections, which align themselves in sequence and move toward a curtain. Your theater has become your train and the curtain slowly lifts to reveal an Audio-Animatronics version of the film you've just viewed. The air reeks of sulfur, as it presumably did during the prehistoric era, the light is eerily blue, and all around you are those darn dinosaurs, the largest Disney robots ever created—and unnervingly authentic. The ride concludes with a final film on the future of energy in a separate auditorium, after your train has once again metamorphosed into a theater. Most amazing of all, you learn that your traveling train has been partially fueled by the solar panels on top of the Universe of Energy pavilion.

Note: Despite its proximity to the front gate, this attraction is not a good choice for the morning; save it for afternoon or early evening, when you'll welcome the chance to sit for a half-hour. Also, the Universe of Energy seats a large number of people at a time, meaning that lines form and dissipate quickly. If the line looks prohibitive, check out nearby pavilions and return in 30 minutes. You may be able to walk right in.

CommuniCores East and West Future World is also the home of CommuniCore East and CommuniCore West, two crescent-shaped plazas full of shops, restaurants, and technological exhibits. The attractions look intimidating, but most kids get the hang of them quickly and enjoy playing with the computers, touch-sensitive TV screens, and robots. Although you probably won't have time for the CommuniCores if you're trying to tour Epcot in one day, visitors with more time are often surprised by how fun the interactive exhibits can be once they get the hang of the technology. Kids of all ages rated Expo Robotics, an exhibit in which a robot actually draws your picture, highest of all CommuniCore exhibits, and the resulting profile sketch is a terrific choice for "show and tell" when the kids are back in school.

Note: The CommuniCores were expanded and re-vamped in 1994, and now feature interactive games that put Nintendo to shame.

WORLD SHOWCASE

Pretty by day and gorgeous by night, the World Showcase is comprised of the pavilions of eleven nations—Mexico, Norway, China, Germany, Italy, America, Japan, Morocco, France, the United Kingdom, and Canada—stretching around a large lagoon. Some of the pavilions have full-scale attractions, listed below; others have only shops and restaurants. Demonstrations, music, and shows are scheduled throughout the day, and the characters, dressed in appropriate international garb, frequently appear in the afternoons.

Most important from an educational and cultural perspective, each pavilion is staffed entirely by citizens of the country it represents. Disney goes to great pains to recruit, relocate, and, if necessary, teach English to the shopkeepers and waiters you see in these pavilions, bringing them to Orlando for a year and housing them with the representatives from the other World Showcase nations. It's a cultural exchange program on the highest level. (One Norwegian guide told me her roommates were from China, Mexico, and Canada.)

These young men and women save the World Showcase from being merely touristy, add an air of authenticity to every aspect of the experience, and provide your kids with the chance to rub elbows, however briefly, with other cultures. So even if pavilions such as Morocco or Japan don't have a ride or film, don't rush past them; stop for a honeyed pastry or an origami demonstration and chat with the young person behind the counter.

World Showcase Attractions

O Canada!

This 20-minute CircleVision 360 film is gorgeous and stirring—and impossible to view with kids under 6. In order to enjoy the effect of the circular screen, guests are required to stand during the presentation, and strollers are not allowed into the theater. This means babies and toddlers must be held, and preschoolers, who can't see anything in a room of standing adults, often clamor to be lifted up as well. So we regretfully suggest that families with young kids pass up this presentation, as well as the equally lovely *Wonders of China.*

Possible Solution: Canada and China are both located near the World Showcase Plaza, where the afternoon character show is held. If one adult volunteers to stay with the kids during the show, the other will have ample time to slip over to Canada or China and see one of the films. Another possibility: If you're dining at Epcot during your parents' night out, this is also a good time to take in those World Showcase attractions that just aren't oriented toward kids.

Impressions de France

What a difference a seat makes! Like all the Epcot films, *Impressions de France* is exceedingly well done, with lush music and a 200-degree wide-screen feel. It's fairly easy to get in, even in the afternoon, and no one minds if babies take a little nap.

The American Adventure

This multimedia presentation, combining Audio-Animatronics figures with film, is popular with all age groups. (Surprisingly, teenagers rated this patriotic show as their second favorite Epcot attraction, right be-hind Body Wars.) The technological highlight of the show comes when the Ben Franklin robot actually walks upstairs to visit Thomas Jefferson, but the 30-minute presentation is packed with elaborate sets that rise from the stage, film montages, moving music, and painless history lessons.

Note: The American pavilion becomes quite crowded in the afternoon, but since it's located at the exact mid-point of the World Showcase Lagoon, it's impractical to skip it and work your way back later. If you're faced with a half-hour wait, enjoy the excellent Voices of Liberty preshow or have a snack at the Liberty Inn next door.

Wonders of China
See *O Canada!*

Maelstrom
This Norwegian boat ride is a hit with kids of all ages. Your Viking ship sails through fjords and storms, over waterfalls, and past a threatening three-headed troll . . . all within four minutes. Riders disembark in a North Sea coastal village, where a short film is presented. The Norway pavilion is the newest of the World Showcase nations and can draw large crowds. Ride Maelstrom before 11 A.M., or just before the park closes, when most people have lined up to await Illumi-Nations.

El Rio del Tiempo: The River of Time
There's rarely a wait at this charming boat ride, located inside the romantic Mexico pavilion. Reminiscent of It's a Small World in the MK, El Rio is especially appealing to younger riders.

GENERAL INFORMATION ON
EPCOT RESTAURANTS

1. Among the families we surveyed, there was a great difference of opinion as to which Epcot restaurants are best. "We loved Alfredo's," writes one family, "but the Coral Reef was a big disappointment. It was overpriced and you can get the same view for free upstairs at the Living Seas." "The Coral Reef was our absolute favorite," writes another family. "Alfredo's, on the other hand, is a waste of time." (Alfredo's and the Coral Reef are the most expensive, most popular—and most controversial—Epcot eateries. Perhaps because reservations are so hard to come by, diners enter with exalted expectations and leave either profoundly disappointed or convinced they've had a mountaintop experience.)

2. If you are staying on-site, you can make reservations for both dinner and lunch up to three days in advance through Guest Services in your hotel. Such foresight may be necessary if you're aiming to get into the Coral Reef on a Friday night in July.

If you're not staying on-site, make your reservations first thing in the morning at the WorldKey Information Center in the Earth Station under Spaceship Earth. Visitors who have no reservations sometimes get seated by simply showing up at the restaurant door, especially if they try a large restaurant like the Biergarten or eat dinner very early.

3. If you'd like to try several Epcot restaurants, remember that lunchtime selections are just as impressive as dinner, and the fare is much cheaper.

4. Kids are welcome at any Epcot eatery, although some are more entertaining for youngsters than others.

(See the following section for details.) High chairs, booster seats, and kiddie menus are universally available.

5. Likewise, casual attire is OK anywhere in the park. It may seem strange to eat oysters with champagne sauce while wearing a Goofy sweatshirt, but you'll get used to it.

6. The Epcot restaurants take their reservations seriously. If you show up at the Mitsukoshi at 12:45 for a 12:30 reservation, expect to be told "Sayonara."

7. Be careful when booking for France, which is home to two sit-down restaurants: Chefs De France, which is at street level, and le Bistro de Paris, upstairs. Many visitors get these confused and risk losing their reservation by showing up at the wrong place.

8. Be bold. Your hometown probably has good Chinese and Italian restaurants, but how often do you get to sample Norwegian or Moroccan food?

9. Epcot dining isn't cheap. Dinner for a family of four at a restaurant described as "moderately priced" will still run about $50 dollars without drinks or wine. But, as throughout WDW, portions are large, even on items ordered from the kiddie menu. Two children can easily share an entree; for that matter, so can two adults.

10. If you want to save both time and money, stick to the fast-food places for meals—but make a reservation at a sit-down restaurant for a truly off time, say 4 P.M. or 10 P.M., and just have dessert. You can soak up the ambiance of le Bistro de Paris or check out the underwater scenery of the Coral Reef for an investment of 30 minutes and 10 bucks.

FULL-SERVICE RESTAURANTS AT EPCOT CENTER

How much is this place going to cost? Is the service so slow we'll miss IllumiNations? Is it hard to get reservations? Is there anything to keep the kids entertained while the adults sip their sake? Read on for an overview of the suitability of the full-service restaurants for kids. If you have fussy eaters in tow, keep in mind that all the full-service restaurants post menus outside their doors.

Disney imposes price controls at the Epcot eateries, so there is little variation in cost among the sit-down restaurants. Adult entrees at lunch will run about $10, dinner entrees about $15. Children's portions at lunch are about $5, at dinner, about $8. If you wish to cut the cost of Epcot dining, go at lunch instead of dinner, leave off wine or alcohol, and choose a restaurant, such as the Nine Dragons in China, in which patrons are encouraged to share entrees.

Note: See Section 8, "Disney World After Dark," for more information on the most romantic and adult-oriented of the Epcot restaurants.

Chefs de France (France)

Booking: Difficult.

Suitability for kids: Moderate. It's fun to watch the crowds go by, but the tables are close and the waiters move at quite a clip, so there is no place for children to stand and stretch their legs.

le Bistro de Paris (France)

Booking: Difficult.

Suitability for kids: Low. This is one of the more romantic Epcot restaurants, with dim lighting and leisurely service. Try it on the night you leave the kids back at the Mouseketeer Club.

Rose and Crown Pub (United Kingdom)

Booking: Easy.

Suitability for kids: High, especially if you eat outside and can watch the FriendShips go by on the lagoon.

Comments: Pub atmosphere, charming service, mediocre food.

Mitsukoshi (Japan)

Booking: Easy.

Suitability for kids: High.

Comments: Diners sit at large common tables while chefs slice and dice in a flamboyant fashion. If there's a Benihana in your hometown, you get the idea. The night we visited, ladies were circulating among the tables making origami souvenirs for the kids.

Alfredo's di Roma (Italy)

Booking: Very difficult.

Suitability for kids: Moderate. Most children like Italian food and the kiddie menu is well conceived, but the restaurant is very crowded and service is slow.

Marrakech (Morocco)

Booking: Easy.

Suitability for kids: Moderate. Exotic surroundings, and kids enjoy the belly dancers. The unfamiliarity of the food may pose a problem, but the children's portions are not as spicy as those served to the adults, so if the kids can be persuaded to give it a try they may find that roasted chicken tastes pretty much the same the world over.

Nine Dragons (China)

Booking: Easy.

Suitability for kids: Moderate. The service is fast, and the staff is quite happy to accommodate special requests, such as "Can you hold the sweet and sour sauce on the sweet and sour chicken?"

Comments: The ambitious menu here extends far beyond the typical Chinese fare at your favorite takeout place back home. Experimenting with an unknown dish such as Red Bean Ice Cream can lead to some very pleasant surprises.

San Angel Inn (Mexico)

Booking: Fairly difficult at lunch.

Suitability for kids: High. The service is swift and friendly, and kids can browse among the market stalls of the Mexico pavilion or ride El Rio del Tiempo while waiting for the food.

Comments: One of the best bets at Epcot.

Biergarten (Germany)

Booking: Easy.

Suitability for kids: High. There's plenty of room to move about. The atmosphere is rousing and noisy, with yodelers and an oom-pah-pah band.

Akershus (Norway)

Booking: Moderate.

Suitability for kids: Moderate. There's a buffet, so you get your food fast and have the chance to see things before you make a selection. But most of the food is apt to be unfamiliar to the kids, and there's a lot of fish, so picky eaters may rebel.

Comments: A fine spot for hearty eaters, since you can load up at the hot and cold buffet tables. Also a good chance to sample a variety of unusual dishes. Although diners were a bit nervous about the Akershus when it first opened, it's growing more popular—and harder to book—each month.

Le Cellier (Canada)

Booking: Doesn't apply, since Le Cellier is a cafeteria, and takes no reservations.

Suitability for kids: High. The menu features foods hearty enough to please a lumberjack—pork pie, meatball stew, cheddar cheese soup, and, in case your blood sugar is a little low from too much touring, Maple Syrup Pie. If the kids rebel against anything too exotic, but the parents can't face another burger, head for the neutral territory of the Canadian cafeteria.

The Garden Grille Room (Land pavilion)

Booking: Tough to book at lunch, easy at dinner.

Suitability for kids: High. Easily recognizable American dishes. The booths are large, which lets you stretch out. The restaurant rotates, allowing diners to watch scenes from the Living with the Land boat ride below.

Comments: The only full-service restaurant at Epcot offering breakfast. Try the crepes.

The Coral Reef (Living Seas pavilion)

Booking: Extremely difficult.

Suitability for kids: Moderate. One whole wall is glass, giving diners an unparalleled view of the Living Seas tank; and since the restaurant is arranged in tiers, literally every table has a good view of the fish. The children's menu is the priciest at Epcot.

Comments: If you want to sample fresh seafood while in Florida, there are innumerable Orlando restaurants that are cheaper and easier to get into.

DECENT FAST-FOOD RESTAURANTS AT EPCOT CENTER

Fast food is a somewhat relative term at Epcot, where long lines are the norm during peak dining hours. But the choices are far more varied and interesting than those in the MK. And the views are so charming—especially at the places in Mexico, Japan, and France—that Epcot blurs the distinction between fast food and fine dining.

1. The skewered chicken and beef at the Yakitori House in Japan is excellent, and the little courtyard outside gives the feel of a Japanese tea garden. *Note:* As is the case in many of the World Showcase eateries, a child's combination plate is more than adequate for an adult, especially if you'll be snacking in a couple of hours.

2. The Cantina de San Angel in Mexico serves tortillas and tostadas at tables clustered around the lagoon.

3. You'll find open-faced salmon or ham sandwiches and unusual pastries at Kringla Bakeri og Kafe in Norway. The Kafe is also a good stop for breakfast, especially for guests of the Yacht and Beach Clubs,

the Swan, or the Dolphin, who enter Epcot through the back door.

4. If your kids are suffering from hamburger withdrawal, there's always the Liberty Inn at the American pavilion, or the Odyssey Restaurant. Pizza is available in the Sunshine Terrace.

5. Simply want a snack? You can't beat the Boulangerie Patisserie in France for pastries. The Odyssey Restaurant offers at least five choices of homemade pies daily, such as Florida Key Lime or Chocolate French Silk. Since the characters appear at the Odyssey several times in the afternoon, it's a very good place to take a break.

6. If you find yourself in Future World at lunchtime, or your party can't agree on a restaurant, visit Sunshine Season in the Land pavilion. The food court here features plenty of choices, including clam chowder, quiche, barbecue, stuffed potatoes, scooped out pineapples filled with fruit salad, and killer chocolate chip cookies.

7. The tables for many of the fast-food places are outside, so if it's raining, head for Sunshine Season in the Land pavilion, the Odyssey Restaurant on the bridge connecting Future World to the World Showcase, or either the Stargate Restaurant or Sunshine Terrace in CommuniCores East and West.

8. La Maison du Vin offers wine tastings throughout the afternoon and evenings. The fee is minimal, and you get to keep the souvenir glass. If you find something you like, the bottles can be sent to Package PickUp for you to retrieve as you exit the park.

EPCOT CENTER EXTRAS

Character Sightings

- Visit with the gang around 8:30 or 9 A.M. in the Stargate Restaurant or Sunshine Terrace.

- The characters also appear in the afternoon at the Odyssey Restaurant. Look for posted times at the restaurant door.

- Often the characters visit World Showcase nations between 2 P.M. and 4 P.M. Pluto wears a serape, Minnie a can-can ensemble, Daisy Duck a kimono, Goofy bagpipes and a kilt, and Mickey is decked out as a Canadian Mountie.

- Twenty or more characters arrive at the mouth of the World Showcase Lagoon by double-decker bus around 5 P.M. daily for a loud, cheerful musical extravaganza and 20-minute autograph-signing session afterward. Check your entertainment schedule for exact showtimes.

Special Shows

- Singers, dancers, jugglers, and artisans from around the globe perform throughout the World Showcase daily. Most of these presentations (which are detailed in your daily entertainment guide) are not especially oriented toward children, although kids over 7 will catch the humor of the Renaissance Street Theater in the United Kingdom or the Teatro di Bologna in Italy.

- Sometimes very special performers, such as Chinese acrobats or stars of the Moscow circus, are showcased in Future World. These acts draw high ratings from kids in every age group.

IllumiNations

This display of laser technology, fireworks, syncopated fountains, and classical music is a real-life *Fantasia,* and an unqualified WDW classic. Very popular, very crowded, and a perfect way to end an Epcot day, IllumiNations takes place on the World Showcase Lagoon, and the performance coincides with the park closing time. Try to watch from the Mexico or Canada pavilion, so you'll be able to beat most of the crowd to the exits afterward. (If you're staying at the Swan, Dolphin, or Yacht and Beach Clubs, and thus leaving via the "back door" exit, try the benches in the America and Italy pavilions.)

Shopping

You'll see things at Epcot that aren't available anywhere else in WDW. German wines, silk Chinese robes, a collection of piñatas that would put any Mexican marketplace to shame, and an entire shop devoted to English teas are all within strolling distance of each other. You don't want to end up actually carrying those hand-knit Norwegian sweaters and that Venetian crystal around the park with you, however, so if you make major purchases, have them sent to Package PickUp near the front gate. They'll be waiting for you there at the end of the day.

AFTERNOON RESTING PLACES AT EPCOT CENTER

- Universe of Energy
- *Circle of Life* or Food Rocks, in the Land pavilion
- The American Adventure
- *Impressions de France*

- Any of the restaurants, since the service is leisurely at lunchtime

BEST RESTROOM LOCATIONS AT EPCOT CENTER

The restrooms within the Future World pavilions are always crowded, and those within the CommuniCores aren't much better. But there are places where you can make a relatively quick potty break:

- The Odyssey Restaurant (Baby Services is also located here, so you can take care of everyone's needs with one stop).
- The restroom behind Kringla Bakeri og Kafe in the Norway pavilion.
- The restroom between the Morocco and France pavilions.
- The restroom near the Group Sales Booth in the Entrance Plaza (near the monorail, and a good place to stop as you exit the park).
- Within Future World, the restroom near the Garden Grille room is your best bet. In fact, most of the sit-down restaurants have their own restrooms, which are less crowded than the big "public" facilities.

THE EPCOT DON'T-MISS LIST

- Spaceship Earth
- Body Wars and Cranium Command in the Wonders of Life pavilion
- Universe of Energy
- It's Fun to Be Free in the World of Motion pavilion

- *Honey, I Shrunk the Audience* in the Journey Into Imagination pavilion
- Journey Into Imagination
- The Living Seas (if you're not touring Sea World later in the week)
- The American Adventure in the America pavilion
- Maelstrom in the Norway pavilion
- *Impressions de France* in the France pavilion
- IllumiNations

THE EPCOT WORTH-YOUR-WHILE LIST

- *The Making of Me* in the Wonders of Life pavilion
- Living with the Land in the Land pavilion
- Horizons
- Image Works in the Journey Into Imagination pavilion
- El Rio de Tiempo in the Mexico pavilion
- *Wonders of China* in the China pavilion
- *O Canada!* in the Canada pavilion
- The afternoon character show at the World Showcase Lagoon
- Food Rocks in the Land pavilion

THE SCARE FACTOR AT EPCOT CENTER

Maelstrom in Norway

This new ride sounds terrifying: you encounter a three-headed troll, become caught in a North Seas storm, and narrowly miss going over a waterfall backward. The reality is much more tame than the description. Kids seem especially enchanted by the fact that you ride in Viking ships, and the much-touted "backward plunge over a waterfall" is so subtle that passengers in the front of the boat are not even aware of the impending danger.

Final verdict: Fine for all.

Journey Into Imagination

Surprisingly, several parents of preschool children reported that the kids were frightened by the googly-eyed purple Figment. This attraction, while one of the more child-oriented in Future World, does have a dark segment that explores the world of mystery.

Final Verdict: Most kids adore Figment, but if one of yours is a bit put off, one parent could always wait with him in Image Works while the rest of the family rides.

Universe of Energy

Again, preschoolers have a range of reactions. The dinosaurs are extremely real looking, and some of them bend fairly low over your passing theater car, dripping vines from their mouths. Most kids are such dinosaur junkies that they only scream when it's time to get off, but some children are genuinely frightened.

Final Verdict: Probably fine for everyone, unless you have a very young child who has trouble distinguishing reality from illusion.

Body Wars in the Wonders of Life Pavilion

The Disney PR people must love the word "plunge," for this ride too is described as "plunging through the hu-

man immune system as you dodge blood cells and anti-
bodies at breakneck speed in a race against attacking or-
ganisms that threaten to destroy your craft and you!"
Makes you breathless just to read it, huh? The ride is indeed thrilling, but most of the effects are visual, with relatively little actual movement.

Final Verdict: Body Wars was rated highly among
families responding to the survey—although a few people did mention that the visual effects gave them motion
sickness, and a few others were put off by the general
theme of the ride. ("All that blood," moaned one father.)
In general, the ride should be fine for kids over 7, but if
you have doubts about whether your child is up to it, use
the "baby swap" method, with one parent riding first
while the other waits with the child. If the first parent
feels that the child can handle the ride, the second parent and child can enter just after him. If he feels it was a
bit much, the second parent can pass the child through
and then ride alone.

6

★★★★★★★★★★★★★★★★★★★★

Disney–MGM
Studios
Theme Park

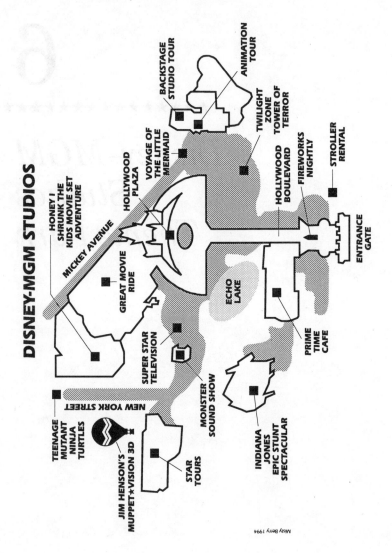

DISNEY-MGM STUDIOS

HONEY I SHRUNK THE KIDS MOVIE SET ADVENTURE

MICKEY AVENUE

HOLLYWOOD PLAZA

VOYAGE OF THE LITTLE MERMAID

BACKSTAGE STUDIO TOUR

ANIMATION TOUR

TWILIGHT ZONE TOWER OF TERROR

HOLLYWOOD BOULEVARD

FIREWORKS NIGHTLY

STROLLER RENTAL

ENTRANCE GATE

GREAT MOVIE RIDE

ECHO LAKE

PRIME TIME CAFE

SUPER STAR TELEVISION

MONSTER SOUND SHOW

NEW YORK STREET

TEENAGE MUTANT NINJA TURTLES

JIM HENSON'S MUPPET★VISION 3D

STAR TOURS

INDIANA JONES EPIC STUNT SPECTACULAR

Misty Berry 1994

GETTING TO THE DISNEY–MGM STUDIOS THEME PARK

Compared to the MK, getting to MGM is a snap.

1. Shuttle buses run approximately every 15 minutes from the TTC, Epcot, and all on-site hotels.

2. If you're staying off-site and have a car, note that the MGM parking lot is small. If you get there at opening time, you can forgo the parking lot tram and walk to the front gate.

3. If you're staying at the Swan, Dolphin, or Yacht and Beach Clubs, you're a 10-minute water-taxi ride from the MGM gates.

YOUR FIRST HOUR AT MGM

1. Once you're through the gate, one parent can handle stroller rental at Oscar's Super Service Station while the other picks up an entertainment schedule at Guest Relations or Crossroads of the World. *Note:* Unlike those at Epcot and in the MK, MGM strollers are the lightweight "sling" kind and are easy to load onto the Backstage Studio Tour tram.

2. If your kids are old enough and bold enough for a really big-deal ride, go straight to the Twilight Zone Tower of Terror on Sunset Boulevard.

   Younger kids? If an early show of the wildly popular *Voyage of the Little Mermaid* is scheduled, you should head there the minute you enter the gate. An attendant can tell you if an 8:30 or 9 A.M. show is planned.

3. Pause at the Hollywood Junction Red Car Station, where Sunset Boulevard meets Hollywood Boule-

vard, to make reservations for either the SciFi Drive-In or the 50's Prime Time Cafe. *Note:* These two popular eateries are often closed for reservations within fifteen minutes of the park opening. If you're not staying at an on-site hotel and are thus unable to make your reservations by phone, it is imperative that you make them first thing in the morning at the restaurant reservation booth. Sample menus for all MGM restaurants are on hand at the booth.

4. Board the Great Movie Ride.

5. Board Star Tours.

6. If you haven't had breakfast, check out the pastries at Starring Rolls.

MGM TOURING TIPS

1. With the exception of the new and popular *Voyage of the Little Mermaid,* save theater-style presentations, such as SuperStar Television, the Indiana Jones Epic Stunt Spectacular, and the Monster Sound Show for afternoon or evening. Tour continuous-loading attractions such as the Tower of Terror, the Great Movie Ride, and Star Tours early in the day.

2. Whatever's newest is hottest, especially at MGM: the Tower of Terror, the Aladdin parade, *Voyage of the Little Mermaid,* the Teenage Mutant Ninja Turtles, and the Beauty and the Beast stage show are all mobbed. The earlier shows are more manageable than those in the afternoon, although waits of 30 minutes at *The Little Mermaid* are common even in the morning. To get a good seat for Beauty

and the Beast, show up 20 to 30 minutes before showtime.

3. Save the tours for after lunch or early evening, when you'll welcome the chance to sit.

4. During peak seasons, the Disney people post a gigantic blackboard at the end of Hollywood Boulevard, keeping visitors updated on approximate waiting times at various attractions. Consult it whenever you're in doubt about what to do next.

   Note: If you're at MGM very early as a result of the Surprise Morning Program, the blackboard will also tell you which attractions are operative; the whole park doesn't open early for the Surprise Mornings, but at least six or seven major attractions will be ready to ride.

5. Your entertainment schedule not only provides showtimes, but also gives you information on the Celebrity of the Day and what shows are filming. If the "All New Mickey Mouse Club" or any other Disney Channel shows are in production on the day of your visit, Guest Relations can tell you how to become a member of the studio audience. *Note:* Many of the shows require that audience members be 12, and for some shows, 17.

6. MGM is small and easily crisscrossed, so don't feel obligated to tour attractions in any particular geographic sequence. Those 4- and 5-year-olds who would need a stroller in the MK or at Epcot can do without one here.

7. If you miss an attraction like the popular Indiana Jones Epic Stunt Spectacular in the afternoon, return in the evening. It's also easier to get tapped for SuperStar Television at one of the less-crowded evening shows.

8. After the dinner hour, popular restaurants such as the SciFi Drive-In sometimes will accept walk-ins, especially if you're just dropping by for dessert. As at the other theme parks, the restaurants are still serving food up to an hour after the park officially closes, so if you didn't make it into one of the big-deal eateries earlier in the day, now's your chance.

MGM ATTRACTIONS

Twilight Zone Tower of Terror

Hold on to your stomachs, because just as we go to press, MGM is set to debut a major new thrill ride. The Twilight Zone Tower of Terror combines the spooky ambiance of a decaying 1930s-style Hollywood mansion with sheer thrills. Guests will be seated in a cage "freight" elevator that will ascend—you guessed it—13 stories. On the way up, the elevator will stop on two floors—once to reveal a never-ending hallway, once to reveal a hallway that literally vanishes before your eyes.

But it's the third stop that will get you. The elevator will move forward, the doors opening onto a panoramic view of the park from over 150 feet in the air. Then you freefall. It only takes three seconds to hit the bottom, but they say your life truly does flash before your eyes.

MGM's last few offerings have been geared toward kids, and the Tower of Terror is a clear effort to draw the interest of the preteens and teens in the family. As with all new attractions, it will debut with plenty of media coverage, and will undoubtedly draw long lines. Ride it early in the morning or be prepared to face truly terrible lines.

The height requirement is 44 inches, and the Tower will be entirely too much for kids under 7.

The Great Movie Ride

Housed in the Chinese Theater at the end of Hollywood Boulevard, the Great Movie Ride debuted as an instant classic. Disney's largest ride-through attraction, it loads steadily and fairly swiftly, but draws large crowds and is best toured either early in the morning or in the last hour before the park closes. *Note:* Most of the waiting area is inside the Chinese Theater; if you see a line outside, rest assured there are hundreds more tourists waiting inside, and skip the attraction for the time being.

Each tram holds approximately 30 riders, and your tour guide provides an amusing spiel as you glide past soundstage sets from *Casablanca, Alien, The Wizard of Oz,* and other great films. The Audio-Animatronics figures of Gene Kelly, Julie Andrews, and Clint Eastwood are among Disney's best.

Things suddenly turn ugly as your car stalls and the movie scenes come to life. Depending upon which car you've boarded, you're about to be overrun by either a gangster on the lam from James Cagney or a desperado trying to escape John Wayne. Your tour guide may be gunned down or your tram taken hostage, but don't fret too much. In a later scene, drawn from *Indiana Jones and the Temple of Doom,* expect another stunning twist of fortune that reestablishes justice and guarantees a happy ending.

Star Tours

Motion-simulation technology and a slightly jostling cabin combine to produce the real feel of flight in Star Tours, the MGM version of the highly acclaimed Disneyland ride. With the hapless Captain Rex at the helm, your crew is off for what is promised to be a routine mission to the

Moon of Endor. But if you think this mission is going to be routine, you don't know diddly about Disney. "Don't worry if this is your first flight," Rex comforts visitors as they board. "It's my first one too." One wrong turn later and you're ripping through the fabric of space at hyperspeed, headed toward combat with the dreaded Death Star.

George Lucas served as creative consultant, and the ride echoes the charming as well as terrifying elements of his *Star Wars* series. The chatter of R2D2, C3PO, and assorted androids make even the queues enjoyable. Star Tours is the best of both worlds, with visual effects so convincing you'll clutch your armrails, but actual rumbles are so mild that only the youngest children are eliminated as potential crew members. *Note:* As in Body Wars at Epcot, Disney attendants are happy to help families traveling with children under 3 break up their party so that everyone except the baby gets to ride.

SuperStar Television

Want to belly up to the bar at "Cheers"? Ride the range with the Cartwrights? Be discovered by Ed Sullivan or chat with Carson? You get your chance at the highly inventive SuperStar Television, where special effects integrate the actions of audience volunteers with footage from well-known TV shows.

To volunteer your services as an actor, show up at the preshow holding area about 20 minutes before the stated performance time. (Showtimes for SuperStar Television, the Monster Sound Show, and the Indiana Jones Epic Stunt Spectacular vary from day to day, so consult your trusty entertainment schedule.) If your kids would like to join the cast of "Gilligan's Island" or be interviewed by Howard Cosell, there's no secret to getting selected. Work your way to the front of the crowd and shamelessly wave your arms. They aren't looking for shy people here. And kids tapped to perform remembered SuperStar Television as the highlight of their MGM day. If you aren't chosen in one casting section you can always exit the holding area without seeing the show and try again later.

Once you are selected, you'll be taken backstage for costuming and a brief rehearsal while the rest of the gang files into the 1,000-seat theater. Most volunteers respond ably and the results are usually quite funny. Because of the large seating area, SuperStar Television is a good choice for midafternoon, but if you don't catch it then try the evening shows, which are never crowded.

The Monster Sound Show

This theater is the smallest at MGM, so check the size of the line before you queue up to watch this funny movie featuring Chevy Chase and Martin Short. Audience volunteers add sound effects to the short film, and when the tape is rolled back the mistakes are screechingly funny. Most kids love this show—and the SoundWorks exhibits as you exit are also a good way to kill some time. (Especially neat are the Phonic Funnies, which let you dub your own voice onto films starring Snow White or Roger Rabbit.) The Monster Sound Show is generally a fine choice for afternoon.

The Magic of Disney Animation Tour

Don't be put off by the name. This 40-minute tour is fast-paced and the preshow, featuring Walter Cronkite and Robin Williams, is hilarious.

Like the Backstage Studio Tour next door, the Animation Tour is divided into two parts. The walking tour gives you a chance to see Disney animators at work. The tour winds up with a theater production featuring animated Disney classics, which greatly appeals to preschoolers.

A good choice for afternoon, although if you don't mind missing the sight of artists at their desks, the evening tours are also a good choice since they're rarely crowded.

Indiana Jones Epic Stunt Spectacular

Next to Star Tours and the Tower of Terror, this is the favorite MGM attraction of teens and preteens. You may think the lines are the most spectacular part of the show but, because the 2,000-seat theater is so huge, people standing as far back as the 50's Prime Time Cafe are usually seated. Line up about 20 minutes before show-time, and be aware that afternoon shows are sometimes a mob scene. If so, try again during one of the last two seatings of the evening.

As in the other theater presentations, audience volunteers are chosen. (Your odds of being tapped seem to improve if you are sitting near the center front.) Professional stunt people recreate daring scenes from the *Indiana Jones* series, and it's a great chance to learn how those difficult and dangerous stunts end up on film.

The Backstage Studio Tour

This is a major attraction; if you stop to play in the Honey, I Shrunk the Kids Adventure Zone and see the Ninja Turtles, and then move on to the Special Effects segment, the tour will take about two-and-a-half hours to complete. Your best time to queue up is in the afternoon, when everyone's energy has begun to flag.

The tour begins with a tram ride that scoots you through wardrobe and prop departments and then past huge outdoor sets representing a typical small town and large city. You'll see the exterior of the home where the Golden Girls "live." The highlight of the tram segment is a stop in Catastrophe Canyon, where you'll be caught in a flash flood, an oil explosion, and an earthquake. (Prepare to get wet.) Later you'll ride behind the Canyon and see how the disasters were created.

After you disembark from your tram, pause for a restroom break or a snack at the Studio Catering Company. Visitors under 10 will undoubtedly be drawn to the new Honey, I Shrunk the Kids Adventure Zone, which is perfectly located to split the lag time between the tram tour and the walk-through tour. If you missed the Ninja Turtles in the morning, check to see if they have a show coming up soon.

The Honey, I Shrunk the Kids Adventure Zone

The Adventure Zone is based on the popular Disney movie of the same name. "Miniaturized" guests scramble through a world of giant Legos, nine-foot Cheerios, and spiderwebs three stories high. Kids are generally so entranced by all the tunnels and neat little hiding areas that many a parent has had to go in to retrieve his tots—and then found he didn't want to leave himself.

Note: Kids 2–5 can enjoy the Junior Adventurers area, with a downsized maze and slide where they can play in safety away from the rougher antics of the older kids. It is strongly recommended that toddlers stay out of the three-story spiderweb, which requires you to climb all the way through before exiting—a daunting task for little legs. Families with preschoolers must stay alert inside the adventure zone—when a child enters a tunnel or climbs to the top of a slide it's often difficult to judge exactly where she'll emerge. Ergo, the attraction really should be retitled "Honey, I Lost the Kids."

Honey, I Shrunk the Kids has received high marks since opening in the spring of 1991. The only complaint? It needs to be about four times larger!

Note: You don't have to take the tour to get to the Adventure Zone. Either enter the animation courtyard and take a sharp left down Mickey Avenue, or take a sharp left at the Great Movie Ride and enter the backlot area via the *MuppetVision 3-D* Plaza.

Teenage Mutant Ninja Turtles

The turtles appear on the backlot several times daily for a brief show and autograph-and-picture-taking session. The area where each turtle will be meeting and greeting his fans is clearly marked; if you're aiming to get more than one autograph, one parent should queue up in one of the four lines while the other waits with the kids at the base of the stage. Consult your entertainment schedule for showtimes.

Note: If you don't want to take the production tour, you can get to the turtles by entering the backlot via the *MuppetVision 3-D* Plaza. Just look for the hot air balloon with Kermit's picture and begin strolling that way about 20 minutes before the stated showtime. The first show of the day is generally the least crowded.

Inside the Magic: The Special Effects and Production Tour

You can begin the walking segment of the Backstage Studio Tour at leisure, moving ahead to see a naval battle and a storm at sea created in the special-effects water tank, and viewing real soundstages where Disney shows such as the "All New Mickey Mouse Club" may be in production. Two kids from the audience are chosen to reproduce the infamous flying-bee scene from *Honey, I Shrunk the Kids,* which is a big hit with all the children in the audience, not to mention the lucky pair selected.

Next, you'll watch Bette Midler in a clever four-minute film called *The Lottery,* then walk through the soundstage where the film was made, checking out the props and special effects equipment up-close. Finally, in the post-production segment of the walking tour, you'll sit back in a theater and enjoy previews of new Disney/Touchstone releases.

The tours are a big deal, and you'll probably want to stop for a snack and a rest afterward. But Disney does a good job of mixing in humor with the more technical information, as well as using big-name stars like Goldie Hawn and Mel Gibson as "teachers," so most kids hold with the tour better than you might expect.

Voyage of the Little Mermaid

Using puppets, animation, and live actors to retell the beloved story of Ariel and Prince Eric, *Voyage of the Little Mermaid* is currently the hottest show at MGM. Come early or prepare for an hour-long wait.

The special effects in this show are the best Disney has to offer: during the brilliant storm scene, you'll feel that you're really under water, and the interplay between the cartoon characters and live actors is ingenious. Toddlers may find certain scenes too real for comfort, but everyone else is certain to be dazzled.

MuppetVision 3-D

Look for the hot air balloon with Kermit's picture, and you'll find the *MuppetVision 3-D* movie, which has all the thrills of *Honey, I Shrunk the Audience* at Epcot, but stars the kid-pleasing Muppets. The 3-D glasses in themselves are a kick, and the movie is charming and funny—and loud. Although the ride tested highly among kids ages 2–5, some parents reported that kids under 2 were unnerved by the sheer volume of the finale.

Beauty and the Beast Stage Show

Still red-hot after two years in production, this 25-minute show recreates musical scenes from the beloved film of the same name. Be at the theater at least 20 minutes before showtime to guarantee a seat, and 30 minutes if you expect to be near the stage. The earliest show of the day is the least crowded, although even it is crowded aplenty. Since the theater is outdoors, afternoon shows can get very uncomfortable in the summer. If you miss the early show, wait until evening. Families pressed for time should consider bringing fast food with them to the show.

Note: The Beauty and the Beast show has been staged in three different theaters during its MGM run: as we go to press, it is showing in the new Theater of the Stars on Sunset Boulevard, which is larger than earlier theaters and may cut down on the crowd problem.

Aladdin Parade

Stake out curb space 20 minutes in advance to assure a good view of the adorable Aladdin parade. Kids familiar with the movie will chortle at the sight of the Genie, Abu-turned-elephant with Aladdin and Jasmine aboard, and the haughty Jafar reduced to a street sweeper.

The show is short but fun, and if the kids clamor to see more of the Aladdin characters later, head for the

Animation Courtyard and Soundstage Restaurant, where the gang's on hand throughout the day. *Note:* At busy times a special "Breakfast with Aladdin" is served at the Soundstage Restaurant. You can reserve seating as you enter the theme park gates or contact Guest Services at your hotel to see if it is running during the time you're visiting.

Disney Channel Filming

On given days Disney Channel shows may be in production on the MGM backlots. If so, a sign will be posted at the front gates telling which show is taping and when, and instructing you to go to Guest Relations if you want to be in the studio audience. *Note:* Many shows require that members of the audience be at least 12, others as old as 17.

In the case of the game shows you may even get tapped to be a contestant, but the odds are statistically against it. Watching a taping is time-consuming and involves a lot of sitting, so visitors on a tight touring schedule or those with kids under 12 are advised to skip the taping sessions. The one possible exception to the rule is if you happen to visit on a day when they're taping the "All New Mickey Mouse Club." If your kids are fans of this show they may leap at the chance to meet the young stars.

Coming Soon: Sunset Boulevard Expansion

Sunset Boulevard, the newest section of MGM, is due to expand with two new action rides, both oriented toward kids. "Roger Rabbit's Toontown Trolley" and "Benny the Cab" should keep the little kids spinning happily in circles while the older ones tackle the Tower of Terror.

MEETING THE CHARACTERS AT MGM

MGM is a great place to meet the characters. They appear more frequently than in the MK or at Epcot, there are fewer kids per square foot vying for their attention, and certain favorites—most notably the Aladdin characters, the Muppets, Beauty and the Beast, the Little Mermaid, and the Ninja Turtles—appear only at MGM. Get your camera ready and check out these locations.

- A variety of characters greet visitors as they enter the park, usually around 8:30 or 9 A.M. The same characters return to the entrances around 3 P.M.

- An even larger variety of characters can be found on Mickey Avenue from midmorning on. Mickey and company hang out here for visits; the shift changes about every 30 minutes, so keep checking.

- The Aladdin gang appears in the Animation Court in midmorning and at the nearby Soundstage Restaurant throughout lunch. If "Breakfast with Aladdin" is scheduled, it offers your best shot of getting a picture and autograph with these popular characters.

- If a parade or ceremony is scheduled for the star of the day, the characters will be there in full force. The Aladdin parade, needless to say, features all the characters from the film.

- Periodically the *Star Wars* characters can be found outside the Star Tours ride.

- The Muppets are sometimes "on location" outside *MuppetVision 3-D*.

- The Teenage Mutant Ninja Turtles have their own show at least six times a day. An autograph and picture session follows.

FULL-SERVICE RESTAURANTS AT MGM

Although, like the rest of WDW, MGM is hardly a bastion of haute cuisine, the food here is fun, with a far greater variety than you'd find in the MK and more punch to the service. Make reservations by phone if you're staying on-site; otherwise, you can make them at a special booth on Sunset Boulevard each morning for the 50's Prime Time Cafe, the SciFi Drive-In, Mama Melrose's Ristorante Italiano, and the Hollywood Brown Derby. The booth is a real time-saver, because you can make lunch and dinner reservations simultaneously and see sample menus from all of the eateries.

As at Epcot, the food is expensive and the service extremely slow, especially at peak dining hours. If you just want to see the inside of the Drive-In or Prime Time Cafe, make your reservation for 3 P.M. or ten minutes before the park is slated to close and just have dessert. *Note:* As at Epcot, beer and wine are available.

1. *50's Prime Time Cafe*
The Cafe, with its kitsch decor and ditsy waitresses dressed like June Cleaver, is almost an attraction in itself. Meatloaf, macaroni, milkshakes, and other comfort foods are served in a fifties-style kitchen, while dozens of TVs blare clips from classic sitcoms in the background.

"Hi, kids," says your waitress, pulling up a chair to the formica-topped table. "You didn't leave your bikes in the driveway, did you? Let me see those hands." Assuming that you pass her clean fingernails inspection, "Mom" will go on to advise you on your food choices. "I'll bring peas with that. Vegetables are good for you."

The camp is lost on young kids, who nonetheless love the no-frills food and the fact that Mom brings around crayons and coloring books, then hangs their artwork on the front of a refrigerator with magnets. But it's baby-boomer parents raised on the sitcoms that the restaurant spoofs who really adore the place. The tacky Tune-In Lounge next door is decorated in exact replicas of the furniture my parents had in their den 35 years ago. Much of MGM is dedicated to nostalgia, but this is nostalgia on a small and extremely enjoyable scale. You can fill up at lunch or dinner for about $8 per person, and the S'mores, so huge that they cover the pink Fiestaware plate, can be split by the whole family for dessert.

2. *The Hollywood Brown Derby*

Terrific Cobb Salad as well as veal, pasta, and fresh seafood are served at the Derby where, not surprisingly, caricatures of movie stars line the walls. Service, however, is extremely slow, making this a bad choice for families with young kids. Lunch for an adult will run about $10, dinner $15. *Note:* If you do opt to dine here, request an outside table. The passing crowds will keep the kids entertained while you're waiting for your food.

3. *The Hollywood and Vine Cafeteria of the Stars*

This large, attractive art deco cafeteria offers a wide variety of salads and desserts and an outstanding rotisserie chicken. The line moves fast, and it's nice to see what you're getting. Lunch or dinner will be about $8, breakfast a bit less. (Breakfast is a popular meal here, with fruit plates, eggs and bacon, pancakes, and all the traditional breakfast foods on line; it's a good alternative to Starring Rolls if you want more than a pastry to start the day.) Reservations are not necessary.

4. *The SciFi Drive-In*

At least as campy as the 50's Prime Time Cafe, the SciFi seats diners in vintage cars while incredibly hokey movie clips run on a giant screen and carhops whiz by on roller skates. Standard drive-in fare such as milkshakes and popcorn are on the menu, but more elaborate dinners like seafood salads and mesquite chicken are also offered. Kids adore the setting and give the SciFi high marks. (Even the food is cutely named: a shortcake dessert is dubbed "When Berries Collide.") Dark and relatively quiet, even at high noon, the SciFi is an excellent way to refresh and regroup after a morning of vigorous touring. Adults should expect to pay about $10 for lunch or dinner and, once again, portions are enormous.

5. *Mama Melrose's Ristorante Italiano*
This rather new restaurant is tucked away near the *MuppetVision 3-D* Plaza and serves "gourmet" brick-oven pizza and a wide variety of pasta dishes. Expect a rather wacky New York ambiance—sometimes Mama herself turns up to inspect the premises—and fairly quick service. The pizzas are a reasonably inexpensive alternative for lunch; if everyone wants pasta, expect to pay about $10 a head.

DECENT FAST-FOOD PLACES AT MGM

1. *Soundstage Restaurant*
Decorated like the town of Agrabah from the popular movie *Aladdin,* the Soundstage Restaurant is in Animation courtyard and contains a small food court with pizza, salads, soup, and sandwiches. Aladdin, Jasmine, the Genie, and Jafar are often on hand midday to greet diners.

2. *The Backlot Express*
Located near Star Tours, the Express lives up to its name and serves up burgers and chicken within minutes. This large restaurant is a good place to grab a bite during the most crowded hours of the day.

3. *Min and Bill's Dockside Diner*

The diner, which is near Echo Lake, serves subs and fruit plates.

4. *The Studio Catering Co.*

Most people aren't aware that this snack stand, tucked away in the middle of the Backstage Studio Tour, even exists. So while the masses amble on to the second stage of the tour and the kids explore the nearby Honey, I Shrunk the Kids Adventure Zone, parents can have a drink in peace.

5. *Dinosaur Gertie's*

Kids can't resist this big green tyrannosaurus. Gertie's is the place to get ice cream while waiting in line for the Indiana Jones Epic Stunt Spectacular.

6. *Starring Rolls*

This is your best bet for a fast breakfast, as well as a great spot to pick up cookies, brownies, and pastries before the Aladdin parade or the closing fireworks.

7. *The Commissary Restaurant*

Next to the Great Movie Ride, the Commissary serves salads, stirfry, and a Mickey Mouse box lunch for kids. The counter service is swift and the food reasonably varied, making the Commissary a good choice for those who just can't face another burger but haven't the time or patience for full-service dining.

8. If you're looking for a fast, healthy snack, stop by the fruit stand at Echo Lake Produce.

THE MGM DON'T-MISS LIST

- Star Tours
- The Great Movie Ride
- The Magic of Disney Animation Tour

- The Indiana Jones Epic Stunt Spectacular
- *Voyage of the Little Mermaid*
- Beauty and the Beast Stage Show
- The Aladdin parade
- SuperStar Television
- Twilight Zone Tower of Terror (for the older, braver crowd)

THE MGM WORTH-YOUR-WHILE LIST

- The Monster Sound Show
- The Backstage Studio Tour
- Inside the Magic: Special Effects and Production Tour
- Live appearances by the Teenage Mutant Ninja Turtles
- *MuppetVision 3-D*
- Honey, I Shrunk the Kids Adventure Zone

THE SCARE FACTOR AT MGM

The Great Movie Ride

The ride begins innocently enough, as you drift past recreations of scenes from classic films. But everyone in my tram, no matter what their age, gave a collective gasp when one movie set "turned real" and our tram driver was killed in a 1930s-style gangsterland shoot-out. After collecting the jewelry of a couple of the riders, the gangster commandeered our tram for the rest of the ride. "Is this supposed to be happening?" wailed one boy who looked about 7, echoing the thoughts, no doubt, of many of the riders. (If your tram manages to elude the gangster, you'll be held up instead by a rootin' tootin' cowboy who blows up the town bank in an explosion so real that even riders in the back of the tram feel the blast of heat.) Danger lurks throughout the ride in the form of the alien (from the movie of the same name), and the green-faced Wicked Witch of the West, who appears in a cloud of quite-convincing mist.

Final Verdict: A couple of scenes are startling and intense, and this ride will have your family debating "How did they do that?" for weeks afterward. Although aspects may scare kids under 4, the fact that the tram driver eventually reappears does underscore the fact that it's all "only pretend."

Catastrophe Canyon

As part of the Backstage Studio Tour, you experience how artificial disasters are created in an outdoor set. Your tram shakes with an earthquake and narrowly misses being swept away by a flood and rock slide. The tour guide explains how it's all done.

Final Verdict: Most children find the Canyon the most fun part of the Backstage Tour.

The Monster Sound Show

Despite the somewhat scary-sounding title, this is really a funny film starring Chevy Chase and Martin Short, with volunteers from the audience providing sound effects.

Final Verdict: Not scary at all.

Star Tours

The warnings posted at the entryway are a bit paranoid, for most kids love this attraction, especially if they've seen the *Star Wars* movie series.

Final verdict: Fine for kids over 5, unless they are prone to motion sickness. If so, skip this attraction, since the flight-simulator technology is capable of persuading your stomach that you're really moving.

Voyage of the Little Mermaid

The storm sequence is very true to the movie that inspired it, with lightning, thunder, and overhead jets of water combining to convince viewers that they are "under the sea." In addition, the sea-witch Ursula appears onstage.

Final Verdict: Unless your child is young enough to be frightened by noise, or was terrified by the storm scenes in the movie, he or she should be able to handle the show. A significant number of kids in the 2–5 age range named *Voyage of the Little Mermaid* as their favorite MGM attraction.

MuppetVision 3-D

Not scary, but loud. Several parents reported that babies and toddlers were put off by the cannon explosions at the end of the film.

Twilight Zone Tower of Terror

Even if the atmosphere doesn't get you, the 13-story drop at the end of the ride is bound to draw a scream. This ride is still so new as we go to press that we were unable to survey riders, but from the description it sounds far too intense for kids under 7, and a bad idea for anyone prone to motion sickness.

7

★★★★★★★★★★★★★★★★★★★★

The Rest of the World

PLEASURE ISLAND

"It's New Year's Eve every night!" is the theme at Disney's Pleasure Island Nightclub Theme Park. This complex of clubs, restaurants, and shops comes alive at 7 P.M. each evening. Adults 18 and over pay one admission price for unlimited entry to two dance clubs, two comedy clubs, a country and music bar, a jazz club, and a seventies-style disco. A different featured band puts on a show each evening, winding down just before midnight, when a street party culminates in the New Year's Eve countdown, complete with champagne, fireworks, and confetti.

Pleasure Island has undergone substantial changes in pricing and policy since it debuted in 1989, and to some degree Disney is still tinkering with the concept. Originally several types of tickets were offered—you could buy one-, two-, or all-club passes, depending on how many bars you planned to hop. Also, in the original plan, teenagers were allowed into two of the clubs that were alcohol-free and youth-oriented in their choice of music and entertainment. Being able to take teenagers along was nice for many families, but ensuring the kids didn't get into the drinking clubs and handling all those different types of tickets ultimately proved too complicated for the Disney people.

In its latest incarnation, Pleasure Island is geared strictly toward adults, and one $11 admission has replaced the ticketing system. (Kids over 4 are admitted with a parent, but there's very little for children to do on Pleasure Island, so few families take this option.) Most patrons prefer the single admission price system; you don't have to pre-guess how many clubs you'll want to visit in an evening, and the single admission pass makes it easier to go from club to club, revisiting favorites several times. Best of all, if you have a Five-Day Super Duper Pass you have unlimited free admission to Pleasure Island for seven straight days from first use. (Even if you don't have the five-day ticket, you still shouldn't have to pay full price—there are numerous discount coupons to be found in the freebie pick-up magazines. And if you just want to see the shops and restaurants of Pleasure Island, there is no admission charge until 7 P.M., when the clubs open.)

Pleasure Island Touring Tips

1. If you choose Pleasure Island for parents' night out, get an in-room sitter for the kids. Most hotel services close down at midnight, and if you stay for the fireworks and street party you won't be back until after that. With an in-room sitter the kids can go to bed at their usual hour. (If your hotel doesn't provide in-room sitting, call Fairy Godmothers at (407) 277-3724, or one of the other sitting services listed in the "Disney After Dark" section of this book.)

2. Visit Pleasure Island after your least demanding touring day. There isn't much walking at the island, but dancing is murder on already puffy feet. Pleasure Island is a good follow-up to a day spent at Typhoon Lagoon; since it isn't a major park, you won't lose a day on your multiday passport.

3. You won't be pressured to drink in the clubs, but if you do, you'll soon learn that the alcohol is expensive.

4. Even if you don't dance, Pleasure Island is worthwhile. Nearby barstools let you watch the dancers, and the comedy clubs and live bands are very good.

5. If your kids are too old to be left with a sitter and too young to tour nightclubs, remember that a

10-screen theater lies across the bridge from Pleasure Island. Bring the kids with you only as a last resort—this is adult-oriented entertainment, crowded and rowdy, and really no place for kids.

Pleasure Island Touring Plan

1. Arrive about 7 P.M. Either eat on the elegant *Empress Lilly* riverboat, which is moored at the Disney Village Marketplace beside Pleasure Island, or at the Portobello Yacht Club, which specializes in upscale Italian dishes. If you'd like a more casual meal, grab some barbecue at the Fireworks Factory.

2. Take in the Comedy Warehouse first. (The dance clubs don't gear up until later.) This 30-minute show, a combination of improvisation and Disney spoofs, is proof positive that comedy doesn't have to be profane or vulgar to be funny. And because so much of the material truly is improvised, some guests return to the Comedy Warehouse several times in the course of the evening, seeing an essentially different routine each time.

3. Move to the Neon Armadillo across the street for country and western music with a live band. The free line dance classes are a blast, especially after all the participants have had a few Electric Lemonades.

4. For something completely different, try the Adventurers Club, a lavish, eccentric hideaway based on British hunting clubs of the 1930s. You won't be in the bar for long before you realize that some of your fellow patrons are actors . . . and the bar stools are sinking and the masks on the walls are moving. Every 30 minutes or so a seemingly-spontaneous comedy routine erupts among the actors; the séance routines are especially

memorable. The biggest hoot is the twice-nightly New Members Induction Ceremony, during which hapless bar inductees are encouraged to learn the club salute, club creed, and all-purpose theme song.

Unfortunately, many people just walk in, peruse the bizarre decor of the place, and leave before they have a chance to really get into the particular brand of comedy. Give it time! The Adventurers Club is definitely worth an hour of your evening. There's nothing like this back home—unless you're from the Congo—and the club is a favorite among Orlando locals.

5. Next, stop by the new Jazz Company, which features live music and vocalists and draws an interesting crowd. The Jazz company has a great selection of wine, many offered by the glass, and so many upscale munchies that if you plan to spend a lot of time here, you may not need to eat supper first. The tables are small, the music relatively subdued, and the clientele more mellow—making this the most romantic of the Pleasure Island clubs.

6. At 8-Trax polyester and disco are still king. It's fun to watch the thirtysomethings sitting in their bean bag chairs, valiantly pretending they don't remember the words to old Bee Gees hits. At other times the club spins back even farther in time to late sixties psychedelia. Sometimes special guests—such as former cast members from the Brady Bunch—appear, adding even more camp to the atmosphere.

7. Finally, divide your remaining hours between the two dance clubs. The Rock 'n Roll Beach Club offers a live band and an informal pool-shooting, beer-drinking, resort-style ambiance; Mannequins is darker and wilder and features canned music, strobe lighting, and a tricky revolving dance floor.

8. Be sure to be back outside for the street party (11 P.M. during the off-season, midnight during the summer and holidays) and countdown to New Year's. Flat-out bizarre entertainment can be found all up and down the street; on a recent evening when I visited, there were female body builders posing in bikinis, a velcro wall begging to be leapt against, and a Russian mime troupe.

9. Then grab a cappuccino and sit in the cobblestone courtyard at D-Zertz. You may feel like dancing more, or you may decide it's time to head home to the kids.

DISCOVERY ISLAND

Just a short ride across Bay Lake is thoroughly unmodern, uncrowded Discovery Island, an 11-acre zoological park. There you'll find walking trails, lush natural vegetation, beaches perfect for picnicking, and hundreds of varieties of animal life. Of special interest are the trained birds at Parrots Perch and the Galapagos sea turtles at Tortoise Beach.

Discovery Island launches leave from the MK and Fort Wilderness campground. If you have a five-day passport that allows you unlimited access to the minor theme parks, you may enjoy taking a break at Discovery Island. In fact, if you're touring in the MK and would like to escape the bustle of the parks for a few minutes, buy some fast food inside the MK park, then take the launch to Discovery Island for an impromptu picnic. If you don't have a five-day ticket, don't spend the time and money ($8 adults, $4.50 kids 3–9) to visit the island; similar zoological parks are undoubtedly closer to your home.

Kids taking "A True-Life Adventure," a Wonders of the World program, will spend a very productive afternoon on the island learning about the conservation of natural plant and animal habitats. For students signed up for the Wonders program, no ticket is necessary.

Children age 8–14 can also participate in Kidventure, a less structured class designed to expose youngsters to the nature trails of Fort Wilderness and the zoological and botanical gardens of Discovery Island. This is a real hands-on program—children learn to identify animal tracks and make track casts—and is offered on Wednesdays year-round, and more frequently during the summer. The cost is $27. Call (407) 824-3784 for reservations and more information.

RIVER COUNTRY

Billed as an "ol' swimming hole perfect for splashin' and slidin'," River Country has been completely overshadowed by the 1989 opening of the much larger and more high-tech Typhoon Lagoon. But River Country remains the better choice of the two Disney water parks for families with young kids, or anyone who doesn't swim very well—the park rarely gets as crowded as Typhoon Lagoon, draws far fewer preteens and teens, and the water level in the center of Bay Cove is only about chest-deep on an 8-year-old.

Bay Cove, the largest section of River Country, features an enormous heated pool surrounded by man-made boulders, as well as swing ropes, two water slides, and White Water Rapids, an exhilaratingly bumpy inner-tube ride down a winding 230-foot-long creek. The nearby swimming pool offers two small but steep slides that shoot riders into mid-air; they smack the water eight feet below with such force that they can barely stagger out of the pool and make it up the stony steps to try it again. And again.

Preschoolers will prefer the Ol' Wading Pool, a roped-off sandy-bottomed section of Bay Cove with four small slides cut into a wall of boulders, designed specifically for preschoolers. Since older kids are kept out of this section and the slides empty into a mere 18 inches of water, parents can relax on the many lounge chairs scattered along the Ol' Wading Pool beach.

Again, the five-day ticket lets you in gratis, but individual tickets are available at $14 for adults and $11 for kids. Or, you can buy a combo ticket for River Country and Discovery Island at $18 for adults and $13 for kids. River Country is a fine place to picnic, and there are a couple of fast-food stands on-site.

While Typhoon Lagoon can take up a whole day, a swift-moving 10-year-old can try out every attraction at River Country in two hours flat. For this reason, it's a good water park to drop into for a couple of hours (especially if you have the five-day ticket) when the theme parks are sweltering and everyone needs to unwind a bit.

If you're coming by car or taking a shuttle from the TTC, be aware that the River Country parking lot is quite far from the park. You'll catch a shuttle from the parking lot, drive through Fort Wilderness, and be let out near the gates. Those coming from Fort Wilderness, or those who have taken the launch from the Magic Kingdom to Fort Wilderness, have only a short stroll to the River Country entrance. Once you're inside, the park is small and easily navigated.

River Country Touring Tips

1. Although the oversized swimming pool is heated, making fall and spring swimming a delight, River Country is sometimes closed during December,

January, and February. Call 824-4321 for details on hours of operation.

2. If you don't have a five-day ticket, buy your River Country admission tickets at either Guest Relations at your hotel or at one of the major theme parks. As the park grows crowded, management sometimes abruptly suspends ticket sales, but if you already have a ticket in hand they'll let you in.

3. Families not returning to their hotels midafternoon can use River Country to break up a day in the MK. Stow your bathing suits in one of the lockers beneath the railroad, and then, when the park heats up and fills up in the afternoon, exit the MK and take the launch marked "Campground and Discovery Island." (The 15-minute boat ride is so pleasant that it almost constitutes an afternoon getaway in itself.) If you're staying off-site, this option is less time-consuming than returning to your hotel pool. After a few hours in the cool waters of River Country, you can hop back on the launch and be in the MK within minutes.

4. Many families swear that the perfect time for a River Country visit is on a summer night; the park stays open until 8 P.M., but crowds thin about 5 P.M., meaning shorter waits for the slides and a nearly empty pool.

5. Horseback riding is located near the River Country parking lot. If you're planning to try the trail rides during your Disney stay, it makes sense to combine the horseback riding with an afternoon at River Country.

   For younger kids, the pony rides and Fort Wilderness petting zoo are located right at the River Country main entrance. The ponies are available from 10 A.M. to 5 P.M., cost $3 to ride, and are incredibly gentle.

6. If you think obtaining a rental life vest will better qualify an unsteady swimmer for the slides and tube ride, forget it. The lifeguards have the final say over who is allowed to ride what, and a life vest often tips them off that a child really isn't capable of handling the major slides.

7. If you enter River Country early in the morning, head for White Water Rapids first. Because the tube retrieval system is time-consuming, this is the first attraction to draw long lines.

TYPHOON LAGOON

Disney has dubbed its 56-acre Typhoon Lagoon as the "world's ultimate water park," and the hyperbole is justified. Where else can you slide through caves, picnic with parrots, float through rain forests, and swim (sort of) with sharks? Typhoon Lagoon was opened in 1989 as the largest water park in the world and was instantly so popular that it is now hard to get in. In fact, Typhoon Lagoon is so hot that slipping away from the theme parks in the afternoon to visit no longer qualifies as a getaway—the pools are as crowded as the parks.

The good news about the popularity of Typhoon Lagoon is that River Country and the hotel pools are less busy than they were four years ago. Also, for anyone with a five-day ticket, Typhoon Lagoon is free for seven days following first use. Otherwise, admission is $22 for adults and $18 for children 3–9, entirely too much to pay for a morning of splashing around.

Note: It is extremely difficult to get into Typhoon Lagoon during peak touring times, and the park occasionally becomes so swamped with swimmers that it closes its gates. On four separate days during Easter week 1993, the park became so crowded that no one was admitted after 10 A.M., to the great dismay of families who had put on their bathing suits, swabbed themselves with sunscreen, and prepared for a day of swimming. Worse, the closing of the Lagoon is sometimes rather abrupt, and busloads of people keep pulling up all day, only to be turned back at the gate. If you're visiting during a holiday or during midsummer, plan to arrive at Typhoon Lagoon before the 9 A.M. opening time.

Typhoon Lagoon Attractions

Where River Country offers the low-key ambiance of a small-town swimming hole, Typhoon Lagoon provides tropical splendor as well as attractions that are definitely exciting to kids 7–11:

- *Humunga Kowabunga:* Two water slides that propel riders down a mountain at 30 mph. It's a bit like riding Space Mountain without a car. No kids under 48 inches are allowed. *Note:* If you're female, a one-piece suit is your best bet. A young Disney employee informed me that the most desired duty in all of Typhoon Lagoon is to stand at the bottom of Humunga Kowabunga, helping riders out of the shute—apparently at least one woman per hour loses her bathing suit top during the descent.

- *Storm Slides:* Three curving slides that deposit riders in the pool below. Kids of any age can ride, but it's suggested they be good swimmers, because although the pool isn't deep, you do enter the water with enough force to temporarily disorient a nervous swimmer. Most kids 7–11 (and some younger) love these zesty little slides, but if you're unsure if yours are up to it, wait at the edge of the pool where the slide empties so you can help them out. *Note:* Each of the three slides—the Rudder Buster, Jib Jammer, and Stern Burner—offers a slightly different thrill, although none is necessarily wilder than the others.

- *Mayday Falls:* White-water tubing. A Disney employee helps you load into the giant rubber tubes and gives you a gentle shove.

  What follows is a zippy, giggly journey that makes you feel like you're about to lose your tube more than once. No kids under 48 inches are allowed. *Note:* If you rent your own tube, you can take it on Mayday Falls; since most of the line is people waiting for the tubes, those with their own tubes can proceed directly up the mountain, cutting their wait time in half.

- *Keelhaul Falls:* A corkscrew tube ride that's full of thrills. Kids under 48 inches are provided with their own smaller tubes, and lots of kids as young as 4 reported that they loved this ride. *Note:* If you opt to rent tubes you can take them on this ride, thus shortening your wait. Kids under 48 inches, however, must queue up for the smaller tubes.

- *Gangplank Falls:* Four-passenger rafts in white water. Slower, milder, but much bumpier than Mayday or Keelhaul, Gangplank is a good choice for families with kids too young for the other white-water rides. Gangplank Falls loads slowly, however, and the ride is short, so hit it early in the morning, especially if you think your kids will want to go down more than once. *Note:* If the kids are small, sometimes more than four people are allowed into a raft.

- *Surfing Lagoon:* Machine-made waves up to six-feet high in a 2.5-acre lagoon. The waves come at

90-second intervals, and are perfectly designed for tubing and bodysurfing. *Note:* Every other hour the pool is emptied of tubes and the wave machine is cranked up to allow for bodysurfing. A foghorn blast alerts you as to when a big 'un is underway. Although the Surfing Lagoon lets anyone in, don't take small children too deep during the hours designated for bodysurfing, or every 90 seconds 400 shrieking teenagers will bear down upon your head.

- *Whitecap Cove and Blustery Bay:* The Surfing Lagoon has two small, roped-off coves where smaller waves lap upon toddlers and shaky swimmers. If you opt to rent tubes, the little ones should keep theirs in this area.

- *Castaway Creek:* A meandering 2,000-foot stream full of inner tubes. Guests simply wade out, find an empty tube, and plop down. It takes about 30 minutes to encircle the rain forest, and there is a bit of excitement at one point when riders drift under a waterfall. But there are numerous exits along the creek, so anyone who doesn't want to get splashed can hop out before the falls. In general, a very fun, relaxing ride, appropriate for any age or swimming level. *Note:* If you opt to rent your own tube, you can take it into the creek and thus not have to wait for an empty one to happen by.

- *Shark Reef:* A saltwater pool where snorkelers swim "among" exotic marine life, including sharks. The sharks and fish are behind plexiglass, of course, and suiting up to snorkel is time-consuming. Only stop at the Reef if you have a whole day to spend at Typhoon Lagoon. *Note:* The sharks are small and not too numerous, so anyone expecting the casting call for *Jaws* will be disappointed. Most of the fun is in getting to view the brightly colored fish up close. If your kids are unsure, the underwater viewing area will give them a greater feel for what snorkeling is all about. Take them down to the viewing area first to observe the marine life and other snorkelers; then let them make up their own minds.

Note: The Shark Reef is only open during summers and holidays.

- *Ketchakiddee Creek:* A water-playground sized for preschoolers with geysers and bubblers in the shape of crocodiles and whales, as well as slides and even a small white-water raft ride. No one *over* 48 inches is allowed to ride, which is a pleasant change from most of the park rules, although parents are encouraged to enter into the area and help their kids, and lifeguards are everywhere. Lots of chairs are set out nearby for adults.

- *Mt. Mayday Scenic Trail:* This footpath leads almost to the top of Mt. Mayday, where the shipwrecked *Miss Tilly* is impaled, and offers great views of the slides and rides below.

To Rent or Not to Rent?

Tubes can be rented as you enter the park for a price of $6, with $1 refunded when you return the tube at the end of the day. Having your own tube is necessary if you wish to ride the waves in the Surfing Lagoon, and shortens the wait at Mayday Falls, Keelhaul Falls, and Castaway Creek. If your kids are determined to tube in the lagoon or are addicted to the white-water tube rides and want to go on them over and over, tube rental is worth the price. The drawbacks to rental? The tubes are cumbersome and hard to transport from ride to ride; and, except for the Surfing Lagoon, tubes are available free anywhere you need them, assuming you're willing to wait five or ten minutes. If your kids aren't old enough to carry their own tubes, don't even consider renting—you won't be able to get around the park.

Note: The rental decision doesn't have to be made immediately upon entering the gates. Typhoon Lagoon has plenty of tubes, and if your kids decide they want one around noon, you can always return to the rental stand. Also, a family of four can make do with two tubes; since they aren't needed for every ride you can keep swapping them off, with Mom and Jeremy going to Storm Slides while Dad and Jake take the tubes to the lagoon. And since no one is allowed to take a tube into the Surfing Lagoon during the hours designated for bodysurfing, you can use that time to try out the white-water rides.

Double tubes are available for $12, but these are far less practical. Although cute to look at and fun in Castaway Creek, you can't use the double tubes on Mayday Falls or Keelhaul Falls at all, and they are so large that you have basically committed yourself to dragging a small boat behind you all day.

If you opt for tube rental, use Castaway Creek as a means of getting around the park. Rather than dragging your tubes along the narrow pathways, whacking everyone you meet on the head as you pass, hop into Castaway Creek, which encircles the park with exits near all the major attractions, and float to your destination.

Typhoon Lagoon Touring Tips

1. The Lagoon draws a rowdy teenage crowd, which means young kids and unsteady swimmers may get dunked and splashed more than they like.

Some of the rides prohibit kids under 48 inches tall, so if your children are very young you may be better off at River Country or your own hotel pool.

2. The Lagoon is extra-packed on weekends, since it's a favorite with locals as well as tourists.

3. In the summer, evenings are a better bet than afternoons. Call 824-4321 for hours of operation.

4. Many visitors arrive with their swimsuits on under their shorts and shirts, which does save time. It's also a good idea to bring your own towels, since towel rental is $1 per towel and they're small. There are plenty of lockers near the main entry, which rent for $5 with a refundable deposit. The locker keys come on rubberized bands that slip over your wrist or ankle so that you can easily keep them with you while in the water. If you're planning to rent tubes, life vests, or towels, save time by sending one parent ahead to get the stuff while the other rents the locker and slathers the kids with SPF 24.

5. Don't bother bringing your own snorkels, rafts, or water wings. Only official Disney equipment is allowed in the pools.

Typhoon Lagoon provides life vests for free, although they do require a $25 deposit. (This can be taken as a credit card imprint and will be destroyed when you return the vest unharmed.)

6. Snorkeling equipment can be picked up for no charge at Hammerhead Fred's near the Shark Reef. An instructor runs you through the basics before letting you loose in the saltwater pool.

7. If you have very small kids along, there are several small shallow pools along the Surfing Lagoon in

which babies can sit and splash in just a couple of inches of warm water.

8. Typhoon Lagoon is an excellent place for teenagers to go on their own. They can catch a shuttle from any on-site hotel or the TTC.

9. The Lagoon is a good place to picnic, although there are also several places to get fast food.

10. If your kids have rubberized beach shoes with non-skid bottoms, be sure to throw them in your beach bag. The sidewalks can be slippery and the pavement can be hot.

11. The Lost Kids Station is across a bridge and so far from the main water areas that lost children are very unlikely to find their way there on their own. Instruct your children, should they look up and find themselves separated from you, to tell one of the Disney employees. (They all wear distinctive bright red bathing suits.) The Disney people will escort the children to the Lost Kids Station, and you can meet them there.

12. There are two approaches to touring Typhoon Lagoon: you can go once and stay all day, or come several days for just a few hours at a time.

    The main advantage of going on only one day is that you save commuting time. Also, by getting there early in the morning, you can hit the major slides and raft rides before the crowds build. Disadvantages? That's a lot of water activity to cram into just one day.

    The advantage of going on several days is that Typhoon Lagoon can cool you off and de-stress you after a morning in the theme parks. Most kids, especially those over 7, love the park so much that they'll want to come more than once, and if you have a five-day ticket, cost is no problem. Disadvantages? You have to go through the logistical hassles of parking, lockers, and tube rental more than once, and this is frankly too large of a park (more than four times the size of River Country) to tromp around every day of your visit. Also, by going every afternoon, you'll be arriving at the most crowded time of the day, when long lines have formed for major attractions. And during the summer you'll run the risk of arriving after the park has reached peak capacity and has been closed to visitors. (*Note:* If you don't have the five-day ticket, and thus have to pay $76 bucks just to get a family of four through the gates, your choice is a simple one—you have to cram it all into one day or go broke.)

Possible solutions are to select a day fairly early in your WDW visit and make this your "big" trip to Typhoon Lagoon—the time when you circle the park and try out everything. After that, return on a couple of subsequent days and only go to one attraction. Come back for an hour or two on Tuesday, for example, and spend the whole time in the lagoon itself. On Thursday you can go directly to the slides. If it's summer and crowds are a problem, consider coming in early evening instead of the afternoon. Call (407) 824-4321 to inquire about hours.

13. Whichever touring method you choose, be sure to visit Typhoon Lagoon early in your WDW visit. Several families reported that they saved it until late in their trip and then found it was the highlight of the whole vacation for their kids. "If we'd known how great it was, we'd have come every day," lamented one father. "As it turns out we only

went once—on the morning of the day we were due to fly out."

14. If you have the five-day ticket and it's summer, consider visiting both River Country and Typhoon Lagoon—they're very different experiences. Visit River Country on the afternoon you tour the MK, because of its proximity to that park. Save more time for Typhoon Lagoon.

15. Typhoon Lagoon is generally closed during January and February.

DISNEY VILLAGE MARKETPLACE

For serious shopping—with twice the selection and half the crowds you'll find in the theme parks—stop by the Disney Village Marketplace. Mickey's Character Shop, with stuffed toys, character-theme clothing, watches, books, and every form of Disney memorabilia you can imagine, is a good place to start. The Christmas Chalet is another must-see, both for the wide variety of Disney ornaments and the incredible tree in the middle of the shop. Team Mickey, featuring sporting equipment and clothes, is full of unusual souvenirs—a softball "autographed" by all the characters makes a special gift for a young athlete.

Chef Mickey is a popular restaurant and a good choice for families who'd like to save the time and expense of a character breakfast. Mickey, dressed in a tall chef's hat and starched white apron, continually circulates among the tables, stopping for autographs and pictures. Those seeking more upscale dining can try the *Empress Lilly*, a permanently moored steamboat with three fine restaurants, or the Portobello Yacht Club, which serves Italian with a nautical flair. Pleasure Island is a short walk across the bridge from the marketplace, and a 10-screen theater lies just beyond another bridge.

The marketplace has a small playground and sand area to keep younger kids entertained, and if kids 12 and older get restless, they can venture down to the dock at the Buena Vista Lagoon to rent one of the little Water Sprite speedboats. If you're staying off-site, the marketplace marina is your best option for boat rental. The cost is $11 a half-hour and younger kids can ride with an adult. The boats appear to be flying, but in reality don't go very fast and are a fun, safe diversion for all ages. (Canopy boats are also available for rent at $17 a half-hour in case the whole family would like to get into the act.) The marina area is so engaging that I've spent hours roaming the marketplace getting a jump on Christmas shopping, only to have my family greet me at the end of my spree with those astounding words "What? You're finished already?"

DISNEY EXTRAS: THE PARADES, FIREWORKS, DINNER SHOWS, AND CHARACTER BREAKFASTS

Don't pack your schedule too tightly. Disney works many wonderful extras into the day, and it would be downright criminal to miss them.

1. *Parades:* If you love a parade, you've come to the right place.

Included in the festivities are:

- The 3 P.M. parade in the MK.
- SpectroMagic, the electrical parade, which runs at both 9 and 11 P.M. during the busy season in the MK.

- Electric Water Pageant, visible from the beaches of the Seven Seas Lagoon from 9 to 10:20 nightly.
- The Aladdin parade at MGM. Usually at 1 P.M., but showtimes vary, so check your entertainment schedule.
- Special parades sometimes are planned at Epcot and MGM. Consult your daily entertainment schedule for times.
- Mind-blowing holiday parades at Easter, July 4th, and Christmas.

Note: SpectroMagic has replaced the popular Main Street Electrical Light Parade, which is currently playing at EuroDisney in Paris. SpectroMagic runs only periodically during the off-season, so call (407) 824-4321 to see which evenings during your visit the parade is scheduled, and make sure you plan to stay in the MK until closing on that date. If you're going in the summer, when two parades run, remember that the 11 P.M. parade is never as crowded as the 9 P.M. parade.

2. *Fireworks:* A 5- to 10-minute display is shown above Cinderella Castle at 10 P.M. nightly during the on-season. Just before the fireworks begin you'll see one of the Magic Kingdom's niftiest—but least advertised—little extras, Tinkerbell's Flight. A young gymnast, dressed in tights and zestily hacking the air with a magic wand, slides down a wire suspended from the top of Cinderella Castle to a rooftop in Tomorrowland.

Fireworks close the day year-round at Pleasure Island and during the on-season at MGM.

Note: As Robert Smith, a travel consultant with Destination Orlando in Worchester, Massachusetts points out, the best place to watch the MK fireworks is not in front of the Cinderella Castle, as everyone assumes. The fireworks are actually fired from behind 20,000 Leagues

Under the Sea, and excellent viewing can be had from the cafe tables in the Fantasyland section. The fireworks are also visible from some locations in the MK resorts; ask if you'll have a view when you book your room.

3. *IllumiNations:* Don't miss this laser, fountain, light, and music extravaganza at closing time each evening at Epcot.

4. *Dinner shows:* All the dinner shows should be booked before you leave home by dialing (407) W-DISNEY. Reservations are accepted at the time you book your room for on-site guests, and 30 days in advance for off-site guests. They are especially crucial for the Hoop-dee-Doo Musical Revue. The on-site dinner shows are:

- *Hoop-dee-Doo Musical Revue.* By far the most popular of the Disney dinner shows, the Revue plays three times nightly (5, 7:15, and 9:30 P.M.) at Pioneer Hall in Fort Wilderness. You'll dine on ribs and fried chicken while watching a hilariously hokey show that encourages lots of audience participation. $35 for adults, $27 for kids 12–20, and $18 for kids 3–11.

- *Polynesian Revue.* You'll enjoy authentic island dancing and not particularly authentic island food at this outdoor show at the Polynesian Village Resort. The two seatings are at 6:45 and 9:30 P.M. Prices are $33 for adults, $25 for kids 12–20, and $17 for kids 3–11. A better choice for families with young kids is Mickey's Tropical Luau, which features the characters and the Polynesian dancers, and is presented at 4:30 P.M. Prices are $29 for adults, $23 for kids 12–20, and $13 for children 3-11.

Note: If you're staying off-site and don't want to return to the WDW grounds in the evening, or if you've waited too late to book a Disney show, be advised that Orlando is chock-full of engaging family-style dinner shows that can be easily booked on the afternoon of the show. See "Off-Site Dinner Shows for the Whole Family" in Section 10 for details.

8. *Character Breakfasts:* Again, you'll make life easier by phoning (407) W-DISNEY for reservations before you leave home. The character breakfasts take at least a couple of hours and probably should be skipped if you're on a very tight touring schedule—or are watching the pocketbook carefully. But families who stayed at WDW for four or five days gave the breakfasts very high marks, especially if they scheduled them near the end of their stay when the kids had had plenty of time to warm up to the characters. Families who schedule their character breakfast on the last day of their visit also note that it doesn't "mess up the day" so badly, since the last morning of your trip is usually broken up anyway by the 11 A.M. check-out time at most Orlando hotels.

If your time is tight and you'd still like to try a breakfast, select one of the continuous-seating breakfasts at the on-site hotels. The continuous-seating breakfasts offer buffets, and only accept reservations during the most crowded times of the year, such as Christmas or Easter week.

The food is pedestrian at the character breakfasts, but who cares? Since it takes a while to meet all the characters (usually six or seven circulate among the diners) and eat, either come early or, if you're opting for the *Empress Lilly,* try to book the first seating of the day. Prices generally run about $12 for adults, $8 for children. The more elaborate Sunday brunch at the Polynesian is also more expensive: about $19 for adults, $11 for kids. *Note:* Several of the character breakfasts are suspended in the off-season, and the times and prices are always subject to change. To avoid disappointment, call (407) W-DISNEY before you leave home to find out which ones are running during the time you'll be at WDW.

Character breakfast locations are as follows:

- The *Empress Lilly* riverboat, moored between the Disney Village Marketplace and Pleasure Island, is the site of Breakfast à la Disney at 8:30 and 10 A.M. each morning. This is the easiest location for families staying off-site. A standard bacon-and-eggs meal is served to everyone, so picky eaters may resist. Make reservations by phoning (407) W-DISNEY or 828-3900.

- The Contemporary Cafe at the Contemporary Resort serves a continuous breakfast buffet from 7:30 to 11 A.M. and does not take reservations.

- The Beach Club offers continuous seating at the Cape May Cafe, where Admiral Goofy and crew hang out from 7:30 to noon. No reservations are accepted.

- There's a continuous seating buffet from 7:30 to noon at 1900 Park Fare in the Grand Floridian. No reservations are accepted.

- Minnie's Menehune runs at the Polynesian during the busy seasons from 7:30 to 10:30 A.M. No reservations are accepted.

- Breakfast with Aladdin—a popular new addition to the roster—is a fast-food–style breakfast served at the Soundstage Restaurant at MGM. You can either make reservations as you enter the park—get there early!—or book through Guest Relations at your hotel.

- During busy seasons other breakfasts are scheduled. A Winnie the Pooh breakfast is held at the Vacation Club on Wednesdays. A Sunday brunch is served at the Dolphin, and a Wednesday and Saturday character breakfast is featured at the Swan. Additionally, the Buena Vista Palace, the Hilton, and the Grosvenor, all located in the Disney Village Hotel Plaza, offer breakfasts during the busy season. For information on these breakfasts that are scheduled less regularly, call (407) W-DISNEY.

6. *Dinner with the Disney Characters:* If your family isn't much for breakfast, you can also see the characters in the evening. 1900 Park Fare in the Grand Floridian runs a buffet from 5 to 9 P.M. at a price of $18 for adults and $9 for kids 3–11, and the characters are in attendance.

Staying off-site? Willing to settle for "only" Mickey? Your easiest evening option is to visit Chef Mickey, a high-quality restaurant in its own right, located on the lagoon at the Disney Village Marketplace.

7. *Jolly Holidays Packages, featuring the Very Merry Christmas Party:* Walt Disney World is at its most magical during the holidays: hours are extended, special parades and shows debut, and a new meet-the-characters show and party is planned. The Very Merry Christmas Party requires a special ticket. It is also included in a Jolly Holidays Package, a special all-inclusive holiday deal. Call (407) W-DISNEY for details.

Note: It is quite possible to celebrate Christmas at Disney without getting caught in the crush. The decorations go up just after Thanksgiving and the special shows, package getaways, and holiday parties begin soon thereafter. A family visiting early in December can see all the special stuff—except for the Christmas Day parade— without having to face the harrowing holiday crowds. If school schedules rule out an early-December trip, note that the week before Christmas is considerably less hectic than the week between Christmas and New Year's.

Last Christmas when my family visited, we were agog at the hotel decorations. Aladdin's hometown of Agrabah was reconstructed out of gingerbread at Port Orleans— the Yacht and Beach Clubs hosted the gingerbread homes of the Little Mermaid and Belle. The on-site hotels hosted fun little parties for their guests, with visits from Santa, stockings for the children, eggnog and cookies, and Victorian carolers giving a homey feel to a hotel holiday. Each hotel has its own theme trees, as well— and the sweeping pink poinsettia tree at the Grand Floridian is a classic.

THAT SPORTIN' LIFE: ON WATER

Most on-site hotels have lovely marinas with a variety of watercraft to meet the needs of every age group. Since the fees at WDW are "adjusted" frequently, it's not a bad idea to call the marina of the hotel where you're staying and confirm prices. If you're visiting at a peak season, reserve a boat in advance. The two major recreational lagoons in WDW are the Seven Seas Lagoon, which is in front of the MK and serves Fort Wilderness and the MK resorts, and the Buena Vista Lagoon at the Disney Village Marketplace. In addition, the Yacht and Beach Clubs share a lagoon with the Swan and the Dolphin, and the Caribbean Beach Resort, Port Orleans, and Dixie Landings all have their own lagoons and watercraft as well.

Note: You do not have to be a guest of an on-site resort to rent the boats, although the marina will ask for either a resort ID or a WDW ticket, along with a current driver's license for the larger boats. If you're staying off-site and don't want to to bother commuting to an on-site hotel, try the Disney Village Marketplace where water sprites and canopy boats are available.

1. *Water Sprites:* Those zippy little speedboats you see darting around the Buena Vista and Seven Seas Lagoons can be rented for $11 a half-hour. Drivers must be 12 years old, although kids of any age will enjoy riding alongside Mom and Dad. Water sprites can be rented at the marinas of the Polynesian, Contemporary, Grand Floridian, Wilderness Lodge, and Fort Wilderness. If you're staying off-site, it's probably easier to rent one at the Buena Vista Lagoon between the Disney Village Marketplace and Pleasure Island.

2. *Sailboats:* The Polynesian, Contemporary, Grand Floridian, Yacht and Beach Clubs, Caribbean Beach Resort, and Fort Wilderness marinas all provide sailboats, ranging from the two-person Sunfish for $10 an hour to the six-person Capri for $15 an hour. Some styles of boats are easier to manage than others, but the marina employees will be happy to help you select the boat that best suits your skill level.

3. *Pontoon boats:* If your party is larger or less adventurous, head for one of the MK resorts and try touring the Seven Seas Lagoon in a motor-powered pontoon for $35 an hour. Similar canopy boats are available at the Disney Village Marketplace, MK resort marinas, Yacht and Beach Clubs, Vacation Club, Wilderness Lodge, Dixie Landings, and Port Orleans for $18 per half hour.

4. *Pedal boats:* These small people-powered crafts can be rented at either the Seven Seas or Buena Vista Lagoon for $8 an hour. The Yacht and Beach Clubs, Swan and Dolphin, Port Orleans, Wilderness Lodge, and Fort Wilderness also have pedal boats, with the option of a half-hour rental for $5, which is preferable since the legs tire quickly in these vehicles.

5. *Canoes and rowboats:* If you'd like to try fishing in the canals around Fort Wilderness, rent a canoe for either $4 an hour or $9 a day at the Bike Barn. Rowboats rent for $5 a half-hour at the Yacht and Beach Clubs marina, Port Orleans, and Dixie Landings.

6. *Waterskiing:* A boat, a driver, and full equipment can be rented at Fort Wilderness, the Polynesian, the Grand Floridian, and the Contemporary marinas. The cost is $70 an hour, and reservations should be made at least three days in advance by dialing the appropriate marina.

7. *Fishing:* Angling is permitted in the canals around Fort Wilderness—but not in the lagoons or lakes. Rods and reels can be rented at the Bike Barn. You can either drop a line from shore, or take a canoe or pontoon boat deeper into the canals. Guided two-hour expeditions leave three times a day, and up to five people can be accommodated for a $110 fee, including the boat, the guide, the equipment, and snacks.

If your kids just want to play around with the idea of fishing, you can drop a line for catfish at Ol' Man Island in Dixie Landings. Or try the catch-and-release excursion that leaves twice a day from the Disney Village Marketplace Marina. Call 828-2461 for reservations.

8. *Swimming:* All the WDW hotels have private pools, but the Contemporary and Dolphin pools are best for serious swimmers because they have special lanes reserved for laps: The newer hotels—the Swan and Dolphin, the Yacht and Beach Clubs, Port Orleans, and Dixie Landings—boast more elaborately themed pool areas that almost qualify as mini-water parks. Upon completion, the pools at the All-Star Resorts promise to be very clever—if you'd like to swim in a guitar or across a baseball diamond, here's your chance.

THAT SPORTIN' LIFE: ON LAND

1. *Tennis:* Several on-site hotels have courts, which can be reserved 24 hours in advance. Call:

The Contemporary	(407) 824-3578
Village Resort Villas	(407) 824-3741
Yacht and Beach Clubs	(407) 934-7000
Swan and Dolphin	(407) 934-6000
Grand Floridian	(407) 824-2433

The tennis courts at Fort Wilderness and the Vacation Club operate on a first-come first-serve basis.

There is considerable variation in fees. A court costs $10 an hour at the Contemporary, $12 at the Grand Floridian, Swan, and Dolphin, but is free at the Village Resort Villas, the Vacation Club, and the Yacht and Beach Clubs. If you'd like private lessons, or want to participate in a clinic, consider staying at either the Contemporary or the Grand Floridian. The Contemporary has lessons for $37 an hour or $20 a half-hour. You can also get a very reasonable package for $25 that gives the entire family court time for the duration of your stay. The Contemporary also runs clinics that include video-taped analysis of your play by the club pro. Call 824-3578 for details.

The Grand Floridian, while not the tennis haven that the Contemporary is, also offers lessons at $35 an hour.

2. *Golf:* There are now five courses actually on the WDW grounds, with greens fees running about $75 for WDW hotel guests and $85 for those staying off-site. (With such pricey fees, anyone planning to golf a lot should consider the World Adventure or some other

package. Or, try playing in the early evening when twilight fees drop to as low as $40.)

The five courses are the Palm and Magnolia, two fairly demanding courses located near the MK; the Lake Buena Vista Course, which is near the Disney Village Resort Villas; and the two brand new courses, Osprey Ridge and Eagle Pines, which share the Bonnet Lakes Golf Club. Beginners and kids are better off at the nine-hole Oak Trail near the Magnolia, which is a walking course with fees of $20 for adults and $10 for anyone under 17.

To reserve a tee-off time or arrange for participation in a golf clinic, dial (407) 824-2270. WDW guests can make tee-off and lesson reservations up to 30 days in advance; those staying off-site can (and should) make reservations seven days in advance.

3. *Running:* Jogging trails cut through the grounds of nearly every WDW hotel. Consult Guest Services for a map. Fort Wilderness has a 2.3 mile exercise trail complete with posted period stops for chin-ups, sit-ups, and a host of other tortures. The sprawling Caribbean Beach Resort and the Wilderness Lodge, with its invitingly shady trails, are also good choices for runners.

4. *Horseback riding:* Guided trail rides leave the Fort Wilderness grounds five times a day. Surprisingly—and disappointingly—children under 9 are forbidden, even though the horses are gentle and the pace is slow. The cost is $16. If younger kids really want to saddle up, they can take a short pony ride at the petting zoo at Fort Wilderness. Rides are offered from 10 to 5 during the on-season, and cost $3. Call (407) 824-2832 or 824-2433 before you leave home for reservations and information.

5. *Spas:* The Contemporary, Grand Floridian, Swan, Yacht and Beach Clubs, Vacation Club, and Dolphin all

have health clubs. The general cost is $5 per visit or $10 for your entire stay—well worth it when you consider some of the health clubs have whirlpools and saunas, which can be nice finishes to a day spent walking around the theme parks.

If working out is really important to you, stay at the Disney Dolphin, whose Body by Jake health club is hands-down the most complete. The equipment is state-of-the-art, the class schedule is varied, and you can even book a session with a personal trainer.

6. *Cycling:* Bikes ($4 an hour or $8 a day) or tandems ($5 an hour) can be rented at the Bike Barn in Fort Wilderness, the Villa Center at the Village Resort Villas, or at Dixie Landings, Port Orleans, the Vacation Club, the Wilderness Lodge, and the Caribbean Beach Resort. If you're driving and staying at one of the really big resorts, most notably the Caribbean Beach Resort or Dixie Landings, consider bringing bikes from home. The sidewalk system is extensive, and cycling is a practical way of getting around.

7. Still have energy to burn? Get up a volleyball or basketball game at Fort Wilderness. The Yacht and Beach Club offer volleyball and croquet.

8

★★★★★★★★★★★★★★★★★★

*Disney
After Dark*

DISNEY WORLD AFTER DARK: WITH THE KIDS

Is there life in WDW after 8 P.M.? Sure there is. The crowds thin, the temperature drops, and many attractions are especially dazzling by dark. Orlando is actually a kiddie version of Las Vegas—a town that naps but never sleeps—where miniature golf courses and McDonald's stay open all night. During peak seasons the major theme parks stay open until midnight, so it's easy to have fun at night. But, needless to say, the particular kind of fun you'll have depends on whether or not the kids are with you.

Evening Activities for the Whole Family

1. *SpectroMagic in the MK*

The latest incarnation of Disney's ever-popular Main Street Electrical Parade, SpectroMagic blends lasers, lights, and fireworks for a dazzling display. Spectro-Magic runs only on selected evenings during the off-season, but every night during the on-season. In the busiest weeks there are two showings—the 11 P.M. is rarely as crowded as the 9 P.M. parade. The parade is a don't-miss: if you're visiting during the off-season, plan your schedule to assure you'll be in the MK on one of the evenings it's slated to run.

2. *The Electrical Water Pageant*

If you're staying on-site, the Electrical Water Pageant may actually float by your hotel window, since it is staged on the Seven Seas Lagoon, which connects the Polynesian, Contemporary, Grand Floridian, and Fort Wilderness resorts. Times do vary with the seasons, but generally the Pageant is visible at 9 P.M. at the Polynesian, 9:20 from the Grand Floridian, 9:45 from Fort Wilderness, and 10:05 from the Contemporary. Dial 11 for Guest Relations at your hotel for exact times. If you're not staying on-site, simply ride the monorail to the resort of your choice. The Electrical Water Pageant plays every night, even during off-season.

Especially striking vantages can be found at the Top of the World Lounge in the Contemporary, and on the beach at the Polynesian. Although this is a much shorter and less elaborate show than SpectroMagic, nothing can beat the effect of multicolored lights twinkling on darkened water. Besides, by 9 P.M. most kids would rather sprawl on a beach than camp on a curb.

3. *Movies*

If you're staying on-site, check out the offerings in the theater of the Contemporary Hotel. Two different Disney classics show each night at 7 and 9 P.M. For information about what's playing, call (407) 824-4500. Movies are also shown at the evening campfire at Fort Wilderness and at the Vacation Club, and in many Orlando hotels the Disney Channel is available 24 hours a day.

The 10-screen theater adjacent to Pleasure Island is a good place to park older kids and teens while parents try out the clubs.

4. *Arcades*

It's no secret that kids flip for arcades, especially the mammoth Fiesta Fun Center in the Contemporary Resort. Even hardcore pinball junkies are bound to find games they've never seen before.

5. *IllumiNations at Epcot*

IllumiNations can be viewed from anywhere around the World Showcase Lagoon at Epcot closing time. With fireworks, laser lights, stirring music, and even choreographed fountains spurting in three-quarter time, IllumiNations is state-of-the-art. *Note:* The fireworks are loud enough to frighten some toddlers.

6. *Fireworks*

A rousing fireworks display can be seen from anywhere in the MK at about 10 P.M. during the on-season. The show is short but exciting, and at holiday times a more extensive fireworks extravaganza is presented. *Note:* Be there a few minutes earlier to witness Tinkerbell's Flight.

Fireworks also close Pleasure Island each night, and MGM is currently signing off with a more elaborate than usual display called "Sorcery in the Sky."

7. *The Rides at Night*

Those attractions with the two-hour lines at noon are far more accessible by night, so it's worth revisiting any ride you passed by earlier in the day. In the MK the Big Thunder Mountain Railroad is much more fun in the dark; Splash Mountain feels like a totally different ride, and Cinderella's Golden Carousel is especially magical at night.

At Epcot it is almost always easy to tour the Journey Into Imagination and see the Land pavilion after 7 P.M. (In fact, any Future World attraction is easily boarded during the dinner hour, when everyone heads out to dine in the World Showcase.) At MGM, try SuperStar Television or the Indiana Jones Epic Stunt Spectacular; not only are the shows less crowded, but volunteer wannabees stand a better chance of being chosen during the evening shows, especially at SuperStar Television.

8. *Night Swimming*

Both Typhoon Lagoon and River Country run extended hours in the summer, and the crowds are far thinner after 5 P.M. It stays hot in Orlando well into a summer evening, and, since you don't have to worry about heat exhaustion or sunburn, many families with young kids actually prefer evening swimming. *Note:*

Water Mania and Wet 'n Wild, Orlando's other large water parks, also run long evening hours and drop their rates considerably after 4 P.M. Hotel pools stay open very late as well, some until after midnight.

DISNEY WORLD AFTER DARK: WITHOUT THE KIDS

Why would any decent parent seek a sitter while on a family vacation? Consider the following scenario.

Meaghan's sucking the inside of the mouth. Loudly. Mom keeps making everyone stop while she readjusts the strap of her shoe to accommodate the blister she picked up halfway around the World Showcase Lagoon. You spent $148 to get through the gates of Universal specifically to ride those highly-publicized high-tech rides you've heard so much about, and Devin spends the entire afternoon feeding quarters into the same arcade game that's in the local mall back home. Dad has been singing the first line—and only the first line—of "Zip-A-Dee-Doo-Dah" since Thursday. You've asked to see the kiddie menus from nine different restaurants in nine different Epcot countries, and you end up at the American pavilion fast-food joint because Kristy won't eat anything but a hot dog. It's 108 degrees, this trip is costing $108 an hour, and that infernal sucking sound is getting on the last nerve you have left. In short, you have third-day-itis.

And it's only the second day of your trip.

Although it may seem un-American or even sacrilegious to suggest building time apart into the middle of a family vacation, the truth is that everyone will have more fun if you occasionally break up the group for a while. Even the most devoted of families aren't accustomed to being together 24 hours a day—for every meal, every ride, every potty stop. Every minute. Some of the hotels in Orlando have responded with programs designed to get the kids involved with other kids so that parents can have some peace and privacy. Kristy can eat her hot dog, Meaghan can give herself hickeys, and Devin can play Cosmic Invaders 77 straight times without parental glares. The adults can dare to order a meal that will take three hours to enjoy, and linger over their coffee. Everyone returns refreshed and recharged, with some happy stories to tell, and you can start the next day actually glad to be together again.

If you decide to schedule at least one parents' night out during your trip, you'll soon learn that Orlando offers an array of child care options. Several of the on-site hotels have full-fledged kids' clubs, and where else on earth can your child be bedded down by a real-life Mary Poppins? Among the off-site hotels, there is a large range in cost and quality among the offered programs; many of the off-site programs are free of charge to hotel guests (at least during certain hours), which can mean big savings for parents.

The key point is to make your plans before you leave home, either by selecting a hotel which has a kids' club or by arranging for an in-room sitter. If you suddenly get an urge for fine dining at 4 P.M. on a Saturday in July, it will be hard to find a sitter. But if you've checked out your options in advance, it's a breeze.

In-Room Sitters

You'll need to arrange for an in-room sitter if any of the following conditions apply:

1. You have a child under the age of 3. Very few of the organized kids' clubs will accept children under this age, and most require they be potty-trained.

2. You plan to be out after midnight. Most kids' clubs close down at midnight, some as early as 10 P.M. Parents headed for Pleasure Island or Church Street Station, where the action doesn't begin to heat up until 10 P.M., need in-room sitting.

3. Your kids are exhausted. If you know in advance that you plan to employ an all-out touring schedule, or your children fall apart after 8 P.M., hire an in-room sitter who can put them in bed at their usual time. Most of the kids' clubs at least try to put preschoolers down in sleeping bags by 9 P.M. (the Hilton actually has beds inside Vacation Station), but this can involve moving them, and possibly waking them, when parents return.

If you decide you'll need in-room sitting, begin by contacting your hotel. Many hotels are happy to arrange the sitting for you through one of the licensed and bonded agencies listed below, and this saves a bit of hassle.

Want to make your own plans? For those staying on-site, KinderCare provides trained sitters for all the Disney hotels. Call 827-5444 at least eight hours in advance. The rate is $9 an hour for two kids.

At least three independent services in town dispatch sitters to off-site hotels:

Super Sitters	(407) 382-2558
Fairy Godmothers	(407) 277-3724
ABC Mothers	(407) 857-7447

These services stay busy during the summer months, so it's not a bad idea to book them before you leave home. Rates are typically $6 an hour, with a four-hour minimum, and an extra-child charge of $1 an hour per child. A $5 transportation fee is also common, meaning that in-room sitting for two kids for four hours runs $33. Not a cheap option, but for many parents it's well worth the cost.

The independent services can be quite inclusive, with service available 24 hours a day, seven days a week. For families willing to pay the extra bucks, sitters will take the kids out to a fast-food place for supper, or even to area attractions. One resourceful divorced father took his two daughters along on a business trip to Orlando; while he sat in meetings, a Fairy Godmother trotted the girls around the theme parks.

KinderCare Child Care Center

KinderCare offers a "learn while playing" developmental program for children 1–12 years in age. The set-up is similar to the hundreds of KinderCares nationwide. It's a daytime program; you drop the children off at the facility, which is on the WDW grounds, and pick them back up a few hours later. Call (407) 827-5437 for details. The center primarily exists for the use of Disney employees, but visiting children are accepted on a day-by-day basis as space permits. You do not have to be a guest at an on-site hotel to use the service, and the cost is $26 for a 10-hour day, or $5.50 an hour.

On-Site Kids' Clubs

There are Mouseketeer Clubhouses at both the Contemporary (824-3038) and Grand Floridian (824-2985) for kids 3–9, and a Sandcastle Clubhouse (934-8000) in the Yacht and Beach Clubs for kids 3–12. The Cubs Den at the Wilderness Lodge is for kids 3–12. Camp Dolphin (934-4241) welcomes kids from 3–12, and Camp Swan (934-1621) is for children 3–12. (The programs at the

Dolphin and Swan are more complete than the others listed above, especially at the Dolphin, where families can get a "lifetime membership" in Camp Dolphin for $35 and arrangements can be made for the kids to be served dinner.) The important thing to remember is that children who are staying in any of the Disney hotels, not just the resorts that happen to have the kid's clubs, are welcome.

The Polynesian Resort offers a twist—a "dinner theater" for kids 3–12 in the Neverland Club, including a full meal and entertainment. Animals and birds are often brought over from Discovery Island, a character drops by, and the evening is wrapped up with ice cream and games. The cost is $7 per child per hour, with a minimum three-hour visit. The Neverland Club is open from 5 P.M. to midnight. Reservations can be made at (407) 824-2170. Several families surveyed specifically mentioned what a swell evening this was for their kids; one father vividly described how his timid and stranger-shy 4-year-old was so won over by the drop-in visit from Alice in Wonderland that she screamed and clung to the Neverland Club doorframe when her parents returned at the end of the evening to pick her up!

The Clubhouses are well stocked with Disney-themed toys—as well as computers, video games, arcade games, and large screen TVs. The cost at all clubs except the Neverland Club is $4 per hour for the first child; additional kids cost $2 per hour. There's a four-hour maximum visit and reservations are required. The clubhouses are open from 4:30 P.M. until midnight, and cookies and milk are served at bedtime. Again, kids must be toilet trained. Even Mary Poppins has her limits.

Note: Prices, policy, and planned entertainment change quickly at the kids' clubs, so confirm all the above information when you make your reservations.

Off-Site Kids' Clubs with Fees

Several off-site hotels, most notably the Hilton and Buena Vista Palace at the Disney Village Hotels, and the Stouffer Orlando just across from Sea World, have their own versions of kids' clubs, with wide-screen TVs, video games, and wading pools to entertain the children while parents do the town. These programs are well run and flexible—Shamu's Playhouse at the Stouffer, for example, offers a wide range of organized activities and accepts kids as young as 2 from 8 A.M. to 11 P.M. Generally, it is not required that you be registered at the hotel in order to take advantage of the program, although this policy can change during busy seasons when the programs are filled. The typical cost is $5 an hour, with $1 for each additional kid.

Another advantage to these hotels is that they have fine dining establishments right on the hotel property. Haifeng and Atlantis at the Stouffer and Arthur's 27 at the Buena Vista Palace are outstanding restaurants with leisurely, adult-paced service. They provide a nice break from the typical theme park dining experience, where you frantically color pictures of Pluto and juggle sugar packets in an effort to keep the kids entertained until the food arrives. If you're looking for something a bit funkier and more casual, the Hilton has recently opened the Florida Fin Factory, a Key West–style seafood place. All of the hotels mentioned are equipped to either escort the kids to the resort coffee shop for a simple meal or order room service so the kids can eat while the parents dine.

At various times the hotels have offered special deals, such as three hours of complimentary child care for parents dining in the hotel's flagship restaurant. This perk seems to come and go, and 24-hour notice is always required, so call to check. Even if you wind up having to pay for the service, this is a good option if you feel a bit nervous about leaving your children back at the hotel you're staying at with a strange sitter. By dining at a hotel with on-site child care, you have the security of knowing that the kids are in the same building. It also softens the blow of being left behind for your children, since they're going "out" too.

A hotel that offers a slightly different spin on the idea is the Hyatt Regency Grand Cypress. (The Hyatt is known throughout the entertainment industry for the quality of its children's programs.) Daily during the on-season and on weekends year round, Camp Hyatt offers kids 5–12 a wide range of outdoor and craft activities. Kids 3–5 are welcome in the ChildCare Center, a less-structured program, and the cost for either Camp Hyatt or the Child-Care Center is $5 an hour or $25 a day. Since the staff is around from 8 A.M. to 10 P.M. during the on-season, parents can take in a round of golf at the resort's outstanding course, play tennis, or simply relax by the dramatically-landscaped pool. If you need child care during dinner hours, both Camp Hyatt and the ChildCare Center are operative during the evening on weekends, and Hemingway's, the hotel's seafood restaurant located in a grotto on top of the pool waterfall, is a romantic getaway.

But the Hyatt doesn't stop there. Rock Hyatt, oriented toward teens, gives your 15-year-olds the opportunity to hang out with their own kind after a stressful day of having to be nice to their younger siblings. Rock Hyatt is free and runs on the weekend year-round and daily during the summer.

For more information on the kids' clubs call:

Stouffer Orlando Resort	(407) 351-5555
Hilton at Disney Village	(407) 827-4000
Buena Vista Palace	(407) 827-2727
Hyatt Regency Grand Cypress	(407) 239-1234

Off-Site Kids' Clubs Without Fees

Parents who'd like to go out more than once during their vacation, or whose kids just enjoy being around other children, should look for a hotel with a complimentary kids' club. Interestingly, this is not one of those times where you get what you pay for—one might think free child care means a lackluster program, but just the opposite is true. Hotels that are committed enough to families to provide a free kids' club are also committed enough to do the job right. The Holiday Inn at Main Gate East and the Sunspree Holiday Inn at Lake Buena Vista, Embassy Suites at Exit 27 off I-4, Sonesta Village, and the Delta Orlando all have hotel mascots, programs that combine outdoor activities with restful activities, and beeper service to keep you in contact and give you additional peace of mind. And, since most of the activities for the kids are free, you're shaving as much as $35 off the cost of a parents' night out.

These perks are not reflected in the cost of the rooms, either. The Holiday Inns and Delta Orlando start as low as $89 a night, and with villas starting as low as $125, Sonesta Village and Embassy Suites are very reasonable options for families needing more room.

Note: The programs are free unless food is involved. All the hotels listed above will arrange to feed kids during the 6 P.M. to 9 P.M. time frame when parents may wish to dine on their own; the cost for supplying the meals is quite reasonable, and the food is always something like pizza or tacos that kids like, generally followed by make-your-own ice cream sundaes. There also may be a cost if a craft is involved. At some programs, such as those at the Delta Orlando or Embassy Suites, the kids learn to tie-dye T-shirts or make other fairly involved crafts. If out-of-the-ordinary supplies are required, that cost is passed along to parents. As with the food, however, the hotels try to keep the costs reasonable.

For details call:

Sonesta Village	(407) 352-8051
Delta Orlando	(407) 351-3340
Holiday Inn Sunscape at Lake Buena Vista	(407) 239-4500
Holiday Inn Main Gate East	(407) 396-4488
Embassy Suites	(407) 239-1144

DINING WITHOUT THE KIDS

Certain on-site restaurants are more enjoyable without children, so once you've found a sitter, reserve a table for two at one of these establishments.

At Epcot

Chefs de France or Bistro De Paris

Chefs de France features nouvelle cuisine, meaning the sauces are lighter and the preparation simpler than traditional French fare. This is still heady stuff: grouper with lobster sauce, roast duckling with prunes, salmon-and-tarragon soufflé. The atmosphere is elegant and understated, and the service unrushed. Chefs is definitely one of the most expensive eateries in Epcot: dinner runs about $100 for two.

The Bistro upstairs is slightly less pricey and just as good. Although the atmosphere is still lovely—high ceilings, brass, and etched glass abound—and the service still attentive, Bistro de Paris represents hearty, casual French dining. Waiters are more than willing to advise you on selections and, as is true at Chefs, it's impossible to go wrong with any of the desserts.

Romance factor: B for Chefs de France, which is "on the street," A for Bistro de Paris, which is quieter and darker.

Marrakesh

Ready to take a walk on the semi-wild side? The music, architecture, and menu in the Moroccan restaurant are truly distinctive, proving beyond a doubt that you aren't in Kansas anymore. You'll be served lamb, couscous, and honeyed chicken by waiters in floor-length robes while belly dancers weave among the tile tables. (The effect of these dancers on husbands is somewhat akin to the effect meeting Mickey has on toddlers. They're stunned while it's happening, but later remember the experience fondly.)

Romance factor: C. The tables are very close together, lots of families bring the kids, and the place can become quite loud.

San Angel Inn

The menu here goes far past the tacos and enchiladas most Americans consider Mexican, and the atmosphere is unparalleled. The restaurant overlooks El Rio del Tiempo, the boat ride that encircles an Aztec pyramid beneath a starry sky. The darkness of the Mexico pavilion, which simulates midnight even at high noon, and the murmur of the Rio are hypnotic. Throw in a couple of margaritas and you may never leave.

The molé poblano and any of the grilled seafood dishes are consistently good. The friendliness of the service make the San Angel a good choice even when the children are along.

Romance factor: B.

L'Originale Alfredo di Roma Ristorante

The Alfredo in question is the gentleman who created fettucine Alfredo. This is the most popular restaurant in the World Showcase, usually the first to book up despite the fact that it seats 250 people. The restaurant is entertaining in itself; you can watch the cooks through a large window as they crank out pasta, the walls are adorned with clever trompe l'oeil murals, and the waiters and waitresses provide impromptu concerts, ranging from mildly bawdy Italian folksongs to Verdi.

Most diners, however, have kids along, making the place a little too loud and crowded for romance.

Romance factor: C.

The Coral Reef

Tucked away under the Living Seas, this Future World restaurant is expensive, about $100 for a couple at dinner.

Unfortunately, the Coral Reef is less romantic than the World Showcase restaurants. The room is simply too large to feel cozy and, as at Alfredo's, most families bring their kids, figuring—and rightly so—that little Nathaniel and Erica can stay busy watching the skindivers while Mom and Dad crack a lobster.

Romance factor: C.

Outside Epcot

There are a few places in the World so elegant and so removed from the classic Disney image that you'll never feel sticky fingers creeping over the top of the booth behind you. Kids are rarely seen at the following establishments, which require ties and jackets for men and something other than jeans for women.

Victoria and Albert's, at the Grand Floridian Resort

Where Disney has built a reputation on providing pleasure to the masses, this 50-seat restaurant proves there is also room in WDW for highly individualized service. When Henry Flagler built the railroad that opened Florida to the oil magnates of the late 1800s, Queen Victoria and Prince Albert sat upon the British throne. Now, in one of those "only Disney would go to such trouble" details, all hosts and hostesses in the restaurant are named either Victoria or Albert.

Your menu will have your own name handwritten on the top. Waiters describe the selections for the evening, and the chef often circulates among the tables. At the end of a six-course meal, guests are presented with long-stemmed roses, Godiva chocolates, and handwritten menus. This is the most expensive restaurant in WDW, hands down—the fixed price dinner is $80 per person, $105 with wine—but it's so special that you'll be talking about it years afterward. On the evening we visited, the salad was a floral arrangement in a crouton vase—until Victoria tapped the side of the crouton, releasing the greens into a fan-shaped pattern on the plate. And the coffee service was more elaborate than a Japanese tea ceremony. Call (407) 824-2391 for reservations.

Note: Victoria and Albert's is the only full-service restaurant in WDW that is not included in the World Adventure or any other package dining plans.

Romance factor: A+.

The Empress Room, aboard the *Empress Lilly* riverboat at the Disney Village Marketplace

It's fun to board this permanently moored reproduction of an 1880s steamwheeler. The *Empress Lilly* actually contains three restaurants, ranging from the casual New Orleans–style jazz bar of Fisherman's Quarters to the elegant Louis XV decor of the Empress Room. In contrast to Victoria and Albert's, the Empress Room offers a large menu, with the emphasis on seafood. Unusual dishes such as venison, pheasant, and quail are also available. The service is top-notch, although a little less formal than at Victoria and Albert's.

Reservations can be made up to 30 days in advance by calling (407) 828-3900. The Empress Room seats no guests after 9:30, so plan accordingly. After you finish, Pleasure Island is just a short walk away.

Romance factor: A.

Outside Walt Disney World

Excellent dining abounds beyond the Walt Disney World gates, and many of the fancier restaurants are in hotels. Dux in the Peabody offers an intimate environment, unusual seafood and game selections, and an outstanding list of California wines, many available by the glass. Arthur's 27, the rooftop restaurant of the Buena Vista Palace, has an award-winning menu and a reputation for consistency in both service and food quality. The huge Hyatt Regency Grand Cypress, a gorgeous destination in itself, is also home to Hemingway's, offering the outstanding cuisine typical to the Hyatts and an atmosphere so lush and tropical it isn't typical of anything at all. Don't feel like dressing up? The soon-to-be-opened Florida Fin Factory in the Hilton promises to be less formal, but emphatically upscale, with an emphasis on fresh seafood and unique preparation.

If you venture past the hotels, you'll find there are plenty of places in Orlando that offer good food, reasonable prices, and friendly, unpretentious service. Pebbles, in the Crossroads of Lake Buena Vista, serves up Key West–style food in a casual atmosphere and, like the Florida Fin Factory, is a good choice if you're going to nearby Pleasure Island after you eat.

Dining of a campier sort can be found at Church Street Station, a dining and shopping complex in downtown Orlando. Rosie O'Gradys and Lilly Marlenes dish up tasty but casual food, huge specialty drinks, and live music. Late in the evening, Church Street becomes a giant party, with patrons moving from one establishment to the next, sampling the various entertainment and bar munchies.

If it's anything like its sister restaurants, the new Planet Hollywood promises to be a popular place to party—either with or without the kids along. And nothing's quite as funky as the Hard Rock Cafe, adjacent to Universal Studios. Both these places rev up late at night, so if you want to get in the true spirit, hire an in-room sitter and eat at 10 P.M.

9

★★★★★★★★★★★★★★★★★★★

*And Another
Thing . . .*

BARE NECESSITIES: DIAPERS, STROLLERS, AND SPECIAL NEEDS

Picky Eaters

1. Try the cafeterias: the Crystal Palace in the MK, Le Cellier in the Canada pavilion at Epcot, and Hollywood and Vine at MGM. The food court in the Land pavilion at Epcot also offers lots of options.

2. Several of the on-site hotels run buffets in the interest of moving people in and out fast, but they're also a draw for families who can't agree on what to eat. 1900 Park Fare at the Grand Floridian and the Contemporary Cafe at the Contemporary are both good choices.

3. Nearly all of the theme park restaurants offer such standards as peanut butter and jelly, albeit at $3 a sandwich. If a kiddie menu isn't posted at the door, ask the hostess if you can see one before you enter the restaurant.

4. Kiddie meals, based on the McDonald's Happy Meal concept, are turning up all around the theme parks and hotel restaurants for about $3.50. You get either a burger, hot dog, or sandwich in a cartoon-covered box, along with fries, a drink, and a prize.

Strollers

1. All kids under 3 need a stroller, for napping and waiting in line as well as for riding.

2. For kids 3–6 the general rule is: Strollers are a must at Epcot, nice in the MK, and not really needed at MGM, where the park is smaller and a lot of time is spent in sit-down shows.

3. Strollers rent for $6 a day, so consider bringing your own from home. If you have an older child who will only need a stroller at Epcot, however, rental isn't a bad option. If you plan to spend time at more than one park, you don't have to pay twice; keep your receipt and show it for a new stroller when you arrive at the next park.

4. The MK and Epcot strollers are sturdy, drop back to form a completely flat bed, and can hold two kids in a pinch. The MGM strollers are the easily collapsible "sling" kind.

5. Tie something like a bandanna or a balloon to your stroller to mark it, thus reducing the probability it'll be swiped while you're inside Peter Pan's Flight. As one mother observed, "Otherwise honest people seem to think nothing about stealing a stroller, but stop when they see they might be taking a personal possession as well."

6. Stroller stolen anyway? In the MK, check in at the Spaceport in Tomorrowland, the Trading Post in Frontierland, or Tinkerbell's Toy Shop in Fantasyland. At Epcot, you can get a new stroller at the World Traveler Shop located between France and the United Kingdom. At MGM, return to Oscar's Super Service. As long as you've kept your receipt, there's no charge for a replacement stroller.

7. If at 8 A.M. your 5-year-old swears she doesn't need a stroller, but at noon she collapses in a heap halfway around Epcot's World Showcase, head for the World Traveler Shop between France and the United Kingdom. The World Traveler is also the place to rent a stroller if you're coming from the Swan, Dolphin, or Yacht and Beach Clubs, and thus using the "back door" entrance.

8. If you have an infant, bring a stroller from home. The rental strollers in the MK and at Epcot are too large and too hard for babies who can't sit at all.

9. Likewise, if you're staying at one of the more sprawling resorts, like the Caribbean Beach Resort, Dixie Landings, or Fort Wilderness, bring a stroller from home. It's likely to be quite a trek from your room to the pool or tram stop.

Baby Services Centers

Rockers, bottle warmers, high chairs, and changing tables are all found at Baby Services—and diapers, formula, and jars of baby food are for sale. (One mother reported that the attendant on duty was even able to diagnose a suspicious-looking rash on her toddler as a reaction to too much citrus juice, evidently a common Florida malady. She later took the child to a doctor and learned the attendant had been right on the money.)

In the MK, Baby Services is beside the Crystal Palace at the end of Main Street. It's inside the Guest Services building at MGM, and near the Odyssey Restaurant at Epcot.

Breast-Feeding

WDW is so casual and family-oriented that you shouldn't feel self-conscious about discreetly nursing in the theaters or restaurants. Some shows, like the Hall of Presidents in the MK or *Impressions de France* at Epcot are dark, quiet, and ideal for nursing. Others, like the Country Bear Jamboree in the MK or the Monster Sound Show at MGM are so loud the baby will probably be distracted.

If you're too modest for these methods or your baby is easily disturbed, try the rockers in the Baby Services centers.

Diapers

Diapers are available at:

- The Baby Services centers
- Stroller rental shops
- The Emporium on Main Street in the MK
- Celebrity 5 & 10 at MGM

The shops don't waste shelf space on such mundane products, so you'll have to ask. Changing tables are available in most ladies' restrooms and now—finally— some mens' as well. You can always use the Baby Services centers to change infants, and there are potty chairs for toddlers as well.

Special Needs

1. Wheelchairs can be rented at any stroller rental stand, and most attractions are accessible by wheelchair. (Epcot has a few of those 3-wheel motorized wheelchairs for rent, which can be very convenient considering the miles you'll cover in a typical Epcot day.) Attendants will be happy to help guests with special needs board and disembark from rides. All the Disney resorts are accessible by wheelchair, but it is impossible to board the monorail by wheelchair in the Contemporary, making it the least convenient for disabled guests. The Polynesian gets points for offering the most transportation options.

Note: Once they're in the theme parks and ready to ride the attractions, guests in wheelchairs are boarded through their own gates and often able to avoid waiting in lines altogether. Some lines have marked wheelchair entrances, and at others you'll have to ask the attendant where to enter.

If someone in your party is in a wheelchair, be sure to request a copy of the *Guidebook for Disabled Guests,* either when you order your tickets in advance or at the wheelchair rental booth. It's a far more specific guide as to how each ride should be boarded.

2. Portable tape players and cassettes for sight-impaired guests are available, as are TDDs for the hearing-impaired. Check with City Hall in the MK, Earth Station at Epcot, and Guest Relations at MGM.

   Deaf guests have a special line to dial (827-5141) for park information.

3. All on-site hotels are equipped to refrigerate insulin.

4. If someone begins to feel queasy or suffers a boo-boo in the parks, head straight for the First Aid Center. If they can't fix the problem, they'll transport you to a place that can within minutes.

5. Likewise, all on-site and most off-site hotels have physicians on call 24 hours a day. Medi-Clinic provides House Med Services 24 hours a day, 365 days a year (648-9234; after September 1994, call 396-1195). A licensed physician will visit you at the hotel.

6. For minor health problems, visit the Medi-Clinic from 8 A.M. to 11 P.M. at the intersection of I-4 and 192 (648-9234; after September 1994, call 396-1195). Transportation can be provided to Medi-Clinic. For more serious illnesses or injuries, head for the emergency room at Sand Lake Hospital (351-8550).

7. No matter where you're staying, of course, in a true emergency you should dial 911.

8. A tip from frequent visitors: If you're traveling with someone in a wheelchair, it's emphatically worth the money to stay on-site. Disney does an excellent job of offering disabled guests a number of transportation options. The ferry and monorail are wheelchair-accessible but, if you need to, you can request a van with a motorized platform. The resorts offer rooms with specially equipped bathrooms and extra-large doors; and specially-designed life jackets are available at some resort pools and both water parks.

9. Another tip from frequent visitors: If you're traveling with someone who has a chronic health problem or disability, rest assured that WDW is one of the most stress-free vacations you could have planned. Because WDW is frequently visited by children sponsored by the "Make a Wish" foundation and other programs like it, the personnel at WDW are accustomed to dealing with a wide variety of challenges and have proven themselves able to accommodate visitors who are quite seriously ill. The key is to make everyone at both your hotel and within the theme parks aware of your presence and the possibility that you'll need special assistance. Then relax. These people will help you in every way they can.

HOW TO GET UP-TO-DATE INFORMATION

If you need information before you leave home:

1. Write to:

    Walt Disney World Guest Information
    P.O. Box 10040
    Lake Buena Vista, FL 32830-0040

2. Subscribe to *Disney Magazine*. You'll receive eight quarterly issues (a two-year subscription) for $14.95. Write to:

   Disney Magazine
   P.O. Box 3310
   Anaheim, CA 92803-3310

Note: Magic Kingdom Club cardholders receive the *Disney Magazine* automatically as part of their package.

If you need information once you check into your hotel:

1. Both on-site and off-site hotels provide a wealth of material upon check-in. Study the maps and brochures your first evening.

2. On-site hotels provide continuous information about park operating hours, special events, and touring tips on Channel 5. Channel 10 offers an especially helpful program called "Disney Nights" that informs you about dinner theaters, evening parades, and special shows.

   Hotels in the Walt Disney World Plaza have similar services on Channel 7. Some of the large off-site hotels have their own entertainment info channels, which keep you up-to-date not only on Disney but all Orlando-area attractions.

3. Magic Kingdom radio is 1030 AM. Epcot is 810 AM. Tune in as you drive into the parks.

4. Guest Services in both on-site and off-site hotels is equipped to answer most questions.

5. If you still have questions, dial (407) 824-4321. A real live person will come on the line to tell you what time Epcot closes on May 7th, the price of Minnie's Menehune Revue for a 10-year-old, and how tall you have to be to ride Splash Mountain.

If you need information once you're in the parks:

1. Check with Guest Services, which is located near the main gate of all three major theme parks.

2. At Epcot, there are WorldKey Information Terminals (which operate like those located behind Spaceship Earth) on the bridges that connect Future World to the World Showcase and in the Germany pavilion. You'll have access to a Disney employee within seconds.

3. Flag down the nearest person wearing a Disney tag. The "cast members" at the theme parks are remarkably helpful and well informed.

SAVING TIME

1. Do as much as you can before you leave home. You should purchase theme park tickets, reserve rental cars, and book shows long before you pull out of your own driveway. Every call you make now is a line you won't have to stand in later.

2. Visit the most popular attractions before 11 A.M. or after 5 P.M.

3. Eat lunch either at 11 A.M. or after 2 P.M. This system will have you eating while everyone else is in line for the rides and riding while everyone else is eating.

4. You will also save time—and money—if you make lunch your big meal of the day. Most families opt to eat a large breakfast and large dinner and snack at lunch; go against the crowds by eating your big meal in early afternoon, when the parks are too hot and crowded for effective touring anyway.

5. Split up. Mom can make the dinner reservations while Dad rents the strollers. Mom can take the 9-year-old to Space Mountain while Dad and the 4-year-old try out Snow White's Adventures. Security in WDW is very tight, so preteens and teens can tour on their own, meeting up with the rest of the family periodically.

6. Be aware that once you cross the Florida state line, there is an inverse relationship between time and money. You have to be willing to spend one in order to save the other. One family proudly listed their cost-saving measures, such as staying 30 miles outside of Orlando and cooking every meal themselves; but it took them six days to tour the three major parks, something most families can manage comfortably in four days. Considering the high cost of admissions, it's doubtful that they saved very much money at all—and they certainly wasted time.

7. If you have three days or less to tour, it is imperative that you go during the off-season. You can see in three days in November what would take six days to see in July.

8. Don't feel you have to do it all. If you study this guide and your maps before you go, you'll realize that not every attraction will be equally attractive to your family. The World won't come to an end if you skip a few pavilions.

9. The full-service restaurants within the theme parks can be very slow. If you're on a tight touring schedule, stick to fast food or sidewalk vendors and order a pizza at night when you get back to your hotel room.

10. If you're staying on-site, make all your dining reservations by phone.

MEETING THE DISNEY CHARACTERS

Meeting the characters is a major objective for some families, and a nice diversion for all. If your children are young, be aware that the characters are much, much larger than they appear on TV and often overwhelming in person. I recently visited WDW with a 20-month-old whose happy babble of "my Mickey, my Mickey" turned into a wary "no Mickey, no Mickey" the minute she entered the MK gate and saw that the mouse in question was a good six feet tall. Kaitlyn's reaction is not atypical; many kids panic when they first see the characters, and pushing them forward only makes matters worse. The characters are trained to be sensitive and sensible (in some cases more so than the parents) and will always wait for the child to approach them. Schedule a character breakfast on the last morning of your visit; by then cautious youngsters have usually warmed up.

Many kids enjoy getting character autographs, and an autograph book can become a much-cherished souvenir upon your return home. You also might want to prepare the kids for the fact that the characters don't talk. As many as 30 young people in Mickey suits might be dispensed around WDW on a busy day, and they can't all be gifted with that familiar squeaky voice. So the characters communicate, and pretty effectively, through body language.

Also be aware that because of the construction of their costumes, the characters can't always see what's beneath them too clearly. Donald and Daisy, for example, have a hard time looking over their bills, and small children standing close by may be ignored. If it appears this is happening, lift your child to the eye level of the character.

Note: As the lists below illustrate, it's easier to see the characters at Epcot and MGM than in the MK. The newer characters appear exclusively at MGM and the character-to-kid ratio is vastly better at Epcot than in the MK. If your kids insist on spending every day in the MK, the chance to see Ariel or Leonardo may lure your 5-year-old away from the MK rides and into one of the other two parks.

Want to actually meet the characters? Want to get close enough for autographs and pictures? If so, try the following locales:

- Mickey's Starland in the MK. (Be sure to line up to see Mickey in his dressing room after the show. The other characters can be found outside, milling around the area near the railroad.)

- The Main Street hub in the MK, just after the park opens.

- Mickey Avenue at MGM. This area of the park is rarely crowded—except with characters! A much better choice for picture-taking than anywhere in the MK.

- The Animation Courtyard and Soundstage Restaurant, where the Aladdin characters appear throughout the day. *Note:* Beauty and the Beast, the Little Mermaid gang, and the Aladdin characters, as of this writing, appear exclusively at MGM.

- The afternoon lagoon show at Epcot's World Showcase.

- The Stargate Restaurant or the Sunshine Terrace at Epcot, just after the park opens.

- The Odyssey Restaurant at Epcot, for several afternoon appearances. If you're trying to save money, a stop at this fast-food place is a good alternative to a character breakfast or dinner.

- The character breakfasts and buffet dinners.
- The Teenage Mutant Ninja Turtles and Muppet characters appear for brief live shows, followed by picture and autograph sessions, at MGM.
- The Neverland Club at the Polynesian is always visited by at least one Disney character around tuck-in time. Compared to the parks, where you get a handshake and picture pose if you're lucky, these are leisurely visits.
- If you're taking the Disney cruise after you leave WDW don't waste too much time trying to meet the characters in the parks. It's much easier to snuggle up to Minnie or Pluto on the boat, where far fewer children are vying for a chance.

If you simply want to *see* the characters, check out the afternoon parade in the MK, as well as SpectroMagic. The MK also runs at least two shows daily during the on-season that feature either the characters or the stars of the All New Mickey Mouse Club. Times are listed in your entertainment schedule.

Epcot offers the afternoon character show at the lagoon. MGM has debuted the extremely popular Aladdin parade, also in the afternoon, as well as scheduled appearances by the Teenage Mutant Ninja Turtles, the Muppets, and other luminaries. Performance times are listed in your entertainment schedule.

PREGNANT?

I've personally toured WDW twice while pregnant and not only lived to tell the tale, but honestly enjoyed both trips. A few precautions are in order:

1. Make regular meal stops. Instead of buying a sand-wich from a vendor, get out of the sun and off your feet at a cafeteria or sit-down restaurant.

2. Most pregnant women are in good condition, but if you aren't accustomed to walking three or four miles a day—an average WDW trek—begin getting in shape at home. By taking 20 to 30 minute walks, beginning a couple of months before your trip, you'll be less likely to get sore or poop out once you're at WDW.

3. Dehydration is a real danger. Drink lots of fluids and consider throwing a juicebox into your tote bag for emergencies.

4. This is definitely an occasion when it's worth the money to stay on-site. Return to your room in midafternoon and put your feet up.

5. If staying on-site isn't feasible, the Baby Services centers have rockers and are good places for mothers-to-be to take a break. And the parks are full of benches. Sit whenever you have to.

6. Standing stock-still can be much more tiring than walking, so let your husband stand in line for rides. You and the kids can join him just as he's about to enter the final turn of the line.

7. Once you're inside the holding area for theater-style attractions, such as Country Bear Vacation Hoe-down or Universe of Energy, attempt to find a bench and sit down. If the benches are taken, sit on the floor near the wall and don't stand up when the Dis-ney attendant gets on the loud speaker and asks everyone to rise; all the people in the holding area will be admitted into the theater, so it's pointless to get up now and mob the turnstile with everyone else. Let them go ahead, then struggle to your feet and

amble through. (This is a good strategy for anyone who is utterly exhausted, pregnant or not.)

8. Use this book to check out restroom locations in advance.

ON A DIET?

Vacation dieting is always tough, and fast food abounds in WDW, which makes it even more difficult. But Epcot Center Executive Chef Keith Keogh and his staff are making an effort to meet the American Heart Association's recommendations for healthy eating by reducing the amount of oil used when frying and substituting yogurt for cream in sauces and salads. Increasingly, fresh fruit (instead of mayonnaise-laden salads) is served with the main course, vegetables are steamed, and meats are broiled.

Fruit stands can be found on Main Street and in Liberty Square in the MK, near Echo Lake at MGM, and between the China and Germany pavilions at Epcot, making it easier for families on the move to select grapes or watermelon instead of chips or ice cream.

The restaurants below are especially good options for visitors looking for healthful fare such as fruit plates, salads, grilled chicken, and broiled seafood.

In the Magic Kingdom

- Crystal Palace Cafeteria at the end of Main Street
- The Lunching Pad in Tomorrowland (for natural foods)
- Sunshine Tree Terrace in Adventureland (for citrus drinks)
- Sleepy Hollow in Liberty Square (for vegetarian meals)

At Epcot Center

- The Garden Grille Room in the Land pavilion
- The Sunshine Surprise food court in the Land pavilion
- The Coral Reef under the Living Seas pavilion
- The Yakitori House and Mitsukoshi Restaurant in the Japan pavilion
- Pure and Simple in the Wonders of Life pavilion (for health foods and juice drinks)
- Nine Dragons in the China pavilion (the best of the full-service restaurants, because the chefs here are willing to adapt recipes, serving sauces on the side or leaving out forbidden ingredients when requested)

At MGM

- The Hollywood and Vine Cafeteria (for chicken on a spit)
- The Backlot Express
- Min and Bill's Dockside Diner (for the fruit plates)
- The Commissary Restaurant (for stir-fry)

BEST BREAKFASTS IN WALT DISNEY WORLD

Wasn't it Archimedes who said "Give me a good breakfast and I can move the world"? The following meals will at least set you up for an active morning of touring:

- Crepes at the Garden Grille Room in the Land pavilion at Epcot.

- Bagels and cream cheese at the Sunshine Season food court, also in the Land.

- Heart-shaped waffles with powdered sugar at Kringla Bakeri og Kafe in the Norway pavilion at Epcot.

- Stellar Scramble at the Stargate Restaurant at Epcot.

- Pastries are available throughout WDW, but especially good at Boulangerie Patisserie in the France pavilion at Epcot. Also check out Starring Rolls at MGM and the Main Street Bakery in the MK.

- Lady and the Tramp character waffles at Tony's on Main Street in the MK.

- And the absolute best is banana-stuffed French toast at the Coral Reef Cafe in the Polynesian Resort. Worth a special trip!

If the best breakfast for you is a fast breakfast, be aware that all the on-site hotels have a food court or coffee shop that opens early. On those mornings when the kids are moving slowly, one parent can always go for juice, cereal, and muffins and bring the tray back to the room. If you're staying off-site, hit one of the drive-throughs on your way into the park.

In addition, it's worth considering the character breakfasts if you have children under the age of 9. (For a detailed discussion of locations, times, and prices, see "Disney Extras: The Parades, Fireworks, Shows, and Character Breakfasts" in section 7.)

Sunday brunch buffets are big business in Orlando—one reason why the theme parks tend to be blissfully uncrowded on Sunday mornings. The off-site hotels are fiercely competitive when it comes to their Sunday buffets, each trying to outdo the others in terms of selection and the size of the spread. If you're in the mood for something special and rather elegant, the Hyatt Regency Grand Cypress is widely considered to have the biggest and best buffet of all.

THINGS YOU DON'T WANT TO THINK ABOUT

1. *Rain:* Go anyway. Short of an all-out hurricane, Disney attractions are open as usual and crowds will be thin. If you get caught in one of those afternoon cloudbursts so common during Florida summers, rain ponchos are available for about $5 in most of the larger shops. Although hardly high fashion, they're better (and safer) than trying to maneuver an umbrella though crowds while pushing a stroller.

2. *First aid:* Next to the MK's Crystal Palace is a first aid center staffed by two registered nurses. Epcot has a first aid center located beside the Odyssey Restaurant; MGM's is in the Guest Services Center. Although most of the patients suffer from maladies such as sunburn, motion sickness, and minor boo-boos, the center is also equipped for major emergencies and, when necessary, transport to Sand Lake Hospital.

It's worth remembering that any medical problem that could occur at home could also occur in the midst of a vacation. I've received letters from people who have broken bones, fainted from the heat, and come down with chicken pox while in Orlando. Their general advice to others is: Seek medical help the minute you even suspect there may be a problem. Although the cost of in-room doctor visits or trips to the Medi-Clinic is high (expect about $100 for an ear infection, including medication), the cost of waiting is invariably higher.

Should you suffer a medical emergency, take comfort in the fact that the Disney people get high points for both their efficiency and their sensitivity. One mother who developed an eye infection from a scratched cornea reported that the nurse at the Epcot first aid center, immediately recognizing the severity of the problem, arranged for her transport to Sand Lake Hospital so that she could see an ophthalmologist. "We only had a long weekend," she writes, "and I would have felt horrible if the kids spent it in a hospital waiting room. But as it was, the nurse handled everything and my husband and children were able to remain in the park touring while I was treated. My husband kept phoning in to the nurse for updates, and I met up with them back at Epcot a couple of hours later, looking like Long John Silver." A woman who suffered a miscarriage while staying at a Disney-owned hotel also offers the highest praise to the staff there, both for their swift medical response and their emotional support.

3. *Lost kids:* Obviously your best bet is not to get separated in the first place. Savvy families have standard meeting spots. *Note:* Everyone designates Cinderella Castle or Spaceship Earth, one reason why those places are always mobbed. Plan to catch up with your crowd at a more out-of-the-way locale such as the flower stall on Main Street or the gardens beside the Canada pavilion.

If you do get separated and your kids are too young to understand the idea of a meeting place, act fast. Lost kid logs are kept at the Baby Services centers at the major parks. More important, Disney employees are well briefed about what to do if they encounter a lost child, so the odds are good that if your child has been wandering around alone for more than a couple of minutes he or she has been intercepted by a Disney employee and is on the way to Baby Services. In real emergencies—if the

child is very young or is handicapped, or if you're afraid
he's been nabbed—All Points Bulletins are put out
among employees. So if you lose a child, don't spend a
half-hour wandering around. Contact the nearest Disney
employee and let the system take it from there.

Note: The one glitch in the system is that sometimes
lost kids are so interested in what's going on around them
that they don't look lost, and thus no Disney employee in-
tercepts them. It's worth taking a couple of minutes to explain to young children that if they get separated from
Mom and Dad they should tell someone wearing a Disney
name tag. The Disney employee can call the child's name
in to Baby Services and, assuming you've contacted Baby
Services to report the child as missing, the attendant
there can tell you where the child is.

4. *Closed attractions:* Because WDW is open 365 days
a year, there is no down-time for refurbishing and re-
pairing rides. Thus, at any given time, as many as four
attractions throughout WDW may be closed for repairs.
If an attraction your family eagerly anticipated is closed,
it can be heartbreaking. The best bet is to call (407)
824-4321 before you leave home and ask which attractions are scheduled to be shut down for maintenance
during the week you're visiting. That way if Space
Mountain or Star Tours is closed, at least you'll know before you get to the gate. There's still a slight chance that
a ride will be malfunctioning and temporarily closed
when you visit, but the Disney people are so vigilant
about repairs that this happens very, very rarely.

5. *Auto breakdowns:* If you return to the parking lot
at the end of the day to find your battery dead or your
tire flat, walk back to the nearest tram stop. WDW roads
are patrolled continually by security vehicles that can
call for help.

The Disney Car Care Center (824-4813) is located near the toll plaza at the MK entrance. Although prices are high, the Car Care Center does provide towing and minor repairs in an emergency. If the car can't be repaired swiftly, don't despair. The day isn't lost. WDW personnel will chauffeur you to any of the theme parks or back to your hotel.

By far the most common problem is forgetting where you parked. Be sure to write down your row number as you leave your car in the morning. Although Pluto 47 seems easy to remember now, you may not be able to retrieve that info 12 brain-numbing hours later.

6. *Running out of money:* The Sun Bank, which has branches all around Walt Disney World, gives cash advances on MasterCard and Visa, and will provide refunds for lost American Express or Bank of America travelers checks. You can also cash personal checks for up to $25 (up to $1,000 if you have an American Express card) or exchange foreign currency for dollars.

7. *Crime:* Florida has received some very bad press over the last year because of crimes against tourists. It's worth noting that the vast majority of these attacks have taken place in the Miami area, several hours south of Orlando.

Nonetheless, use common sense, especially in trying to avoid the most common crime, theft. Make use of the lockers so that you won't have to carry valuables or new purchases around the parks, take cameras and camcorders onto the rides with you, and be extra-cautious at Typhoon Lagoon and River Country, where you may be tempted to leave your wallet in your lounge chair while riding the waves. It's far better to either wear one of those waterproof waist pouches in the water or rent a locker, returning to it whenever you need money. The locker keys are on elasticized cords that slip around your wrist, so there's no hassle to hanging on to them.

Two much more serious crimes were highly publicized in 1992: a break-in and rape at an on-site hotel and a kidnapping from within one of the major parks. The kidnapping turned out to be part of a custody battle and not a random crime, but reports like this remind us that there's always a chance we'll encounter violence while vacationing. Don't let paranoia ruin your trip—statistically, Orlando remains a safe haven for visitors—but do keep your wits about you, making sure that you lock your hotel and rental car doors, and that you stick to major roads while exploring. Most important, be sure your kids know what to do if they get separated from you.

SAVING MONEY

Saving money at WDW is somewhat of an oxymoron, but there are ways to contain the damage.

1. Purchase a Magic Kingdom Club Gold Card. A $49 two-year membership qualifies you for savings of up to 30% at Disney hotels during certain seasons of the year, discounts on theme park tickets, cruises, souvenir purchases, and a host of other benefits.

2. If the cost of flying the whole family down and then renting a car is prohibitive, consider renting a van in your hometown and driving to Orlando.

3. Eat as many meals as possible outside the parks. If you have a suite, fixing simple meals there is clearly your most economical option. Many Orlando hotels offer free breakfasts to guests, and there are

numerous fast-food and family chain restaurants along International Drive and the I-4 exits.

4. If you'd like to try some of the nicer Epcot restaurants, book them at lunch when prices are considerably lower. And remember that restaurant portions are huge, even with kiddie meals. Consider letting two family members share an entree.

5. Except for maybe an autograph book and a T-shirt, hold off souvenir purchases until the last day. By then the kids will really know what they want and you won't waste money on impulse buys.

6. Purchase film, blank videotapes, diapers, and sunscreen at home before you come. These things are all available in the parks, but you'll pay dearly for the convenience.

7. The Caribbean Beach Resort, Port Orleans, Dixie Landings, and Fort Wilderness Campground provide your most economical on-site lodging. Off-site, there are several Comfort Inns and Days Inns along I-4 and International Drive, most offering shuttle service to the parks. Larger families will probably come out ahead by paying for a suite; the Embassy Suites is a good option if you have three or more kids.

8. If you're driving to Orlando and not arriving until afternoon or evening, don't reserve your on-site room until the second day of your visit. It's silly to pay for a whole day of Grand Floridian amenities if you'll be checking in at 10 P.M. Instead, stop your first night at a budget hotel, rise early the next morning and check out, and then go straight to your on-site hotel. They'll let you unload your bags, pick up your tickets and resort ID, and go on to the theme parks.

9. If you move from park to park in your car, save your parking receipt so you'll only have to pay the $5 once. Likewise, be sure to save stroller receipts.

10. If you plan to try any of the minor parks such as Typhoon Lagoon or Pleasure Island, buy the Five-Day Super Duper Pass. Without it, you'll pay separately for each minor park, which can add up very fast. It's wonderful to break up the day with a few hours at River Country or Typhoon Lagoon. Some families reported that they went to one of the water parks every day during their WDW stay—a trick that is easy with a Super Duper Pass but totally unfeasible otherwise.

11. Call 1-900-89MAGIC before you leave home and request a Magic card, which entitles you to savings on restaurants, area attractions, and many off-site hotels. If you belong to the Entertainment Club, stay at one of the hotels listed in the back that offer 50% price breaks to members.

12. The dinner shows are expensive, costing a family of 4 about $100, and even a character breakfast can set you back $40 or more. If the budget is tight, skip these extras and concentrate on ways to meet the characters inside the parks.

    One cost-saving option is to visit the Diamond Horseshoe Jamboree in lieu of the Hoop-Dee-Doo Revue at Fort Wilderness. The shows are a lot alike, but the Diamond Horseshoe is free. (You can order sandwiches if you wish, but even with lunch, the Diamond Horseshoe won't cost more than $25 for a family of four—the Hoop-Dee-Doo would cost that same family $124.)

13. The employees of many of the companies that have exhibits inside of WDW, such as General Electric,

Exxon, etc., are entitled to discounts and benefits similar to those of Magic Kingdom Club cardholders. (Employees of the federal government also qualify for these price breaks.) Most companies don't publicize this benefit, but if your employer does sponsor an exhibit inside WDW, contact the personnel office well before you leave home and see if any discounts are offered on park admissions or on-site lodging.

14. Disney park admission prices are spiraling out of control, with four substantial raises in the last two years. Buy your tickets when you make your hotel reservations and you'll be protected in case Disney decides it's time for another "adjustment."

BEST SOUVENIRS

For serious shopping, leave the theme parks and head to the Disney Village Marketplace. There you'll find a wide variety of stuffed toys, character-themed clothing, Mickey watches, and every form of Disney memorabilia you can imagine. The Marketplace is never as crowded as the shops within the theme parks, and the selection is better. Mickey's Character Shop is the largest store in all of WDW and is a good place to start.

Looking for a slightly unusual souvenir? Consider these:

1. Boldly-colored T-shirts featuring the flags of Epcot countries, available at Disney Traders, near the mouth of the World Showcase Lagoon.

2. Autograph books, which can be purchased nearly anywhere on the first day of your trip. The signatures of the more obscure characters such as Eeyore or the Queen of Hearts are especially valuable.

3. Characters in vehicles, purchased at the small trinket shops near the stroller rental stands. Mickey rides a moveable crane, Minnie a pink roadster, Donald a locomotive, and so on; these figures are the perfect size for a toddler's chubby fist. At $3 apiece, they're one of the few souvenir bargains to be found in WDW.

4. Anything featuring Figment, the googly-eyed purple star of Journey Into Imagination. Available throughout Future World at Epcot.

5. Disney watches, with an outstanding selection to be found at Uptown Jewelers on Main Street in the MK. Check out the Goofy watch—it runs backward.

6. A piñata from the Mexico pavilion at Epcot.

7. Character Christmas ornaments, found in abundance at either Mickey's Christmas Carol in Fantasyland or the Christmas Chalet in the Disney Village Marketplace.

8. Mickey's Character Shop at the Disney Village Marketplace has entire sections of kidswear devoted to Ariel, Belle, Aladdin, and other heroes.

9. Endor Vendors, next to the Star Tours ride at MGM, offers a slick selection of silver and black jackets.

10. Sid Cahuenga's One-of-a-Kind at MGM sells old movie posters and other campy memorabilia.

11. Disney Villains at MGM is devoted to Captain Hook, Cruella De Ville, Ursula the Sea Witch, and the other no-gooders of Disney films. Disney Villains is a welcome break from all the sweetness and light, and teenagers especially enjoy the chance to align themselves with these punky antiheroes.

12. You'll find character cookie cutters or presses that stamp Mickey's visage onto toast and pancakes at

Yankee Trader in Liberty Square in the MK. Eating a Disney-themed breakfast on your first Saturday home is a nice way to fight those post-trip blues.

13. Get character-theme athletic gear at Team Mickey in the Disney Village Marketplace. You'll see some items here that you won't see anywhere else—like Mickey golf balls, softballs, and basketballs, and Little Mermaid ballet tights.

14. And, of course, mouse ears have a sort of retro-chic. Get your name stitched on a pair at the Mad Hatter in Fantasyland.

FAVORITE TEEN AND PRETEEN ATTRACTIONS

The following attractions received the highest approval rating from the WDW visitors we surveyed age 11–16.

In the Magic Kingdom

- Space Mountain
- Splash Mountain
- Pirates of the Caribbean
- Big Thunder Mountain Railroad
- The Mad Tea Party

At Epcot

- Interactive Games in the CommuniCores
- Body Wars
- IllumiNations
- The American Adventure

At MGM

- The Twilight Zone Tower of Terror
- Star Tours
- Indiana Jones Epic Stunt Spectacular
- The Monster Sound Show

In the Rest of the World

- Typhoon Lagoon
- Water Sprites

Note: Families traveling with teenagers should consider staying at the Hyatt Regency Grand Cypress. This hotel's Rock Hyatt program allows kids 13–17 to participate in planned evening activities with other teens, as well as some supervised "field trips"—such as an afternoon of horseback riding. Rock Hyatt runs daily during the on-season, and on weekends year round. Call (407) 239-1234 for details.

SNAPSHOTS YOU CAN'T LIVE WITHOUT

You can rent 35mm cameras at any of the Kodak Camera Centers for a nominal fee. Film and two-hour photo developing are widely available throughout WDW. Needless to say, the prices of both are higher than at home, but it's good to know you can get more film fast if you go into a photo frenzy. *Note:* The employees at the Camera Centers are generally knowledgeable about photography and are a good source of advice if you've borrowed a big-deal camera from Aunt Lizzie and can't figure out how to advance the film.

For those postcard-perfect shots, Kodak has well-marked Photo Spot locations throughout all the major theme parks. But if, like most parents, what you really want to focus on is your own kids, try the following locations.

In the Magic Kingdom

1. Dumbo, just before takeoff. Once he rises it's just too hard to get a good angle on the riders.
2. With Cinderella, in the downstairs waiting area of King Stefan's Banquet Hall.
3. Among the interactive exhibits and cardboard stills in Mickey's Starland.
4. With Mickey, of course, in his Starland tent.

At Epcot Center

1. In front of the entrance fountains, or at the neat anti-gravity fountains at Journey Into Imagination.
2. Leaning against the railings inside the Land pavilion, with hot air balloons in the background.
3. With the characters garbed in spacegear during breakfast at the Stargate Restaurant or Sunshine Terrace.
4. With the characters fetchingly dressed for Mardi Gras at the World Showcase Lagoon show.

At MGM

1. Halfway through the Backstage Studio Tour there's a break for bathrooms, snacks . . . and pictures ala *Who Framed Roger Rabbit?* The kids can even pose

beneath the steamroller that nearly did in the Toontown gang.

2. Also part of the Backstage Studio Tour is the new Honey, I Shrunk the Kids Adventure Zone. Lots of fun shots here, but most families seem to like the camp of posing inside a nine-foot-high canister of Kodak film.

3. With your waitress-mom at the Prime Time Cafe or in your SciFi Drive-In car.

4. With the gossip columnist, budding starlets, autograph hounds, or other "streetmosphere" players on Hollywood Boulevard.

5. In front of Dinosaur Gertie's.

6. On the lawn of the Golden Girls' house, in the middle of Residential Street on the Backstage Studio Tour.

7. Measuring your footprints against those of the real-life stars in the concrete courtyard of the Great Movie Ride.

CAMCORDER TAPING TIPS

1. If you have one of the old-fashioned camcorders, you know they can be heavy and bulky, and it's risky to leave them in strollers while you're inside the attractions. So for the sake of your back, take your camcorder with you on only one day, preferably the last day of your trip when you're revisiting favorite attractions. That way you'll leave with a "WDW Greatest Hits" tape.

2. If you do plan to take your camcorder with you frequently, make use of the lockers located near the

main gates of all three parks. Lockers can be especially helpful if you'll be riding Space Mountain and Big Thunder Mountain, where you'll risk jarring the machine, or Splash Mountain, where there's a very good chance it'll get wet.

3. Don't pan and zoom too much, because sudden camera moves disorient the viewer. If you're filming the kids, say, on the teacups, use the wide-angle setting and keep the camera stationary. Attempting to track them in close-ups as they spin past is too tough for anyone but a pro.

4. Camcorders can be rented at the Kodak Camera Center on Main Street in the MK or at the Camera Center near Spaceship Earth at Epcot. Rental is $40 a day and a refundable deposit of $400 is required. (The deposit is generally taken on a credit card, and the imprint is ripped up at the end of the day when you return the camera undamaged.)

5. If you rent a camera or are borrowing one from home, try to familiarize yourself with the machine before you begin to actually film. Novices tend to use rapid, jerky movements.

6. If you're using vocal commentary such as "We're in Frontierland now, looking toward Big Thunder Mountain Railroad" be sure to speak loudly. The background noise of the parks will muffle your words.

7. Don't point the camera into the sun. This can permanently damage the camera.

8. Camcorder filming is allowed inside attractions, including many where flash photography is forbidden.

9. Film events such as parades, character shows, and theater-style attractions—for example, the Country

Bear Vacation Hoedown or the Indiana Jones Epic Stunt Spectacular. These are especially fun to watch once you're home.

10. Remember to ask each time you board the monorail if the driver's cab is vacant. Sooner or later you'll get the chance to ride up front, and one bonus is the chance to film panoramic views of the parks as you enter.

SPECIAL TIPS FOR EXTRA-CROWDED TIMES

If your schedule is such that you simply have to go Easter Week or in the dead of summer, the following tips will make the trip more manageable.

1. Stay on-site. You'll have the advantage of the Surprise Mornings, and you won't have to hassle with the traffic jams that paralyze Orlando during the on-season. It's also very helpful to be able to make dining reservations in advance.

2. Allow an extra day—or two. First of all, you won't be able to see as much in a single day as you would if you were going at a less-crowded time. Secondly, you'll tire more easily when the crowds are thick and need longer rest periods to recuperate. Many families schedule an entire day "off" from touring in the middle of their week; this is especially helpful when you're going in the busy season.

3. You *must* be at the parks when they open. By 11 A.M. you'll be facing hour-long waits at many rides—and the parks may even close to arriving guests.

4. Read the sections on each park and choose the two or three things you most want to see. Focus on them and be aware that when you're touring at a crowded time, you probably won't get to "see it all." Just make sure that what you do see is the best.

WHAT'S NEW?

Since the summer of 1994, Disney has debuted two new on-site hotels, Wilderness Lodge and the first phase of the All-Star Resorts, and a major thrill ride, the Twilight Zone Tower of Terror. Planet Hollywood, a casual and funky eaterie located near the Disney Village Marketplace, is set to open as we go to press, and should be a good choice for couples headed toward an evening at Pleasure Island. Planet Hollywood is the latest in a family of celebrity-owned restaurants, and will undoubtedly be popular with the teen and preteen crowd as well.

What's on tap for the future? In the next couple of years look for an expanded Sunset Boulevard at MGM, with two new action rides, and more restaurants and shops. A completely revamped Tomorrowland in the MK will be debuting in stages, beginning with the Alien Encounter.

10

★★★★★★★★★★★★★★★★★★

Life Beyond Disney: Universal Studios, Sea World, and Other Orlando Attractions

UNIVERSAL STUDIOS

Should You Visit MGM or Universal Studios?

Proving once again that imitation is the sincerest form of flattery, Universal and Disney-MGM opened studio theme parks a scant 18 months apart. Both parks offer mind-blowing technology, and there is a real split of opinion among the families we surveyed as to which is better. In general, families with children under 10 preferred MGM. A quick scan of the attractions MGM has added since opening—*MuppetVision 3-D, Voyage of the Little Mermaid,* Beauty and the Beast Stage Show, the Aladdin parade, the Honey, I Shrunk the Kids Adventure Zone, and the Teenage Mutant Ninja Turtles—makes it clear that Disney is making a concerted effort to gear MGM more toward younger kids. Universal, in contrast, is best known for high-thrill adventures such as Kongfrontation, Jaws, and Back to the Future, which scare the socks off of preschoolers but delight preteens and teens.

With a $35 adult admission fee and a cost of $28 for kids 3–9, Universal is as expensive as MGM, but many area hotels offer slightly discounted tickets, and anyone flying down on USAir, the official airline of Universal Studios, gets a price break as well. Families surveyed also noticed that Universal seems less crowded than MGM. It is generally conceded at Disney that MGM was too small the day it opened, and although management has tried to control the crowds by keeping MGM open later at night than originally planned, the park can still become claustrophobic. Universal is over twice as large as MGM, and major attractions are spread out geographically. Thus, with the exception of the area around the main entrance gate, few sections of the park ever become unbearably crowded.

Universal does a good job of controlling crowd flow by breaking many presentations into stages. At Murder She Wrote, for example, a group of visitors is admitted into the first theater while the previous group is in theater two, and the group that entered before them is in the third phase of the show. This means that although the total presentation time is 40 minutes, a group is let into the first theater to begin the cycle every 15 minutes, dramatically reducing wait-time. Universal also stages several shows—the Animal Actors and Wild West Show, for example—in theaters so enormous that large groups can be seated at once, assuring that even on the most crowded days anyone arriving at the theater 10 minutes before showtime can see the show.

In the area of measuring how well the parks manage their own technology, the nod has to go to MGM. Universal has been plagued with attraction breakdowns since the week it opened, and in the early days many visitors requested refunds after highly publicized rides either malfunctioned or were closed for hours at a time. (The Jaws ride was shut down completely due to the frequency of malfunctions, but reopened, at last, in 1994.) Although Universal has made great strides since these early months, glitches are still fairly common, so be forewarned that some attractions may be shut down for an hour or two on the day you visit. On one recent day when my family toured, Murder She Wrote, E.T., and Earthquake were all closed down at different times during the course of an eight-hour period. It makes you appreciate the smooth competence of Disney more than ever.

Nonetheless, Universal packs some major punches, and Back to the Future, E.T., Kongfrontation, Jaws, The

Funtastic World of Hanna-Barbera, and Earthquake match or surpass anything offered at WDW. So is Universal or MGM better? Since at this time each park is small enough to be comfortably toured in a day, there's no reason not to see both and draw your own conclusions.

Your First Hour at Universal Studios

1. Parking is easy if you arrive 20 minutes before the main gate opens. (Call either 363-8230 or 363-8000 the day before you plan to visit to confirm hours of operation.) After getting your tickets, you'll wait in a small holding area for about 10 minutes. Hanna-Barbera characters such as Woody Woodpecker and the Flintstones often circulate among the crowd to pose for pictures and give autographs.

2. Generally, guests are allowed through the main turnstiles about 10 minutes before the official opening time. If a Nickelodeon Studios show such as "Super Sloppy Double Dare" or "Wild and Crazy Kids" is filming on the day you're visiting, this will be indicated on a sign outside the main turnstile, along with directions on how to get tickets. *Note:* Watching a taping is time-consuming and may take up as much as two hours from your morning. If your kids are young and will be skipping many of Universal's scary attractions anyway, you'll have the time. But if your children are older and you'll be trying to cram all the big rides into your day, you won't have time to view a taping.

3. After entering the main turnstile, early arriving visitors are allowed part way down Plaza of the Stars and Rodeo Drive, the two major streets in Universal Studios. If you want to see Back to the Future or E.T. first, go down Rodeo Drive as far as you're allowed. If you'd rather see the Funtastic World of Hanna-Barbera, Kongfrontation, or Earthquake first, go down Plaza of

the Stars until you're stopped by the ropes. Jaws, the farthest ride from the entrance, is a 10-minute walk from either direction. Families who haven't had breakfast may have time for a pastry and gourmet coffee at the Beverly Hills Boulangerie before the ropes drop.

4. Once the ropes drop, go directly to the Funtastic World of Hanna-Barbera. Because of its proximity to the main gate, this attraction draws large lines from 10 A.M. on and must be visited early. (It's also a good gauge as to how well your children will handle the flight-simulation technology found at Back to the Future. If the cartoon chase inside Hanna-Barbera makes them frightened or queasy, you should forget Back to the Future, where the special effects are even more intense.)

5. After you've saved Elroy, try to convince the kids not to linger too long in the interactive play area behind the Hanna-Barbera ride. You can always come back again in midafternoon, but now you need to move on to the other big-name attractions as quickly as possible.

6. If your kids are old enough, ride Kongfrontation, Jaws, and Back to the Future in rapid succession. (At this time of day you shouldn't encounter any waits of longer than 15 minutes.) If your kids aren't up to the high-intensity rides, head toward E.T., then the water ride in Fievel's Playland.

7. If you have tickets for a Nickelodeon taping, it's now time to head back toward the Nick Studios gate. If you're not planning to watch a taping, you're probably worn down from the impact of the rides you've taken in and ready for a break. Visit a theater-style attraction such as Ghostbusters, the Horror Makeup Show, the Wild West Stage Show, Murder She Wrote, or the Animal Actors Stage Show next.

Universal Studios Touring Tips

1. The same basic plan you used in the Disney theme parks will also apply here. You need to visit major attractions—Kongfrontation, Back to the Future, E.T., Jaws, Earthquake, the Funtastic World of Hanna-Barbera—either early in the morning or in the evening. Take in the tours and theater-style attractions in the afternoon.

If you miss one of the major continuously-loading attractions in the morning, hold off on it until two hours before the park closes. Midday waits of up to 90 minutes are not uncommon at popular attractions like Back to the Future, but the crowds do ease off a bit during the dinner hour, and by the time the crowd has moved to the lake to watch the Dynamite Nights Stunt Show the lines at major attractions have become much shorter.

2. On busy days a bulletin board located across from Mel's Diner keeps you posted on upcoming showtimes and the approximate waiting times for continuously-loading attractions. Because the park is big and spread out, crowd movement is uneven at Universal, so the board is definitely worth purusing on a crowded afternoon—you may find there's a 40-minute wait at Kongfrontation, but a mere 5-minute wait at Earthquake.

3. If you plan to see Universal in one day, it's unlikely you'll have time for a midafternoon break, such as returning to your hotel or visiting a water park. But the numerous theater-style attractions at Universal offer plenty of chances to rest up, and small kids can nap.

4. If the kids burn out from too much riding or sitting, Universal offers a pleasant alternative to arcades—although, needless to say, the park has those too—in the form of the carnival midway in the Amity Beach section of the park. This section of the park, modeled after the

New England seacoast village that was beset by the great white superstar of *Jaws,* is rarely crowded. The kids can throw balls in a peach basket or try their luck at hoops while munching candy apples and popcorn. Playing the midway is like stepping back into a different era, and a nice mental break from all the pizzazz of the rides.

Fievel's Playground offers the same sort of escape for kids under 10, with boots to climb through, harmonicas to slide down, and squirting canteens to dodge. As in the Honey, I Shrunk the Kids Adventure Zone at MGM, however, the playground can become unbearably crowded—especially around the popular water ride, which can draw lines so long that a 40-minute wait is not uncommon in midafternoon.

5. The theaters that hold the Horror Makeup Show, Hitchcock, the Wild West Show, Ghostbusters, the Animal Actors Show, the Beetlejuice Graveyard Revue, and Murder She Wrote are high capacity, so even if the lines in midafternoon look discouraging, the odds are you'll still be seated. Consult the entertainment schedule that you receive with your ticket or check the posterboard at the attraction entrance for showtimes, and then put one parent in line about 20 minutes before the show is due to start. The other can take the kids for a drink or bathroom break. If you all opt to wait together in line, be aware that Universal has placed trashcans all through the queue areas of the high-capacity attractions in acknowledgment of the fact that visitors on a tight touring schedule may well be eating or drinking in line.

6. It is not necessary to take the Production Tour to orient yourself to the layout of the park, as some people assume. Universal is laid out in sections that correspond to the movie locales of the major rides—Earthquake, for example, is located in the San Francisco section of the

park, while Kongfrontation and Ghostbusters are naturally enough found in the New York section. A quick lap around the park will alert you to the locations of the major attractions, and—if you decide to take it at all— the tram ride can be safely saved for afternoon when you'll welcome the chance to sit.

7. If you plan to see the Dynamite Nights Stunt Show on the lake (which shows at the park closing time), be there at least 20 minutes before showtime. Unlike Illumi-Nations or the fireworks that close the Disney parks, the Stunt Show is a boat race and subsequent explosion that takes place at water level, and unless you're actually standing lakeside, you won't see much.

8. Headed toward Back to the Future or another intense attraction? Universal employees are prepared to help families traveling with a baby or toddler do a "baby swap" so that everyone can ride. *Note:* If there is some question about whether an older child can "handle" a ride, let one parent ride first, then return with the verdict. If the first parent feels the child can handle it, the second parent can immediately board with the child.

Universal only employs height restrictions on one ride, Back to the Future, and even then kids must only be 40 inches to ride. (But just because any kid big enough to sit up is allowed on Jaws or Kongfrontation doesn't mean it's a good idea to take them; consult the ride descriptions for information on the special effects.) Other attractions such as E.T. and the Funtastic World of Hanna-Barbera provide separate stationary seating for kids under 40 inches, thus allowing families to go through the attraction as a group.

9. Presently, Universal is running a special promotion that allows day visitors to reenter the park after 3 P.M.

on another day at no extra charge. The revisit has to be within seven days of the original visit. You can pick up this special second-day ticket at a designated desk near the exit. If you're running short of time, and would really like to watch a Nick Studios taping, or the kids are pooping out, take Universal up on their offer and come back another afternoon.

10. As at the Disney parks, the age of an attraction is one clue to its popularity. Jaws has drawn consistently big crowds since its debut, and Back to the Future is still a major deal after nearly three years in operation. Try to see the new stuff early in the morning.

Universal Studios Attractions

Back to the Future

Flight-simulation technology makes a quantum leap forward—or is it backward?—in Back to the Future, which has drawn rave reviews since opening in the spring of 1991. After a pre-show video, in which Doc Brown (played by Christopher Lloyd of the movie series) explains that bad-boy Biff has sabotaged his time travel experiments, you'll be loaded into six-passenger Deloreans; what follows is a high-speed chase back through the prehistoric era. The cars bounce around a little, but it's the flight-simulation techniques that are the real scream-rippers, far more intense than those provided by Disney's Star Tours or Body Wars. (Passengers who can bear to glance away from the screen will notice that as many as 12 Deloreans, arranged in tiers, take the trip simultaneously, making Back to the Future a sort of ultimate drive-in movie.)

At one point in your trip through the prehistoric era you're even swallowed by a dinosaur, making the ride much too much for kids under 7, although technically anyone over 40 inches is allowed to board. If your child does want to try the ride, brief him or her that the majority of the effects can be erased simply by closing your eyes—and that's not a bad tip to keep in mind yourself if you're prone to queasiness. For those with strong stomachs, however, the ride is pure pleasure—still the hottest thing in Orlando after nearly four years in operation, which is high praise in a town that takes its fun so seriously.

Earthquake

After a preshow hosted by Charlton Heston, visitors will travel through two separate theaters where they will learn how special effects and stunts were done in the movie *Earthquake*. (The special effects and intricate models of San Francisco are somewhat of a revelation to most kids, since few remember the original movie, which was made over 15 years ago.)

Note: Several Universal attractions, most notably Earthquake, Alfred Hitchcock, and Murder She Wrote, require visitors to move from theater to theater in the course of the presentation. It helps the lines outside the attraction to move steadily, but is tough on families lugging a sleeping child. If you do have a youngster doze off during one of the preshows of the theater-style attractions it is easier to hold her than attempt to put her down, since you'll undoubtedly be moving on within a few minutes.

After the preshows you'll be loaded onto your subway for the ride segment itself. Earthquake is a very short ride and less intense than you may have been led to believe from the advertisements. Most kids will hold up through the rumbles, fires, floods, and train wrecks just fine and, as one mother wrote, "it's fun to feel it really happen instead of watching it on a screen." And it's even more fascinating to watch the water recede, the concrete mend itself, and the fires implode when the ride is over!

Kongfrontation

You'll go head-to-head with one of the fiercest monsters in movie history in the justifiably popular Kongfrontation. The long "underground" queue area, meant to emulate the subways of New York, sets the mood with TV cameras overhead reporting to you that the ape is loose and on a rampage. You'll eventually be loaded onto trams (which carry about 30 riders) and lifted above the fiery streets of a city under siege. Riders will confront Kong up close twice, coming near enough to inspect his 4-foot fangs and even feel the hot blast of banana-breath in their faces. This is one real-looking ape, and the ride is simply too intense for toddlers. Some parents of kids as old as 8 reported that the combination of the darkness, the bursts of flames, and, of course, the mega-ape had their kids clutching their arms and ducking their heads.

Older kids love the ride, however, and rate it extremely highly—especially the impressive finale in which Kong grabs your tram car and "drops" you back onto the street. (The actual fall is only about 10 feet; this attraction relies heavily on its atmospheric effects to scare its riders.) As your wounded tram limps to a halt you'll learn that your close brush with disaster has made the evening news. A videocam inside your car filmed your reaction to the drop and the tape is replayed on a TV camera above your head, adding a fun closing to a powerfully fun ride.

Note: The Universal people are no dummies; every major attraction empties through a gift shop selling memorabilia from the movie or TV show the attraction is based on. You can pick up Jetson T-shirts after riding the Funtastic World of Hanna-Barbera, Slimer toys after seeing Ghostbusters, and an ashtray from the Bates Hotel as you exit Alfred Hitchcock. But Safari Outfitters, adjacent to Kongfrontation, is one of the best gift shops in all of Universal Studios. You can even pose clutched in the fist of King Kong himself for a family souvenir shot; the pictures are developed immediately, and at $4.50-per-pose it's a fun and reasonably-priced momento.

The Funtastic World of Hanna-Barbera
This attraction features a high-speed cartoon flight-simulation chase and is very popular with kids in every age group.

In the brief preshow you learn that Dick Dastardly has kidnapped Elroy Jetson and that it is up to you, along with Yogi Bear and Boo Boo, to rescue him. You'll go on into another room to be loaded into cars, which contain six to eight passengers. Since the cars will be lurching about a bit during the movie, children under 40 inches tall, pregnant women, anyone with back or neck problems, or those who are just plain gutless are ushered to stationary seats at the front of the theater. The flight-simulation effects can convince even the most skeptical parents that they're really flying, and most kids squeal with delight as they meet up with other well-known Hanna-Barbera characters such as the Flintstones and Scooby Doo. Needless to say, Elroy is safely back with his family by the end of the ride. After Yogi brings you in for a rather rough landing, you go on to the interactive area, where you can make a choir of birds sing by stepping on a huge piano, and color your own cartoon using computers.

Note: Like Alfred Hitchcock and the other attractions along the Plaza of the Stars, huge lines form by 10 A.M. as late-arriving visitors walk through the front gate and simply queue up to the first attractions they see. Visit the Funtastic World of Hanna-Barbera first thing in the morning, both to avoid the crowds and to use the ride as a gauge for how well your family will handle the more intense flight-simulation ride, Back to the Future.

E.T. Adventure

This charming ride is as technologically impressive and atmospherically seductive as anything at MGM, but because there's nothing scary about it, the entire family can enjoy it as a group.

The attraction begins with a brief preshow featuring Steven Spielburg and E.T., after which you file through a holding area and—somewhat mysteriously at the time —are required to give your name in exchange for a small plastic "interplanetary passport." Then you move into the queue area, which winds through the deep dark woods and is so evocative that it even smells and sounds like a forest. (Universal in general does a bang-up job of setting the moods in the queue areas; Kongfrontation has many visitors in a lather of nerves before they even board the ride, and E.T. is designed to make you feel small and childlike.)

After handing your passport to the attendant, children under 40 inches tall and anyone elderly, heavy, pregnant, or otherwise unsteady are loaded into flying gondolas. Others get to ride bicycles, and the lead bike in each group has E.T. in the front basket. You rise up and fly over the forest in an effective simulation of the escape scene in the *E.T.* movie. After narrowly escaping the police, you manage to return E.T. to his home planet, a magical place populated by dozens of cuddly aliens.

The ride closes on a stunning note, for as you sail past E.T. for the final time, he bids you farewell by name. When you give your name to the attendant before you enter the queue area, your name is computer coded onto the plastic passport. As you give up the passport and are loaded into your group of bicycles, the cards are fed into the computer. The ride thus "knows" who is riding in that particular batch of bicycles, which enables E.T. to say "Goodbye Jordan, Goodbye Leigh, Goodbye Kim," etc., as your family flies past.

Or, maybe it's just magic.

Note: Unfortunately, this "personal goodbye" system is the most frequently malfunctioning part of the ride, so I wouldn't mention it to the kids at all. That way if it works, everyone is extra-delighted, and if it doesn't, the ride is still an upbeat experience.

Ghostbusters

You'll witness a variety of special effects in this show—which is far more sloppy than scary. For the first part of the show Slimer, Gozer, and the Terror Dogs appear to be winning, but after the Ghostbusters get into the act, the bad guys are history. The climax of the show is when the Marshmallow Man is blown away in an ectoplasmic energy blast. Any kid familiar with the movie and cartoon series shouldn't be overly frightened by the ghouls.

Alfred Hitchcock: The Art of Making Movies

You'll pick up 3-D glasses in the holding area, but only part of the film that follows requires them. This rapid-fire montage of classic scenes from Hitchcock thrillers will go right over the heads of most kids who aren't familiar enough with the movies to tense up when they see that *Psycho* shower curtain. The brief 3-D effect, however, is a thrilling adaptation from a scene in *The Birds,* and you don't have to be a Hitchcock buff to get chills down your spine as those ravens appear to be coming right off the screen toward you.

After the movie you'll be directed into a separate theater where audience volunteers will illustrate how the infamous shower scene in *Psycho* was shot. This part is a bit too scary for younger children; if one of the kids would like to see the 3-D movie but skip *Psycho,* ask the attendant to let you walk straight through the second theater and into the interactive area, where you can play with the props until the rest of your party joins you.

The interactive area is interesting, giving volunteers a chance to try out action special effects. And if you miss the Bates Motel Gift Shop on your way out, Mother will be very upset.

Jaws

As the people of Amity Beach learned, that darn shark just won't stay away.

Although closed down for over two years due to malfunctions, the Jaws ride eventually did come back on line in late 1993. The new version, which actually takes you on a boat ride through the harbor of Amity Village, is even more nerve-racking than the old ride. The shark appears several times quite suddenly, the unseen boat before you "gets it" in a gruesome way, and the chase scene culminates in a fiery finale. Between the grenade launches, explosions, fuel spills, and, of course, the shark, the ride is too frightening for kids under 7—even though, as long as a child is big enough to sit up on his own, no height restrictions apply. The boat doesn't move around too much, but the effects may terrorize a child too young to understand the difference between illusion and reality, and the convincing spiel by your boat captain does nothing to reassure them.

It's new, and therefore hot. Go during the first hour the park is open in the morning, or expect long lines.

Note: Interestingly enough, Universal has invested $50-million in the ride, which is over six times what Spielburg spent on the original circa-1975 movie.

The Gory, Gruesome, and Grotesque Horror Makeup Show

This show was formerly titled the Phantom of the Opera Makeup Show, but Universal evidently figured that while not every visiting kid knew who the Phantom was, they all knew what gory and gruesome meant. A witty pair of young actors illustrate certain makeup effects on stage. You'll also see clips from *The Exorcist, The Fly,* and an astounding man-to-beast transformation scene from the little-known *An American Werewolf in London.* While the movie clips and general gore level are too high for preschoolers, most kids over 7 can stomach the show, which is, in the final analysis, an informative illustration of how special effects have become more and more believable through the years.

The Animal Actors Stage Show

If your children are strung out from a combination of 90-degree heat, 3-D birds, and man-eating dinosaurs, the Animal Actors Stage Show will offer a welcome change of pace. The show features apes, birds, and Benji-clone dogs. It takes place in a large open-air arena, so if you show up about 10 minutes before the designated showtime, you'll have no trouble getting seated. Kids in both the 4–7 and 7–11 age group rated the animals very highly. This attraction is also a fun one to videotape and watch again later at home.

Murder She Wrote Mystery Theater

This amusing show, which allows the audience to select the outcome of an episode of the well-known TV series, has been overlooked and somewhat underrated by the crowds, which rush past it on their way to the theme rides. Fans of the TV series will find the attraction especially engaging—they even get to choose a dinner date for their beloved Angela Lansbury. The presentation is so wittily presented and encourages so much audience participation that almost everyone ends up having fun.

As at most of the theater-style Universal attractions, you move from theater to theater as you edit the show, add sound effects, and ultimately select the outcome of the episode. All this moving about makes it hard for kids to nap during the presentation. Although kids under 7 won't get most of the jokes, kids 7–11 will enjoy the attraction far more than you'd guess, especially if they're chosen to come up on stage and help with the sound effects (this possibility becomes more likely if you sit near the front of the theater).

The Wild West Stunt Show

Funny, fast-moving, and full of surprises, this show ranks at the top of the list with kids 7–11 and rates highly with kids under 7 as well. The shoot-em-ups, fist-fights, and explosions are played strictly for laughs, and sometimes the comedy tends to overshadow how dangerous these stunts really are. A good choice for the whole family, and, like the Animal Actors Show, it's fairly easy to get into, even in the crowded parts of the afternoon.

Fievel's Playground

The brand-new Fievel's Playground is very popular, featuring a cleverly-designed play area filled with western-style props—including a harmonica that plays notes as kids slide down it, a giant talking Tiger the Cat, canteens to squirt, cowboy hats to bounce in, spider webs to climb, and a separate ball pit and slide area for toddlers.

The centerpiece of the playground is a 200-foot water ride in which kids and parents are loaded into "sardine cans built for two" and swept through a sewer. The ride is zippier than it looks, will get you soaking wet, and is so addictive that most kids clamor to get back on again immediately. The water ride is very popular and loads slowly, so by afternoon the lines are prohibitive; if you come in the morning it is possible to ride several times with minimal waits, but by afternoon one ride is all you can reasonably expect. *Note:* Fievel's Playground usually opens a couple of hours after the general park. If you ride the big-deal rides and then show up at the playground at the opening time indicated on your entertainment schedule, you'll be able to try the water ride without much of a wait.

Fievel's Playground is great fun, and most kids could happily stay for hours. The only drawbacks are that, like the Honey, I Shrunk the Kids Adventure Zone at MGM, it needs to be much, much larger, and that Universal unwisely lets preteens and teens in. Their rowdy play makes the area downright unsafe for younger kids, especially in the afternoon when the playground is crowded. How about a few reverse height restrictions, guys?

Rocky and Bullwinkle Live

This new stage show—which runs only in the summer—features not only Rocky and his "enormoose" friend Bullwinkle, but also Boris and Natasha (who have headed for Hollywood, since jobs are getting hard to find in the spy business), Dudley Do-Right, and Snidely Whiplash. The distinctive style of humor created by the late Jay Ward is in truth so sophisticated that many of the jokes will go right past the kids. The production is enjoyable on several levels, however, and the kids will giggle at the pure silliness of the situations, while the adults smirk at the satire and in-jokes. The characters hang around after the show for autographs and pictures. Rocky and Bullwinkle both arrive and depart via a bright blue prop plane, which rolls through the streets of the park stirring up a bit of excitement.

Since the show takes place outdoors and is completely exposed to the sun, afternoon performances can be sweltering. Come to the first show of the day or an evening show.

The Beetlejuice Graveyard Revue

A rock-and-roll dance show starring Dracula, the Wolfman, Phantom of the Opera, and Frankenstein and his Bride, the Revue is very popular with the 7–11 age group and teens—although the show is so goofy and upbeat that younger kids certainly won't be frightened by the ghouls.

This is a high-tech show featuring pulsating lights, fog-machines, a spoof of synchronized MTV-style dancing, and wry renditions of rock classics. (My personal favorite is the Bride of Frankenstein's version of "You Make Me Feel Like a Natural Woman.") Since this 15-minute show plays frequently throughout the day, getting in isn't too tough—work it into your schedule whenever it happens to suit you.

Lucy: A Tribute

Fans of "I Love Lucy" should take a few minutes to walk through this exhibit, which houses memorabilia from the famous TV show, including scale models of the Tropicana and the Ricardos' apartment, clothes and jewelry worn on the show, personal pictures and letters from

Lucy and Desi's home life, and the numerous Emmys that Lucille Ball won throughout the years. The "California Here We Come Game" is a treat for hard-core trivia buffs. By answering questions about episodes of "I Love Lucy," game participants get to travel with the Mertzes and Ricardos on their first trip to California. They lost me somewhere in the desert, but perhaps you'll do better.

The Production Tour

Since the preshow film has been scrapped, all that is really left of the Production Tour is a 15-minute tram ride through the streets of the theme park, with your tour guide pointing out painfully obvious facts, such as "We're on the streets of San Francisco now." While some visitors flock to the tour immediately upon entering the park, thinking it will orient them to the location of major park attractions, the tour provides little practical information. And, unlike the MGM tour, the ride spends very little time "behind the scenes." All in all, the Production Tour is skippable, especially for families with young kids.

The Nickelodeon Tour

After being labeled somewhat of a drag by reviewers and families, this tour has been revamped and is now much more fun. Even if you don't decide to take in the filming of a Nick show, your kids will enjoy the 45-minute walk-through tour. They'll see the sets of shows they'll immediately recognize, perhaps get a glimpse of a show in production, and then move on to the popular Game Lab where audience volunteers are slopped and glopped in the best Nickelodeon tradition. Kids 7–11 rated the tour very highly, as did younger kids who were familiar with Super Sloppy Double Dare and the other Nick game shows. Parents unfamiliar with the social significance of Gak may find the Game Lab absolutely bewildering. It's a bit like an old *Three Stooges* movie with some hapless Dad from Illinois cast in the role of Curly.

Note: Even if you don't plan to take in the tour or a filming, drop by the Nick Studios entrance and check out the Green Slime Geyser, which periodically erupts and spews an unearthly-colored substance about the consistency of pudding into the air. Even the bathrooms in the Nickelodeon section have Green Slime Soap in the soap dispensers. For some preschoolers, this is the highlight of the trip.

Screen Test Adventure Studio

The Screen Test Adventure Studio is part attraction, part souvenir stand, and it takes the technology found in MGM's SuperStar Television one step further. Through the use of costumes, mock-up sets, and film splicing, you and your family can fly with William Shatner, Leonard Nimoy, and the rest of the Star Trek crew, and take home a video reminder of your acting debut. (You can also film yourselves visiting major attractions at Universal Studios—in other words, reacting to shouted directions with a blank screen behind you. The backgrounds of Kongfrontation and Earthquake are added later. But on the day I observed, few families selected this option; almost everyone suited up in polyester and headed for the bridge of the Starship Enterprise.)

The cost of the experience is $29.95, with a $6.50 charge for additional videotapes. Up to six members of a family can assume roles and enter into the fun, and the resulting tape does make an unusually clever—if somewhat expensive—reminder of your visit to Universal Studios.

Coming Soon: Jurassic Park

Let's face it, the ride is an inevitable follow-up to a movie about theme park rides—a spoof of a spoof, so to speak.

Universal is paving the way for the attraction with Jurassic Park jeep-style strollers, a booth where you can have your picture taken with a T-Rex, and an exhibit featuring props used in the film.

Shows at Universal Studios

Showtimes are listed on the entertainment schedule that comes with your ticket: Try to take in at least a couple. Kids especially enjoy the Blues Brothers and the Ghostbusters. *Note:* The Ghostbusters street show, which runs only in the summer, is an entirely different presentation from the one inside the Ghostbusters building.

If you're trying to do the whole park in a day, it's a good idea to plan your meals around the musical shows, such as eating your noontime burger at Mel's Drive-In while the Hollywood Hi-Tones croon ballads from the fifties, or taking in a bit of Irish folksinging at Finnegan's Pub along with your evening meal of shepherd's pie and ale. It's like a free dinner show!

The most well-known of the Universal Studios shows is the Dynamite Nights Stunt Show, which is staged at closing time every evening. The show is Universal's answer to the popular Indiana Jones Stunt Spectacular at MGM and involves a high-speed boat chase ending in a fiery explosion. But be aware that you must stake out your position early. One of the best vantage spots is on the small pavilion in front of the Animal Actors Show—if you don't mind getting splashed, that is.

Best Food Bets at Universal Studios

The fastest fast food is simply to purchase a hot dog from one of the many vendors scattered throughout the park, but you'll be missing much of the fun if you eat on the run for all three meals. Universal has many appealing dining choices, and in general the food is far tastier and cheaper than that found within the Disney theme parks. There's not only a good selection, but the lines keep moving, even during the lunch hours of a busy summer day.

In addition, since most families have a one-day Universal ticket and are trying to cram it all into 12 straight hours of touring, few break up the day by actually leaving the park. That means you'll need to rest up a bit in the afternoon or risk having the kids—and maybe the parents—collapse in tears of exhaustion at 6 P.M. A late lunch or early dinner is advised, since it will get you off the streets during the hottest and most crowded touring times of the day, and give everyone a chance to rest and regroup before heading on to those attractions you missed earlier. Below are a few of the more interesting Universal eateries:

1. *The Hard Rock Cafe*

What is there to say? The Hard Rock Cafes, found in major cities all over the world, are justifiably famous for their funky atmosphere, raucously friendly service, and tasty, unassuming food. The one in Orlando is the largest of all, with a correspondingly large collection of pop memorabilia, and even the building is fascinating. (Note the Pink Cadillac crashing into the front of the facade.) Hard Rock T-shirts and sweatshirts are highly valued souvenirs, especially among status-conscious teenagers and preteens, and it would be a shame to visit Universal and not take in the Hard Rock Cafe.

The problem is when to go. The Hard Rock Cafe does not take reservations, and large crowds are the norm from midafternoon on. If you have young kids along, the best bet is to eat a fairly early lunch around 11:30 A.M., when the cafe isn't so crowded that you can't get up and look around. Another crowd-busting option is an early dinner around 4:30 or 5 P.M.

Others swear that the Hard Rock gets better and better as the day wears on, and it's impossible to truly get into the spirit of the place before dark. If adults in your party would like to linger over drinks and listen to the music, this is a good option for a parents' night out. *(Note:* You can enter the Hard Rock Cafe from Universal Studios or from a separate parking lot, so you do not have to have a Universal Studios ticket to enter the restaurant. It is, in fact, popular with Orlando locals, which is one reason why it is always hard to get in.)

If you only want to buy a Hard Rock T-shirt or sweatshirt, you can purchase merchandise without entering the restaurant—just make sure you're in the right line.

2. *Finnegan's Pub*
Friendly, informal, and with the added bonus of having live music during peak dining hours, Finnegan's is a great place to rest up and pig out. It's dark inside, too, even on the most blistering summer afternoons, so kids can stretch out and nap in the booths.

3. *Lombard's Landing*
If you crave a fancier meal, such as prime rib or fresh pompano, Lombard's Landing is a beautiful restaurant on the Fisherman's Wharf section of San Francisco. The service is leisurely and the atmosphere a bit more elegant than most of the park restaurants, so opt for Lombard's only if your kids can be counted on to behave reasonably well (or sleep) through a 90-minute meal. Lombard's Landing becomes quite crowded at dinner, so a late lunch or midafternoon meal is a better bet.

4. *Cafe la Bamba*

A good choice for Mexican, with outstanding margaritas and live music on the patio during lunch and dinner.

5. *Studio Stars*

Big eaters in the party? Studio Stars runs lunch and dinner buffets (adults $10, children $5), which are a good choice if you want more than a burger but you still want to get your food quickly.

6. *Mel's Drive-In*

Unquestionably the place to go for fast food, Mel's offers homestyle burgers and fries, served up with '50s music and a bevy of car hops on roller skates. The drive-in is based on the one in the film *American Graffiti,* and even kids far too young to remember the movie, much less the decade being spoofed, will fall for the table-based jukebox and vintage cars parked outside. If you plan ahead and arrive about 15 minutes before show-time, you can claim one of the outside tables and catch a performance of the Hollywood Hi-Tones, an excellent a cappella group, while you eat.

7. *Louie's*

A nice spot for a fast Italian dinner, especially if you're headed for the nearby Dynamite Nights Stunt Show, Louie's offers spaghetti for kids at a reasonable $3 and a choice of hearty pasta favorites for adults.

If you're just looking for a snack, try the following:

1. *Schwab's Pharmacy*

We can't promise you'll be discovered here, as Lana Turner allegedly was, but the milkshakes are made the old-fashioned way and served up in pedestal glasses.

2. *San Francisco Pastry Co.*

If you need a break after riding Earthquake or Back to the Future, stop off for a brownie, a kiwi tart, or one of the fantastic pastries. The Key West flans with lime are the best.

3. *Cafe Alcatraz*

Sweets aren't your thing? You can always sit by the dock of the bay in the San Francisco district and enjoy a crab or shrimp salad. Just don't leave your salad if you go back for a napkin—those seagulls circling overhead mean business.

Snapshots You Just Can't Live Without

Universal offers a wealth of great photo opportunities, surpassing the Disney parks in the sheer variety of campy locales for an unusual family shot. Your kids would look great in any of the following poses:

1. Perched on the hood of one of the brightly colored vintage cars permanently parked outside Mel's Drive-In.

2. With their heads inside the mouth of the Great White Shark strung up in the Amity Beach section.

3. Vamping and camping it up with Mae West, Charlie Chaplin, the Blues Brothers, or any of the other Hollywood stars who roam Rodeo Drive.

4. In front of the Bates Hotel, located near the Hard Rock Cafe.

5. In front of the globe and fountains outside the main turnstile.

6. In front of the green slime machine beside the Nickelodeon Studios entrance.

7. For $4 you can pose on a bike with E.T. or in the grip of King Kong. Just stop by Safari Outfitters as you exit Kongfrontation, or E.T.'s Photo Spot as you leave the E.T. Adventure.

8. Kodak sponsors Trick Photography Photo Spots scattered throughout the park, the most elaborate of which can be found in the "boneyard" of props in front of the Production Tour. By placing your camera in the indicated spot and arranging your family in front of specially-scaled props, you can turn the kids into the crew of a NASA space shuttle or photograph them in front of the Hollywood Hills.

Favorite Teen and Preteen Attractions at Universal

Most of the visitors 11–17 rated Universal as "grosser and wilder" than MGM—and in this age group, that's a compliment. Attractions especially popular with teens and preteens were:

- Kongfrontation
- Back to the Future
- Jaws
- Alfred Hitchcock: The Art of Making Movies
- The Gory, Gruesome, and Grotesque Horror Make-up Show
- Dynamite Nights
- The Beetlejuice Graveyard Revue

And, not surprisingly, this age group considered a visit to the Hard Rock Cafe an essential wrap-up to a perfect day at Universal Studios.

Universal Studios Don't-Miss List

- The Funtastic World of Hanna-Barbera
- Kongfrontation
- E.T. Adventure
- Back to the Future
- Jaws
- The Animal Actors Stage Show (if you have kids under 10)
- The Wild West Stunt Show
- Fievel's Playground (if you have kids under 10)
- The Nick Tour (if you have kids under 10)

Universal Studios Worth-Your-While List

- Ghostbusters
- Earthquake
- Alfred Hitchcock: The Art of Making Movies
- Murder She Wrote Mystery Theater
- The Gory, Gruesome, and Grotesque Horror Make-up Show
- Dynamite Nights
- Rocky and Bullwinkle Live
- A Nickelodeon Show, if one of your child's favorites is in production on the day you visit

The Scare Factor at Universal Studios

The shows and tours are family-oriented and fine for everyone, but some of the big-name attractions are entirely too frightening for preschoolers.

Universal imposes very few height restrictions and thus gives parents little guidance. Kids below 40 inches are banned from Back to the Future and required to use special seating on E.T. and the Funtastic World of Hanna-Barbara—but beyond these minimal restrictions, parents are the ones who decide who rides what.

Any child old enough to sit on his own can ride Jaws, Earthquake, and Kongfrontation. Universal seems to set the rules based on how physically wild the ride is—and in truth none of the rides listed bounces you around too much. But they're psychologically scary, and a visit to Kongfrontation or Alfred Hitchcock may lead to more bad dreams than even the wildest of coasters. Although obviously individual reactions vary from child to child— my own 4-year-old son adores Kongfrontation—read the ride descriptions and consult the list below to help you decide.

Fine for Anyone:

- The Funtastic World of Hanna-Barbera
- E.T. Adventure
- Animal Actors Stage Show
- Murder She Wrote Mystery Theater
- Earthquake
- Ghostbusters
- Lucy: A Tribute
- Rocky and Bullwinkle Live
- The Beetlejuice Graveyard Revue (*Note:* The monsters aren't scary but the show is very loud. Some toddlers may be frightened.)
- Fievel's Playground, including the water ride

Wait Until Your Kids Are at Least 7 to Try:

- Kongfrontation
- Back to the Future
- Jaws
- Alfred Hitchcock: The Art of Making Movies
- The Gory, Gruesome, and Grotesque Horror Makeup Show

Your Last Hour at Universal Studios

1. If you want to see Dynamite Nights, find a spot around the lagoon at least 20 minutes before showtime. Benches are everywhere, so after you stake out a good spot, one member of your party can go back for snacks so you can enjoy a picnic while waiting for the show.

2. If you don't care to see the lagoon show, you'll find it draws so many people to one spot that it's now much easier to get into rides like Kongfrontation or Jaws, which may have been swamped all day.

3. As you work your way toward the exit, you'll see characters such as the Ghostbusters, the Blues Brothers, and the Hanna-Barbera cartoon gang circulating among the crowds. If you haven't gotten pictures or autographs earlier, here's your chance.

4. Some of the shops and restaurants stay open 20 to 30 minutes past the official park closing time. If the exits seem glutted, stop for a drink or check out the shops until the crowds disperse.

5. If the special tickets that allow you to reenter for free after 3 P.M. are offered, stop by and pick them up as you exit the park.

6. Forget about slipping into the Hard Rock Cafe for a nightcap as you leave. Eleven thousand other people have the same good idea.

SEA WORLD

Opened in 1973, the same year as the Magic Kingdom, Sea World is best known as the home of Shamu and the killer whales. But other exhibits are equally fascinating, such as the Penguin Encounter, where you can observe the tuxedoed charmers both above and below the ice floe, and witness their startling transformation from awkward walkers to sleek swimmers. *Note:* Check your entertainment schedule for feeding time; you'll get to see the trainers slip about on the iceberg with buckets of fish and the penguins waddle determinedly behind them. The birds ingest the fish in one amazing gulp, and you can stand on the top observation level and watch for as long as you like.

If your kids are too cool to like cute, try the Terrors of the Deep exhibit, where you'll encounter sharks, moray eels, and barracudas at close quarters, or Mission: Bermuda Triangle, a motion-simulation ride about a sea dive gone really, really wrong. The Discovery Cove show featuring leaping dolphins and white beluga whales is especially popular with kids, as is the hilarious sea-lions show. The water-skiing show, updated frequently to keep the performance fresh, is always dazzling and amusing. All of the shows take place in enormous open-air theaters, so touring Sea World is as simple as consulting your entertainment schedule (which is also your map) for showtimes and being at the theater about ten minutes early.

Sea World has recently opened an exhibit dedicated to one of Florida's own endangered species, the manatee, as well as a new area simulating the natural environment of the California sea lions. The Budweiser Clydesdales have also joined the Sea World family, and most children thrill at the chance to meet these huge but gentle creatures. *Note:* At certain times of the day, one of the horses is taken out into a paddock and children are allowed to get close enough to have a picture taken. Again, the time is noted on your entertainment schedule.

Sea World is a low-stress experience, much less high-tech and frenetic than the other Orlando parks. It can be easily seen in six or seven hours, and is laid out so that the crowds pretty much flow from one scheduled show to the other. The park is so beautifully landscaped that you often can't see one stadium from the other, and the sense of space is a welcome change after a week spent in the Magic Kingdom or at MGM. But the openness also means that children up to age 5 will benefit from a stroller; fortunately, the dolphin-shaped rental strollers are so cute that most kids climb in without a fuss.

If you're feeling guilty about taking the kids out of school, Sea World offers educational tours (Quick—can you tell the difference between a sea lion and a seal?). "Backstage Information," which explores how endangered marine species and their natural habitats can be preserved, is a 90-minute tour and, despite the heavy-sounding topic, can be enjoyed by kids as young as 9. "Animal Lover's Adventure," also 90 minutes, takes visitors into the animals' habitats and explores what they eat, how their group dynamics work, and how they care for their young. "Let's Talk Training" lasts for 45 minutes and is a better choice for younger kids.

All of the tours are reasonably priced (adults $6, children $5). Tours leave several times a day during the busy season, and reservations are not necessary. Either buy your tour ticket when you purchase your general admission ticket, or, if you get the urge to join a tour after a few hours in the park, return to Guest Relations near the main entrance. *Note:* If more than one tour is scheduled, don't take the first tour of the day. Let the kids explore the theme park for a while and see a few shows during the empty morning hours, then return for the tour in the afternoon as the park becomes more crowded.

Small children at Sea World welcome the numerous chances to get close to the beasties. My 4-year-old son loved feeding the harmless-looking-but-actually-quite-vicious seals, and the vicious-looking-but-actually-quite-harmless stingrays. For $3 you can get three small fish and toss them to the seals, sea lions, or dolphins. The dolphins and stingrays are in shallow tanks so that children can reach over and touch them as they glide by. Running a hand along the flank of a dolphin or flinging a fish into the whiskered mouth of a furiously barking sea lion is a real kick for young children, and the experience will probably stay with them long after the shows and tours have faded from memory.

Another kick for the young kids is Shamu's Happy Harbor, a play area that puts those at MGM and Universal to shame. Shamu's Harbor is not only happy but huge, with an elaborate web of climbing nets, a ship heavy-laden with water-firing muskets, a splashy climb-through area, a variety of ball pits to sink into, and padded pyramids to climb. After a few hours spent in shows and exhibits, stop by and let the kids just play for a while. There's a shaded area with seats below the climbing pits so that parents can relax. A separate play area for smaller kids ensures they don't get tangled up in the webs, whacked by an older kid on a tire swing, or, worst of all, get confused in the mazes and exit far from where Mom and Dad are waiting. Since several of the play areas involve water, some parents let kids wear their bathing suits under their shorts. It provides a nice in-park break on a summer day full of touring.

In the evening, Sea World offers a different show starring Shamu called Night Magic! *Note:* Be sure to take a snapshot of the kids sitting on the huge cast iron Shamu outside his stadium as you enter. The night show is definitely worth waiting around for (or returning to if you've left the park in the afternoon for a rest), but be forewarned: If you opt to sit in "splash zone," the first four rows of the stadium, Shamu's special goodbye wave will leave you not just splashed but drenched straight through to your underwear. Kids adore the surprising blast of sea water, but if you're touring off-season and it's chilly it may be wiser to sit farther back and laugh at the unwary tourists sitting down by the tank.

Sea World admission is $34 for adults and $29 for kids 3–11, but numerous discount coupons can be found floating around Orlando, and sometimes specials drop the price as low as $21 for adults. The park opens at 9 A.M. It is virtually empty until 11 A.M., and can be comfortably toured in seven hours. Have your hand stamped as you leave, spend the afternoon relaxing at your hotel or at one of the water parks, and return for the evening show, the fireworks, and—if you purchased tickets for it earlier in the day—the popular nightly Polynesian luau. Call (407) 351-3600 for more information.

GATORLAND ZOO

The—ahem—unique ambiance of Gatorland Zoo is established by the fact that you enter through a giant blue concrete gator mouth. While most of the hundreds of alligators within are rendered passive by the Florida sun, things do perk up four times a day at the Gator Jumparoo. The gators leap as high as five feet out of the water to retrieve whole chickens from the hands of the trainers. One young cynic surveyed pointed out that the animals jump highest at the first show of the day, aka "breakfast." The Gator Wrestlin' Show and Snakes of Florida are also a hit with kids.

This campy little place, which also has a small zoo and a train ride, can be easily toured in two or three hours. Children can have a souvenir shot taken of them holding either an alligator or a boa constrictor. And while Sea World certainly doesn't serve dolphin, Gatorland suffers no qualms about biting the hand that feeds it. You can pick up a few cans of Gator Chowder at the gift shop, surely a unique "thank you" for those neighbors back home who are watering the plants while you're away. Gatorland Zoo admission is $11 for adults, $8 for kids 3–11. Call (407) 855-5496 or 1-800-393-JAWS.

WET 'N WILD

The atmosphere doesn't stack up to the Huck Finn feel of River Country or the tropical splendor of Typhoon Lagoon, but for families staying off-site, Wet 'n Wild is a great place to cool off without getting back into the Mouse Race.

This was the original water theme park in Orlando, and in terms of sheer thrills, the preteen crowd surveyed claim it's still the best. The six-story plunge of the Der Stuka, the twisting tubes of the Mach 5, or a spiraling descent through the Black Hole are not for the faint of heart. Wet 'n Wild's newest attraction, the Bomb Bay, sends riders on a six-second freefall down a 76-foot slide and is, like the other big-deal attractions, strictly off-limits to children below 48 inches in height. These rides are enough to knock the breath out of even a strong swimmer. Some kids who make the height requirements still aren't up to the intensity of the attractions, so if you have doubts, steer your 8-year-old toward the smaller slides and flumes.

Small children and others who are chicken of the sea can slide along in a Bubba Tub or float down the Lazy River in a big rubber tube. In 1991 Wet 'n Wild opened a $1.5 million children's water playground, billed as a "safe, fun environment for kids 1–10." Now preschoolers and unsteady swimmers have their own wave pool, a miniature raging rapids, and fiberglass flumes designed for riders under 48 inches tall. It's the perfect addition for families whose children range in ages and who need a place that can be both Wet 'n Wild and Wet 'n Mild.

Admission is $21 for adults and $18 for kids 3–9, but your best bet is to arrive in late afternoon or early evening, when prices are cut in half. Discounts take effect at 3 P.M. during the off-season and at 5 P.M. in summer, when the park stays open until 11 P.M. Crowds become far more manageable as the sun goes down, and summer evenings offer live entertainment, poolside karaoke, and the laid-back party atmosphere of a beach club. Wet 'n Wild is located on International Drive, which is exit 30A off I-4. Call (407) 351-1800 for details.

WATER MANIA

A slightly less crowded off-site water park is Water Mania—a better choice for families who are staying near 192 (exit 25 off I-4). Along with the standard assortment of wave pools, slides, floats, and flumes, Water Mania features the new Wipe Out, a specially designed surfboard ride full of body-slamming thrills, and Aqua Xpress, a kid-

die area with a wonderful little train for climbing and slid-
ing. Admission is $21 for adults, $19 for children 3–12,
and there are numerous discount coupons to be found in
brochures and at the Guest Services booths of area hotels.
Call (407) 239-8448 or 1-800-527-3092 for details.

MYSTERY FUN HOUSE

A good place for rainy days, the Mystery Fun House is full
of mazes, sloping floors, and optical illusions. It also houses
a miniature golf course and arcade. Admission for all ages
is $8. Starbase Omega next door charges $6 a head regard-
less of age and features an alien planet with a space-grav-
ity surface, targets, and a laser tag game, which is a great
hit with teenagers who'd like the chance to interact with
other humanoids. Numerous discount coupons are available (some lowering the price as much as 50%), and you
can get a combination ticket for both the fun house and
Starbase Omega. Call (407) 351-3355 for details.

FUN 'N WHEELS

Go carts and bumper boats (and a few standard kiddie
rides) can be found at Fun 'N Wheels, located just off International Drive. The rides are on a pay-as-you-go basis
(the cars cost about $4 per person, the bumper boats
about $3), and the park stays open until 11 P.M. Call
(407) 351-5651 for details.

Still looking for something to do? In addition to Orlando attractions, there's Cypress Gardens to the south,
Cape Canaveral to the east, and Busch Gardens to the
west, all worthwhile and all within a 90-minute drive.

OFF-SITE DINNER SHOWS
FOR THE WHOLE FAMILY

Disney isn't the only company in Orlando offering family dinner theaters. The dinner theaters that follow differ greatly in theme, with some more suitable for children than others. Each offers four- or five-course meals, unlimited beer and wine, and a live show. Prices run about $32 for adults, $21 for kids 3–11, but discount coupons (some dropping the price of an adult dinner as much as $10) can be found all around Orlando at Guest Services booths, family-style restaurants, and in those freebie magazines aimed toward vacationers. There is generally one seating nightly in the off-season, two during the on-season, so you'll need to call for exact showtimes and to make reservations. The halls hold between 400 and 1,000 people; come prepared to buddy up to that couple from Michigan.

1. *Arabian Nights*
The only dinner show to serve prime rib (although the food is only so-so at all of these places), Arabian Nights features over 60 horses, including White Lipizzans and a "mystical unicorn." The highlight of the evening is a high-speed chariot race re-created from the movie *Ben Hur.* 1-800-553-6116 or (407) 396-1787.

2. *Wild Bill's Fort Liberty*
A favorite of younger kids, this Wild West show offers knife throwers, rain dancers, lasso twirlers, and the comical soldiers from E Troop. (If you remember the old "F Troop" TV show you get the general picture.) Barbecue, fried chicken, and corn on the cob are served up chuckwagon style. 1-800-347-8181 or (407) 351-5151.

3. *Medieval Times*
Dueling swordsmen and jousting knights on horseback perform in a huge pit while guests dine on roast

chicken and ribs. Several of the gentlemen surveyed gave a "must see" rating to the serving wenches' costumes. Medieval Times was the favorite dinner theater of kids in the 7–11 age range, largely because the arena is divided into competing teams bearing different colors and the performers do a wonderful job of urging spectators to cheer for "their" knight. 1-800-229-8300 or (407) 239-0214.

4. *Mardi Gras*
Smaller and a bit more distinctive than the others, Mardi Gras offers a highly sanitized version of a New Orleans show, complete with can-can dancers and cabaret singers. The food is not as spicy as French Quarter fare, either; expect fried shrimp and tenderloin. 1-800-347-8181 or (407) 351-5151.

5. *King Henry's Feast*
The portly monarch is searching for his seventh wife— portraits of her six unlucky predecessors hang in the entry hall—as magicians, jugglers, and minstrels offer a kinder, gentler version of Medieval Times. Chicken and ribs are on hand for the revelers. 1-800-347-8181 or (407) 351-5151.

6. *Asian Adventure*
One of the newer entries in the family dinner sweepstakes, the Asian Adventure features acrobatic and balancing acts, martial arts, magic, music—and, of course, a Chinese banquet. (407) 351-5655.

7. *Capone's*
Expect Italian food and mobsters aplenty in this cheerful version of a Chicago prohibition-era speakeasy. Capone's offers musical comedy in the best *Guys and Dolls* tradition, and massive portions of pasta. (407) 397-2378.

8. *Sleuth's Mystery Dinner Show*

And now for something completely different. . . . As you munch hors d'oeuvres and mingle with suspicious characters in an English drawing room, be sure to keep your wits about you: A crime is about to unfold, and it is up to you to collect the clues, interrogate the suspects, and formulate a theory. The family who comes up with the most accurate solution wins a prize. The meal is veddy civilized as well—Cornish game hen with herb dressing. (407) 363-1985.

Of the dinner theater options listed above, Wild Bill's and Medieval Times are the best for young children—they can enter into the raucous action with no fear of disturbing anyone. Older kids will be able to better appreciate the uniqueness of the Asian Adventure, the music and humor of Capone's, and the challenge of the Sleuth's Mystery Theater.

Index

Hawai'i: The Big Island

Making the Most of Your Family Vacation, 4th Edition

by John Penisten

Maui and Lana'i

Making the Most of Your Family Vacation, 6th Edition

by Greg & Christie Stilson

Order
PARADISE FAMILY GUIDES
for a wonderful family vacation!

With an emphasis on family travel and an eye on the family budget, the PARADISE FAMILY GUIDES are the indispensable books for families traveling to the islands. They contain information on the following:

- Over 100 condominiums and hotels listed by price and location on the island, with lodging descriptions including facilities, "kid-appeal," children's activities, baby-sitting availability, beach access, and toll-free reservation numbers.

- Over 70 restaurants listed by price and location, with critical descriptions including hours, menu, children's meals, and phone numbers.

- Beaches and beach activities, with descriptions including accurate directions to both popular destinations and little-known hideaways, facilities available at each site, and different kinds of water recreation.

- Recreation and tours (for air, land, and water), including golf, tennis, hiking, biking, horseback riding, running, snorkeling, shopping, and available rentals.

Ensure a happy, stress-free vacation for moms, dads, grandparents, and kids with the
PARADISE FAMILY GUIDES!

Available October 1994

FILL IN AND MAIL TODAY

PRIMA PUBLISHING
P.O. Box 1260BK
Rocklin, CA 95677

USE YOUR VISA/MC AND ORDER BY PHONE
(916) 632-4400
Monday–Friday 9 A.M.–4 P.M. PST

I'd like to order copies of the following titles:

Quantity	Title	Amount
_____	*Walt Disney World '95* $9.99	_____
_____	*Hawai'i: The Big Island* $12.95	_____
_____	*Maui and Lana'i* $12.95	_____
	Subtotal	_____
	Postage & Handling ($3 for first book, $1 for additional books)	_____
	7.25% Sales Tax (California only)	_____
	TOTAL (U.S. funds only)	_____

Check enclosed for $_____ (payable to **Prima Publishing)**

Charge my   ❏ Mastercard   ❏ Visa

Account No._____ Exp. Date_____

Signature _____

Your Name _____

Address _____

City/State/Zip_____

Daytime Telephone (_____) _____

Satisfaction Guaranteed!
Please allow three to four weeks for delivery.